COMPARATIVE CONSUMER INSOLVENCY REGIMES
—A CANADIAN PERSPECTIVE

All modern legal systems with advanced economies must address the question of how to respond to the needs of insolvent consumers whose burden of debt greatly exceeds their capacity to repay within a reasonable time frame. This study surveys comparatively the insolvency regimes currently in place or likely to be adopted in the foreseeable future in Canada, the United States, Australia, England and Wales, Scotland, Scandinavia and a representative group of Western countries on the continent of Europe.

Modern legal systems have two basic alternatives in providing relief for over-committed consumers. The first, which involves restricting the enforcement of individual creditor remedies, is a method with which this study is not concerned. Where the consumer is seriously insolvent and owes money to many creditors, a different approach is required—a collective solution to debtor's problems—and this, the solution provided by modern insolvency systems, is the focus of this study.

Comparative Consumer Insolvency Regimes— A Canadian Perspective

JACOB S ZIEGEL

Professor of Law Emeritus, University of Toronto

·HART·
PUBLISHING

OXFORD – PORTLAND OREGON
2003

Hart Publishing
Oxford and Portland, Oregon

Published in North America (US and Canada) by
Hart Publishing c/o
International Specialized Book Services
5804 NE Hassalo Street
Portland, Oregon
97213-3644
USA

Hart Publishing is a specialist legal publisher based in Oxford, England.
To order further copies of this book or to request a list of other
publications please write to:

Hart Publishing, Salter's Boatyard, Folly Bridge,
Abingdon Road, Oxford OX1 4LB
Telephone: +44 (0)1865 245533 or Fax: +44 (0)1865 794882
e-mail: mail@hartpub.co.uk
WEBSITE: http//www.hartpub.co.uk

British Library Cataloguing in Publication Data
Data Available
ISBN 1–84113–272–1 (hardback)

Typeset by Hope Services (Abingdon) Ltd.
Printed and bound in Great Britain on acid-free paper by
Biddles Ltd, www.biddles.co.uk

To Roy and Catherine Goode
In deep friendship

Preface

When historians come to write the social, economic and legal history of Western societies in the last quarter of the 20th century, they will surely be struck by the rapid increase in the number of overcommitted consumer debtors and by the equally rapid growth in the outstanding volume of consumer credit. Overcommitted debtors create many problems, legal and non-legal, but the single most pressing question is how to provide relief from the burden of debt. This comparative study examines the consumer insolvency regimes of Canada, the United States, Australia, England and Wales, Scotland, and, collectively, Western European continental countries to see how they have responded to the new challenges either by revising existing insolvency laws or by developing alternatives to traditional bankruptcy solutions.

This book is a revised and updated version of a report prepared by me for Industry Canada in 2000 in preparation for the third round of amendments to Canada's bankruptcy and insolvency legislation.[1] My hope is that the study may also be of interest to a wider readership given the commonality of the problems and the lessons national regimes can learn from each other in devising appropriate solutions, statutory and otherwise.

A study of the legal rules is only a small part of a rich and complex tapestry in which social, economic, legal and political factors are all immensely important for an understanding of contemporary insolvency cultures. It would be presumptuous, however, for me to claim that I have captured all the nuances and subleties distinguishing the different consumer insolvency regimes. That would have required a book several times as long and lengthy research visits to each of the countries under review other than Canada. The subject moreover is very dynamic and each month brings news of a new legislative project, task force reports, empirical studies, and a new set of statistics. In short, this book is a comparative study in progress whose contents will continue to change so long as there are a significant number of consumer insolvents.

I owe a very large debt to the many individuals, organizations and government agencies who have assisted me in the preparation of this study and I hope I will be forgiven if I only list some of them. In Canada, Dave Stewart, senior project leader, Office of the Superintendent of Bankruptcy, and his two associates, Lynda Colley and Stephanie Cavanagh, were outstanding in responding to my requests for a seemingly endless supply of tables and other data. Prof Iain Ramsay of the Osgooode Hall Law School and Prof Saul Schwartz of Carleton University were generous in sharing with me their expertise in the insolvency

---

[1] I retained the copyright to the report.

area. I also benefitted greatly from the opportunity to meet with many trustees in bankruptcy, too numerous to mention by name, both in Toronto and in other parts of Canada. My neighbour Dr Eric Koch gave up several Saturday afternoons helping me translate some of the German language documents.

In Australia, my important sources of information included David Bergman, adviser, policy and legislation, Insolvency and Trustee Service Australia, and other ITSA officials, Prof Rosalind Mason of the University of Southern Queensland (who also allowed me to reproduce a table appearing in chapter 4 of this book), and Jan Pentland, chairperson, Australian Financial Counselling and Credit Reform Association, and Dr Martin Ryan of La Trobe University.

The United States was a particularly rich and vital source of information and assistance. My many contacts there included Prof Jean Braucher of the University of Arizona College of Law, Edward M Flynn, policy analyst, Executive Office for United States Trustees, Prof Karen Gross of the New York Law School, Henry Sommer, a former legal aid lawyer in Philadelphia with deep knowledge of insolvency law problems affecting the poor, and Prof William Whitford of the Wisconsin University Law School, who read an earlier version of the study and made many helpful suggestions. No listing of US sources would be complete without an acknowledgment of the great debt all researchers in this area owe to the remarkable pioneering work of Professors Terry Sullivan, Elizabeth Warren and Jay Westbrook.

My list of English acknowledgments is only slightly shorter and encompasses Registrar Stephen Baister, Royal Courts of Justice, London, Prof Iain F Fletcher of University College, London, Steve Hill, a senior insolvency practitioner in London, Anna Lee of the Lord Chancellor's Office, Peter Joyce, former Inspector General of the Insolvency Service and his successor Desmond Flynn, and Andy Woodhead and Mike Norris, two officers in the policy section of the Insolvency Service. I am grateful too to Dr Jane Phipps, project officer, Oxfordshire Money Advice Project, and Teresa Perchard, head of social policy, National Citizens Advice Bureaux, for providing me with access to some very important recent English reports.

In Scotland, Prof Michael Adler was my academic contact and George Leslie Kerr, former Accountant in Bankruptcy and Maureen McGeown, Deputy Accountant in Bankruptcy were most helpful with reports and other data. In Scandinavia and Germany, my principal contacts were Dr Johanna Niemi-Kiesilainen of the University of Helsinki and Dr Udo Reifner in Hamburg and his colleague Dr Helga Springeer. Dr Reifner and Dr Niemi-Kiesilainen also kindly allowed me to reproduce tables wholly or partially prepared by them and appearing in chapter 7 of this book.

I am also very grateful to the following University of Toronto law school students who, at varying intervals, have provided research and computer assistance over the past four years: Martha Hundert, James McClary, Stephen Parks, Nika Robinson, Sarit Shmulevitz, and Lori Stein. With the help of Dean Ron Daniels, the Cecil A Wright fund at the University of Toronto law school made a substantial contribution to help defray the cost of preparing the manuscript for publication. Similarly, a research grant from the Social Sciences and Humanities Research Council of Canada assisted in covering expenses incurred at a much earlier period, including a visit to Australia.

No list of acknowledgments would be complete without a particularly warm appreciation to two individuals. The first is Jim Buchanan, senior project officer, Corporate Law and Policy Directorate, Industry Canada, who extended the original invitation for me to prepare the comparative report. The second is Richart Hart of Hart Publishing, the incomparable benefactor of so many contemporary Anglo-Canadian authors, who generously agreed to publish a revised version of the study.

Jacob Ziegel
July 2003

Contents

Abbreviations

AFCCRA	Australian Financial Counselling and Credit Reform Association
AIB	Accountant in Bankruptcy (Scotland)
AITA	actual income threshold amount
BA	Commonwealth Bankruptcy Act (Australia)
Bankruptcy Court (US)	US Federal Court of first instance responsible under the US Bankruptcy Code for adjudicating disputes and for supervising and giving directions to trustees and others
BIA	Bankruptcy and Insolvency Act, RSC 1985, c B-3, as amended (Canada)
BIA III.1	Part III Division 1 of the BIA dealing with consumer proposals
BIAC	Bankruptcy and Insolvency Advisory Committee (Canada)
BITA	base income threshold amount
BLAA	Bankruptcy Legislation Amendment Act 2002 (Australia)
BRO	bankruptcy restriction order
CAIRP	Canadian Association of Insolvency and Restructuring Professionals
CIPA	Canadian Insolvency Practitioners Association (name changed in 2001 to CAIRP)
Cork Committee	English government-appointed committee chaired by Sir Kenneth Cork and responsible for the Cork Report
Cork Report	*Report of the Review Committee on Insolvency Law and Practice* (London, Cmnd 8558, June 1982)
DTI	Department of Trade and Industry (British government department responsible, inter alia, for consumer protection and insolvency legislation)
EOUST	Executive Office for United States Trustees
EU	European Union
FCC	Federal Court of Canada
FITA	Federal Insolvency Trustee Agency
GAO	General Accounting Office (United States)
IA	Insolvency Act 1986, as amended (England)
Industry Canada	Canadian government department responsible for the administration of and changes to Canada's insolvency legislation

Industry Canada Report	*Report on the Operation and Administration of the* Bankruptcy and Insolvency Act *and the* Companies' Creditors Arrangement Act (September 2002)
InSG	*Insolvenzgesetz* (German Insolvency Law 1994, as amended)
Insolvency Service	English government agency responsible for the administration and enforcement of the Insolvency Act 1986, as amended
IPA	income payment agreement
IPO	income payment order
ITSA	Insolvency and Trustee Service Australia
IVA	individual voluntary arrangement
LAO	liquidation of assets order
LICO	low income cut off standard
NBRC	National Bankruptcy Review Commission (United States)
NCAB	National Citizens' Advice Bureaux (England and Scotland)
NCBJ	National Conference of Bankruptcy Judges (United States)
NCCUSL	National Conference of Commissioners on Uniform State Laws (United States)
OPPSA	Ontario Personal Property Security Act, RSO 1990, c P 10, as amended (Canada)
OR	official receiver
OSB	Office of the Superintendent of Bankruptcy (Canadian government agency responsible for the administration of the BIA and the appointment and supervision of trustees in bankruptcy)
OT	Official Trustee (Australia)
PITF	Personal Insolvency Task Force (Canada)
R3	Association of Business Recovery Professionals (UK)
RA	reaffirmation agreement
RRSP	registered retirement savings plan
RT	registered trustee (Australia)
SLC	Scottish Law Commission
Task Force Report	Report of the Personal Insolvency Task Force (Ottawa 2002)
TDI	total disposable income

Table of Cases

Canada

England and Wales

United States of America

Table of Legislation

Australia

Canada

France

Germany

Scotland

United States of America

Part A

Introduction

1

Purpose of Study

1. RESPONDING TO CONSUMER OVER-INDEBTEDNESS

A<small>LL MODERN LEGAL</small> systems with advanced economies must address the question of how to respond to the needs of insolvent consumers whose burden of debt greatly exceeds their capacity to repay within a reasonable time frame. This study surveys comparatively from a Canadian perspective the insolvency regimes currently in place or likely to be adopted in the foreseeable future in the United States, Australia, England and Wales, Scotland, Scandinavia and a representative group of Western countries on the continent of Europe, with a view to determining what Canada can learn from them and what they can learn from each other.

The United States has been chosen for comparison because it is Canada's closest neighbour and most important trading partner, because of its cultural influence, and because consumer insolvency problems have received the most intensive scrutiny there. The choice of England has been determined by the fact that historically it has greatly influenced the evolution of Canada's insolvency regime, as well as Australia's and New Zealand's and that of many other Commonwealth countries, and because England and Canada both have free market economies and common consumption patterns. Australia has been chosen because in size, population, demographic, constitutional and economic structure it too has many affinities with Canada, and because its recent legislation shows some striking similarities to Canada's. Scotland is a relevant jurisdiction for comparison because its legislative experience casts important light on one piece of the Canadian puzzle. The continental countries, and Germany in particular, are appropriate jurisdictions for comparison because of their much more stringent approach to consumer insolvencies and their rejection of the 'fresh start' policy long embraced in the United States.

Modern legal systems have two basic alternatives in providing relief for over-committed consumers. One alternative is to impose restrictions on the enforcement of individual creditor remedies, for example, by exempting from seizure household furnishings, tools of the trade, and other essential items required by the debtor for the support of the debtor and the debtor's family and the gaining of a livelihood, by restricting the percentage of the debtor's salary that may be garnisheed and by prohibiting wage assignments. Another familiar example of restrictions on individual remedies is the imposition of moratoria on the enforcement of secured creditors' remedies in periods of acute economic recession, particularly with respect to mortgages on homes.

This individualised approach may be appropriate and effective where the debtor is only facing temporary financial difficulties, but is inadequate where the consumer is seriously insolvent and owes money to numerous creditors. What the debtor needs in such cases is a collective solution to debtor's problems—the solution designed to be provided by modern insolvency systems. This study is exclusively concerned with this second alternative to meeting the needs of contemporary consumers. Today, the economic efficiency and social justice of the collective solution enabling a debtor to petition for the debtor's bankruptcy[1] and to obtain a discharge from the balance of his debts at some point after the bankruptcy seems to us compelling. Nevertheless, the solution is of comparatively recent origin and is still not accepted by a substantial number of countries with advanced economies. Voluntary bankruptcies were only made available to non-trading individuals in England with the passage of the Bankruptcy Act in 1883,[2] and were only introduced in Canada in the Bankruptcy Act of 1919.[3] The celebrated US 'fresh start policy' only became firmly imbedded with the adoption of the national Bankruptcy Act of 1898.[4] Prior to these turning points in legal history and social policy, debtors who failed to pay their debts were much more likely to be imprisoned for non-payment than to be the object of society's solicitude.

For a variety of reasons, for a long time the number of consumers seeking to take advantage of the new insolvency regimes was very modest. As late as 1972, the number of individual non-business bankruptcies in Canada, 3,647, was smaller than the number of business bankruptcies. It grew rapidly thereafter and reached 21,025 in 1980.[5] Between 1985 and 1997, the number of consumer insolvencies increased by over 300 per cent, from 19,752 to 90,034.[6] In 2001, the total

---

[1] Unfortunately, the terminology is not uniform among the different jurisdictions. In the US Bankruptcy Code, the term bankruptcy covers both liquidation bankruptcies and chapter 13 non-liquidation payment plans. In Canada, the term only covers liquidation proceedings and not proposals under Division III, Part 2 of the Bankruptcy and Insolvency Act, RSC 1985, c B-3 (hereafter BIA, Part III 2) or Orderly Payment of Debt Arrangements under Part X of the BIA. Also, some jurisdictions, such as England and Australia, do not distinguish between individual bankruptcies and consumer bankruptcies. The Canadian statistics distinguish between consumer and business bankruptcies but the distinction may not be complete. This is because a substantial number of the consumer bankruptcy figures include bankruptcies by self-employed non-professional individuals. In North America, 'consumer insolvencies' is often used to describe all types of bankruptcy proceedings involving consumers and the expression will be used in this broader sense in this study.

[2] 1883 (UK) 46 and 47 Vict, c 52.

[3] Stat Can 1919, 9 and 10 Geo 5, c 36.

[4] Ch 541, 30 Stat 544 (US 1898) (repealed and replaced in 1978 by the US Bankruptcy Code, US Pub L 95–98, Title 1 §101, USC Title 11 as am).

[5] Office of the Superintendent of Bankruptcy (OSB), *International Consumer Insolvency Statistics* (Ottawa, June 1999) 2 (hereafter *International Statistics*).

[6] There was a drop of nearly 10% in the number of Canadian consumer insolvencies between 1997 and 1998 (from 90,034 to 82,620) and a 3.7% increase in the US figures (from 1,350,118 to 1,398,182) as compared with a 20% increase in the US figures between 1996 and 1997. See OSB, *International Statistics* (n 5 above) at 1, 3, 7. The improvement in the Canadian employment

number of individual filings amounted to 102,539.[7] The US figures tell a similar story. Between 1985 and 1997, the number of consumer insolvencies grew from 341,233 to 1,350,118, also a three-fold increase. The number has continued to climb and reached 1,452,129 in 2001.[8] Still more significant is the increase in the number of consumer insolvencies as a ratio of population. In Canada, the ratio increased between 1981 and 1997 from 0.93 to 3.00 per 1,000 of population, an increase of 223 per cent. The comparable figures for the United States were 1.4 and 5.1, an increase of 264 per cent.[9]

The number of insolvencies in comparable jurisdictions was much smaller. Nevertheless, they too show a very significant percentage increase between 1985 and 1997. During this period, the number of individual insolvencies in England and Wales grew from 6,776 to 24,441 and from a ratio of 0.14 to 0.47, a 235 per cent increase.[10] The number of Australian consumer insolvencies grew from 8,761 in 1986/87 to 22,333 in 1996/97, a 150 per cent increase.[11] The ratio per head of population grew from 0.50 to 1.21, an increase of 142 per cent.[12] By way of comparison with a Scandinavian country, the number of personal insolvencies in Finland grew from 21 in 1985 to 5,454 in 1997.[13] The number of personal insolvencies reached 18,685 in 1995, its highest point. The number of straight bankruptcies was much smaller, and only grew from 21 in 1985 to 184 in 1997.[14]

---

position and the general buoyancy of the Canadian economy may explain the drop in the Canadian figures, although this is only speculation. The 1997 amendments to the BIA, discussed below in Chapter 2, may also have made an impact, particularly on filings by debtors with large student loans. The steep rise in the US insolvency figures throughout the 1990s shows that a robust economy is no harbinger of lower insolvency filings. Prof Ausubel argues that credit industry standards, especially on the credit card side, are more important factors. See LM Ausubel, 'Credit Card Defaults, Credit Card Profits, and Bankruptcy' (1997) 71 *American Bankruptcy Law Journal* 249.

[7] 'Total individual filings' comprises individual bankruptcies and Division 1 and 2 proposals by individuals. There were 87,302 individual bankruptcy filings, of which 9.1% were individual business filings and 90.9% (79,317) were individual consumer filings. There were 1,721 individual Division 1 filings, of which 72.2% (1,243) were individual consumer filings. There were 13,453 individual Division 2 filings and all but 4% of these were individual consumer filings. Email information supplied to author by Stephanie Cavanagh, OSB analyst, on 10 January 2003.

[8] See *International Statistics* n 5 above at 7, and ABI World, Annual Filings US 1980–2002 (www.abiworld.org/stats/1980annual.html). The US consumer insolvency figures cover chapter 7, chapter 11 and chapter 13 filings.

[9] *International Statistics* (n 5 above) at 4, 10.

[10] *Ibid* at 12, 13, 17–18. See further chapter 5 below, Table 5.1, and note carefully that individual insolvencies cover business as well as consumer insolvencies.

[11] *Ibid* at 29. The number of personal bankruptcies amounted to 24,109 in administrative year 2001–02, of which 20,039 were non-business bankruptcies. These figures do not include debt agreements and arrangements under Parts IX and X of the Commonwealth Bankruptcy Act. See further chapter 4 below, Table 4.1.

[12] *International Statistics* (n 5 above) at 32.

[13] *Ibid* at 22. The figure was revised upwards to 8,950 in OSB, *International Statistics* (June 2002) at 8.

[14] *Ibid* at 23. In 2001, the number dropped to 119. *Ibid* (June 2002) at 8. For the important differences between personal insolvency and personal bankruptcy proceedings in Scandinavia and many of the continental European countries, see chapter 7 below.

2. INDUSTRY AND LEGISLATIVE REACTIONS

In Canada and the United States, both industry and legislators have expressed keen concern about the rapid growth in the number of consumer insolvencies. In both countries, the allegation has often been made that it is too easy for consumers to go bankrupt and to shed their debts even when the consumer is in a position to pay off at least a part of the debt. In Canada, this led to the 1997 amendments to the Bankruptcy and Insolvency Act (BIA) requiring mandatory payments of surplus income by the debtor in accordance with the Superintendent of Bankruptcy's ('Superintendent') directive, and giving trustees enhanced roles in recommending terms of discharge under sections 172 and 173 of the Act. These changes were designed to encourage a much larger number of consumer proposals involving payment of at least part of the outstanding debts. Further changes to Canada's consumer insolvency regime are likely as part of the third phase of amendments to the BIA expected to be adopted in the near future.[15]

In the United States, responding to strong credit industry pressure, Bills were introduced in 1997 and 1998 in the House of Representatives and in the Senate.[16] The Bills were approved in the two chambers but lapsed in November of 1998 because the legislators were unable to reach agreement on a compromise Bill before the Congressional elections. Similar Bills, HR 833 and S 625, were introduced in 1999 and a compromise bill was approved by the two chambers and sent to the White House for President Clinton's signature. However, he pocket vetoed[17] the Bill in December 2000 just before leaving office. New Bills, S 420 and HR 333, were introduced in the Senate and the House of Representatives in 2001 in President Bush's first year in office but, because of the tragic events of 11 September 2001, attempts to reconcile the conflicting versions had to be postponed till 2002. Agreement appeared to have been reached on 26 July 2002, but fell apart a few days later.[18] No agreement was reached before the 107th Congress ended in November 2002 and the Bills died.[19] There was considerable uncertainty whether the Bills would be revived in the new session of Congress given the more pressing concerns likely to occupy US legislators in 2003. Nevertheless, it did happen and Rep. F. James Sensenbrenner Jr. introduced HR 975, the new House version of HR 333, on 27 February 2003.[20] All the Bills

---

[15] For further details, see chapter 2.3 below.

[16] See Responsible Borrower Protection Bankruptcy Act, HR 2500, 105th Congress, 1st Session; Bankruptcy Reform Act of 1998, HR 3150, 105th Congress, 2nd Session; and Consumer Bankruptcy Reform Act of 1998, S 1301, 105th Congress, 2nd Session.

[17] A 'pocket veto' is a presidential veto exerciseable by the US president with respect to Congressionally approved Bills when the Congress is not in session.

[18] See American Bankruptcy Institute (ABI) Newsletter, 'Final Agreement reached on Bankruptcy Bill' (26 July 2002); and ABI Newsletter, 'Bankruptcy "Agreement" Hits New Snag' (29 July 2002).

[19] Email message to author from Edward M Flynn, research analyst, Executive Office for United States Trustees (EOUST), 15 January 2003.

[20] American Bankruptcy College news release to members, 28 February 2003.

involved, or involve, means testing and would make consumer debtors ineligible to make a chapter 7 filing if the debtor's income was equal to or better than the median US family income and if the debtor, allowing for prescribed cost of living standards, could have paid an indicated percentage or more of the outstanding unsecured debts within a five year period.[21]

As will be discussed later in this study, there is much controversy among Canadian and US observers about the percentage of insolvent debtors with a significant amount of discretionary income. In Canada, the 1998 study by Schwartz and Anderson[22] showed that there were relatively few debtors filing for bankruptcy with a sizeable discretionary income. Professor Iain Ramsay's study of a large sample of filings in Metro Toronto[23] shows a somewhat higher figure. Still more substantial figures appear in the statistics collected by the Office of the Superintendent of Bankruptcy (OSB) in Canada under the 1997 amendments to the BIA showing the number of consumer bankrupts with surplus income as determined by the Superintendent's directive under the amendments.[24] US analysts, applying the proposed means testing standards in the Congressional Bills to recent US consumer bankruptcy filings, have come up with figures varying between 3 per cent and 15 per cent.[25]

Other Commonwealth jurisdictions, particularly England, Australia and New Zealand, have or had consumer bankruptcy and discharge structures very similar to the Canadian pre-1997 law. Australia adopted important legislative changes in 1991 and 1996 in response to the escalating rates of insolvency filings and further changes were approved in late 2002.[26] In England, as a result of the Insolvency Act 1986, section 279(1), first time individual bankrupts became entitled to a discharge three years after the bankruptcy order (two years in the case of summary administrations)[27] unless the official receiver opposed the discharge. In England, too, there has been a very substantial increase in the number of personal insolvencies since 1987 but on a population basis the number of consumer bankruptcies is still much below the comparable rate in Canada and the United States. This is almost certainly due to the stigma that still attaches to personal bankruptcies in England and the high court and administration fees that must be paid to file a petition in bankruptcy.[28] The available evidence points to the fact that England is currently facing many of the same problems arising from consumer over-indebtedness as have been familiar in Canada and Australia for a

---

[21] The details will be found in chapter 3.5 below.

[22] S Schwartz and L Anderson, *An Empirical Study of Canadians Seeking Personal Bankruptcy Protection* (Ottawa, Industry Canada, 1998). See also S Schwartz, 'The Empirical Dimensions of Consumer Bankruptcy: Results from a Survey of Canadian Bankrupts' (1999) 37 *Osgoode Hall Law Journal* 83.

[23] IDC Ramsay, 'Individual Bankruptcy: Preliminary Findings of a Socio-Legal Analysis' (1999) 37 *Osgoode Hall Law Journal* 15.

[24] See chapter 2.7(c) below.

[25] See further chapter 3.5(b) below.

[26] See Bankruptcy Legislation Amendment Act 2002, No 131, 2002, and chapter 4.2 below.

[27] The period is reduced to one year in the Enterprise Act 2002. See chapter 5.6 below.

[28] For the details see chapter 5.3(a) below.

much longer period. The insolvency provisions in the Enterprise Act 2002 approved by the British Parliament in autumn 2002 are designed to address some of the resulting problems, though their main focus is to encourage more private enterprise in England and to mitigate the consequences of small business failures by liberalising the provisions in the existing Insolvency Act 1986.[29]

The legal position is very different in Scandinavia and many of the Western European continental countries. There, a straight bankruptcy, followed by a discharge order, is either not available at all or is only available as a last resort after all other alternatives have been exhausted. These alternatives usually involve voluntary or statutory debt adjustment arrangements with the creditors. Many of the Western European jurisdictions, such as the Scandinavian countries and Germany, have also established comprehensive debt counselling services, which include negotiations with creditors for the establishment of a payment plan.

This summary therefore shows that modern societies respond differently to the challenges of rising consumer indebtedness and insolvencies. At the same time, it is important to appreciate that we are dealing with a complex interplay of legal, economic and social factors and that national solutions are also deeply affected by historical factors and cultural values.

3. DESIGN OF STUDY

The balance of this study proceeds as follows. Part B provides a non-exhaustive survey of the current insolvency regimes and prospective changes under consideration in Canada, the United States, Australia, England, Scotland, and selected Western continental countries in Europe. The study begins with Canada and uses Canada as a template against which to measure the other jurisdictions. Part C contains an assessment of the lessons to be drawn from the country surveys and what Canada can learn from the experience and approaches of those countries and hopefully also what they can learn from Canada. Part C also contains a functional analysis of leading issues common to the insolvency regimes, including (in part) the economic and social rationales of a discharge policy for consumer debts as applied in the common law jurisdictions.[30]

So far as the country surveys are concerned, the reader should be aware of some methodological difficulties. In the case of the United States, there is an overwhelming volume of materials on all facets of consumer insolvencies. In Canada and Australia, on the other hand, scholarly analysis of the issues is still in its early stages. In the United Kingdom, until quite recently, consumer insolvencies were not regarded as a major legal and social issue and this perception

---

[29] See chapter 5.6 below.
[30] The issues are also examined in some detail in the country survey of the United States, chapter 3.5(b) below.

is reflected in the very modest volume of legal and non-legal literature. In the continental European countries, there is growing recognition of the importance of the problems. However, because of opposition to the discharge philosophy associated with the United States and other common law jurisdictions, until recently the discussion has focused much more heavily on social than on legal solutions.

4. CONCEPTUAL STRUCTURE OF COUNTRY ANALYSES

A conceptual framework is desirable in describing and analysing the various consumer insolvency systems. A uniform approach is not possible because of the fundamental differences between the common law philosophy and the philosophy that has so far animated the continental European countries. So far as the common law jurisdictions are concerned, the differences and similarities between them can best be articulated by asking the following series of questions that constitute the fault lines of many modern bankruptcy regimes:

(1) How does the debtor enter the bankruptcy process, are there preconditions, and who administers and pays for the debtor's bankruptcy?

(2) How much of the debtor's property must the debtor surrender to the bankruptcy estate? Does it include any part of the debtor's income prior or subsequent to the debtor's discharge? What part of the debtor's property is exempt from the trustee's reach, and how are secured claims treated?

(3) When is the debtor entitled to apply for a discharge or is discharge automatic at some point? May the court refuse a discharge or impose conditions for a discharge? In particular, may the court require payment of some or all of the outstanding debts from future income of the debtor? What types of claim are excluded from discharge?

(4) What alternative statutory schemes are in place to enable or encourage a debtor to avoid straight bankruptcy and to enter into an arrangement or compromise of his debts ('plan or proposal') with the debtor's creditors? What are the preconditions for a successful plan or proposal? What are the consequences of the debtor's failure to live up to the terms of the plan or proposal?

(5) Does the regime permit reaffirmation of pre-bankruptcy debts?

(6) What roles do credit or debt counselling and financial education play as part of the debtor's rehabilitation, whether in a straight bankruptcy or as part of a plan or proposal?

A different, much less structured and more succinct approach, is adopted to describe the current non-common law Western European regimes.

Part B

Country Surveys

2

Canada[1]

I N CANADA, AS in the United States and Australia, the federal government is constitutionally empowered to adopt bankruptcy and insolvency legislation.[2] The difference between Canada and the United States is that in Canada's case the federal government is, on paper at least, invested with an exclusive jurisdiction to legislate on questions of bankruptcy and insolvency whereas the US government is only empowered to adopt uniform laws in the bankruptcy area. In practice, Canadian courts have tolerated, though not consistently, a substantial amount of overlap between federal and provincial law in the insolvency area so long as the provincial law is not in direct conflict with federal law.[3] In any event, the federal bankruptcy system is premised on a largely provincially originating substratum of property and other pre-bankruptcy rules[4] so that provincial law exerts a powerful influence on the resolution of bankrupt disputes.

The pre-confederation provinces had a variety of insolvency legislation but it was not uniform and was largely creditor-driven. It contained no provisions for voluntary assignments by debtors to be followed by a discharge. The same was true of the first federal Insolvency Act of 1869,[5] which was modelled on Ontario's Act of 1864[6] and only applied to traders. The 1869 Act was replaced in 1875.[7] The 1875 Act was widely criticised and was repealed in 1880.[8]

---

[1] This chapter borrows heavily from JS Ziegel, 'The Philosophy and Design of Contemporary Consumer Bankruptcy Systems: A Canada-United States Comparison' (1999) 37 *Osgoode Hall Law Journal* 205 and follows its structure closely. The author has also substantially updated and, where necessary, revised and expanded the information in the article.

[2] Constitution Act 1867 (UK), 30 and 31 Vic, c 3, s 91(21). Cf US Constitution Act, Art I, sec 8, clause 4 ('Congress shall have power . . . to establish uniform laws on the subject of bankruptcies throughout the United States.')

[3] See, eg, *Ontario (AG) v Canada (AG)* [1894] AC 189 (PC) (constitutionality of provincial assignment and preferences legislation); *Abitibi Power & Paper Co v Montreal Trust Co* [1943] AC 536 (PC) (validity of special provincial restructuring act); *Donald A Robinson v Countrywide Factors Ltd* [1978] SCR 753 (validity of Saskatchewan's fraudulent preferences legislation); and *Pacaar Financial Services Ltd v Sinco Trucking Ltd (Trustee of)* (1989) 57 DLR (4th) 438 (Sask CA) (validity of s 20(1) of Saskatchewan Personal Property Security Act); and contrast *Reference re Orderly Payment of Debts Act, 1959 (Alberta)* [1960] SCR 571 (validity of provincial wage payment plan); *British Columbia v Henfrey Samson Belair Ltd* [1989] 2 SCR 24 (constitutionality of provincial deemed trust provisions where debtor bankrupt); and *Husky Oil Operations Ltd v MNR* [1995] 3 SCR 453 (constitutionality of provincial retention of payment provisions).

[4] BIA, s 72(1) provides that the Act shall not be deemed to abrogate the substantive provisions of any other law or statute relating to property and civil rights that are not in conflict with the Act.

[5] SC 1869, 32 and 33 Vic, c 16.

[6] SO 1864, 27 and 28 Vic, c 17.

[7] SC 1875, 38 Vic, c 16.

[8] SC 1880, 43 Vic, c 1. For an excellent account of the early Canadian bankruptcy history, see TGW Telfer, *Reconstructing Bankruptcy Law in Canada, 1867 to 1919: From an Evil to a Commercial Necessity* (SJD Thesis, University of Toronto, 1999).

Between 1880 and 1919, Canada had no general bankruptcy legislation at all. Various efforts were made by business interests and Members of Parliament between 1880 and 1903 to promote a new federal Act but these all foundered on one or other of two obstacles: opposition in Western Canada to legislation driven by Central Canada mercantile interests and general opposition to providing a discharge from debts not based on creditor consent. The federal government, it seems, was unwilling to take any initiatives itself and was quite happy to pass on the baton to the provinces.

To bridge the gap, Ontario adopted An Act Respecting Assignments for the Benefit of Creditors in 1885.[9] This enabled a debtor to make an assignment of his assets in favour of his creditors but the Act did not (and constitutionally could not) provide for a discharge. Nevertheless, the concept of a non-pejorative assignment by a debtor has left an enduring mark and remains the method used under the federal Bankruptcy and Insolvency Act (BIA) for a debtor to put himself into voluntary bankruptcy.[10] Despite its limited scope, there was much uncertainty about the constitutionality of the 1885 Act, which was only resolved in Ontario's favour with the Privy Council's decision in *Ontario (AG) v Canada (AG)* in 1894.[11]

The first comprehensive federal Bankruptcy Act was adopted in 1919[12] and finally overcame long-standing creditor opposition to voluntary bankruptcies followed by a discharge of the debtor's debts.[13] The Act was equally accessible to consumer as well as business debtors, and enabled an insolvent debtor to make a voluntary assignment in bankruptcy and to obtain a discharge which, at the court's discretion, could be an absolute, conditional or suspended discharge. The conceptual structure of the 1919 Act remains intact and continues to drive the current BIA. As previously mentioned, voluntary assignments appear to have been used very modestly by consumers in the inter-war period[14] although consumer credit was already a well established phenomenon at the time.

The 1919 Act was extensively revised in 1949.[15] The revised Act introduced two changes of particular importance to insolvent consumers. The first was the introduction of a 'minicode' for the administration of small estates where the debtor's assets amounted to CAN$500 or less.[16] The second introduced the concept of an automatic application for a discharge.[17] The discharge application was deemed to be made at the time of the assignment or the making of a receiving order, and its purpose was to avoid the mischief of large numbers of

[9] SO 1885, 48 Vic, c 10.
[10] BIA, s 49(1).
[11] [1894] AC 189.
[12] SC 1919, c 36.
[13] See TGW Telfer, 'The Canadian Bankruptcy Act of 1919: Public Legislation or Private Interest' (1995) 24 *Canadian Business Law Journal* 357.
[14] Judging by the reported cases, most of the assignments were business related.
[15] SC 1949 (2nd Sess), c 7.
[16] *Ibid*, ss 26(6), 114–116.
[17] *Ibid*, s 127.

bankrupts living in legal limbo for many years because they could not afford to make a formal application for their discharge.

Comprehensive proposals for new revisions were presented by a federal Study Committee in 1970.[18] However, the proposals were never translated into law despite the introduction of several bills between 1975 and 1984. Instead, in 1984, the Mulroney government appointed a committee of insolvency experts to recommend amendments to the existing Act. The Committee reported in 1986. Many of its recommendations were enacted in 1992[19] and have since been followed by a second round of amendments in 1997.[20] A third round of amendments is envisaged for adoption early in the new century.

2. 1992 AND 1997 AMENDMENTS

The 1992 amendments were important because they greatly simplified the procedure for the handling of discharges for personal bankrupts[21] and because they introduced[22] a separate regime for the making of consumer proposals as an alternative to straight bankruptcy. The 1997 amendments added another very significant feature to the treatment of consumer bankruptcies. Section 68 of the Act was completely rewritten to require debtors between the time of bankruptcy and the time of their discharge to pay over their surplus income based on standards issued by the Superintendent of Bankruptcy ('Superintendent'). The details of these changes will be discussed later.[23]

New provisions were also added dealing with the debtor's application for a discharge. Section 170.1 of the BIA requires the trustee's report to the court hearing the discharge application to state whether the debtor has complied with the section 68 payment requirements and whether the debtor chose the bankruptcy route for resolving his indebtedness when the debtor could have made a viable proposal. The trustee's report may also include recommendations with respect to whether the debtor's discharge should be made conditional. If such a recommendation is made, it will be treated as an opposition to the discharge. Another amendment, this one to section 173,[24] adds to the list of circumstances precluding the court from granting the debtor an unconditional discharge if the debtor has failed to comply with a section 68 income payment requirement or if the debtor chose the bankruptcy route when the debtor could have made a viable proposal.

---

[18] *Report of the Study Committee on Bankruptcy and Insolvency Legislation* (Ottawa, 1970) (hereafter 'Study Committee'). John Honsberger, QC, Canada's leading bankruptcy practitioner/scholar, was a key member of the Committee.

[19] SC 1992, c 27.

[20] SC 1997, c 12.

[21] See now BIA, ss 168–170.

[22] See now BIA, Part III, Division II (hereafter BIA, part III 2).

[23] See 2.7 below.

[24] BIA, s 173(1)(m)–(n).

3. PITF RECOMMENDATIONS

In the summer of 2000, the Superintendent established a Personal Insolvency Task Force (PITF)[25] comprising a broad cross-section of members of the Canadian bankruptcy community, including three academics,[26] to explore 'alternative models of personal insolvency processes better geared towards addressing the perceived weaknesses' of Canada's insolvency process and/or redress mechanisms to the existing process in order to ensure:

(1) that Canada's highly privatised bankruptcy system, which was designed for debtors with assets and/or income, can nevertheless remain accessible to debtors with no assets and/or income;

(2) the appropriateness of low-income debtors paying even a modest fee to obtain a fresh start while being subject to the same procedural process as those with high income and/or assets;

(3) that bench-marking is incorporated into the recommendations and that best practices from other countries such as Australia, United States and United Kingdom are drawn on to improve the efficiency and effectiveness of Canada's insolvency system.[27]

The Superintendent also invited the Task Force to address seven other specific issues and to recommend appropriate legislative solutions.[28] In the event, the Task Force focused most of its limited time on these and related questions and very little on exploring the desirability of Canada adopting new insolvency procedures.

The Task Force met over a period of 15 months and issued its report in 2002. Most of the Task Force members were of the view that the Canadian insolvency system was 'basically sound and in need of incremental, rather than fundamental reform.'[29] Nevertheless, the Task Force's 120-page report contains 32 recommendations, a substantial number of which could have a significant impact on the future operation of Canada's consumer insolvency system. The Committee's most important recommendations were the following:

---

[25] The Task Force's original name was Consumer Insolvency Task Force. It was subsequently changed to take account of a fairly significant number of personal insolvencies in Canada that are business-related. Quite often the bankrupt's debts will be an amalgam of consumer and business-related debts. The Office of the Superintendent of Bankruptcy (OSB)'s system is to classify individual bankruptcies as consumer bankruptcies if 50% or more of the debts are personal and to classify them as individual business bankruptcies if the reverse is true.

[26] For PITF's composition, see OSB, *Personal Insolvency Task Force: Final Report* (Ottawa, August 2002), Annex 1 (hereafter PITF Report). (Although dated August 2002, the Report was not published until December 2002.) There were some significant gaps in the Task Force's composition. There were no representatives from Alberta and Saskatchewan. Bankruptcy registrars were also not represented although they discharge the bulk of the judicial work in the consumer bankruptcy area. Private trustees in bankruptcy, on the other hand, were very well represented through five members of the Task Force.

[27] PITF Report (n 26 above) at 79–80.

[28] *Ibid* at 80.

[29] *Ibid* at 7–8.

(1) there should be a reduction in the period of non-dischargeability of student loans from 10 years to five years, with power in the court to reduce the period still further in cases of hardship;

(2) with important restrictions and conditions, Registered Retirement Savings Plans (RRSPs) (these are an important type of tax exempt private retirement savings plan for Canadians) should not be treated as part of the bankrupt's estate;

(3) the BIA should be amended to provide an *optional* federal list of personal exemptions, thereby giving individual bankrupts an alternative to the otherwise applicable provincial exemptions;

(4) non-purchase money security interests in exempt personal property should be avoidable in bankruptcy;

(5) reaffirmation of debts after the debtor's discharge should be closely regulated;

(6) the BIA should be amended to introduce a procedure for the recognition of unsecured debts discharged under a foreign insolvency procedure;

(7) the meaning of income and the allocation of non-periodic payments should be clarified for the purposes of sections 67 and 68 of the Act;

(8) monetary ceilings on the amount of non-business debts should be abolished for the purposes of consumer proposals in Part III, Division 2 of the BIA;

(9) fee agreements between debtors and trustees should be enforceable after a debtor's discharge; and

(10) a bankrupt's obligation to make surplus income payments under section 68 should be extended from nine months to 21 months in accordance with the Superintendent's directive.

Many of these recommendations will be referred to more fully hereafter. Not all of the Task Force's recommendations won unanimous support and dissenting reports were filed by two of its academic members.[30]

4. ADMINISTRATIVE AND JUDICIAL STRUCTURES

In Canada, the actual administration of consumer estates vests largely in the hands of privately appointed trustees. The role of the Superintendent of Bankruptcy and his appointed officials is to supervise the trustees' work and ensure compliance with the BIA and the supporting regulations and directives. In theory at any rate, Canadian bankruptcies are creditor driven and the judicial role is minimised. At the apex of the administrative hierarchy sits the

---

[30] This author was one of the dissenters. The Task Force's draft recommendations were considered in a discussion paper prepared by the Policy Sector of Industry Canada in May 2002. This was followed by a series of public consultations across Canada in the spring of 2002 to receive feedback on the discussion paper, including the Task Force's draft recommendations. See Industry Canada, *Report on the Operation and Administration of the Bankruptcy and Insolvency Act and the Companies' Creditors Arrangement Act* (September 2002).

Superintendent of Bankruptcy, a federally appointed official, who appoints or recommends the appointments of all trustees in bankruptcy and official receivers.[31] Official receivers are full time federal officials and are located in the bankruptcy districts into which Canada is divided.[32] Their functions include receiving assignments in bankruptcy, appointing a trustee if none is designated in the assignment, and conducting inquiries into the causes of a bankruptcy.[33]

In practice, the trustee, who is not a government official, is the most important cog in the administrative wheel.[34] The trustee is required to be licensed by the Superintendent[35] and is usually a chartered accountant specialising in insolvency law. Canadian trustees differ from their US counterparts in two important respects. First, Canadian trustees are drawn exclusively from the private sector and are not public officials although for some purposes they may be treated as officers of the court. Secondly, most consumer bankruptcies are initiated and processed by trustees without the intervention of an attorney. Canadian debtors are free to retain an attorney to prepare the assignment but few consumers would find it efficient or can afford to do so since it would involve the payment of two set of fees, the attorney's fees and the trustee's fees.

Canadian trustees advertise their services widely on cable TV and in the Yellow Pages of the local telephone directory and less frequently on local TV.[36] Canadian trustees frequently operate from more than one office and rely heavily on non-professional staff to help them process large numbers of consumer bankruptcies.[37] As a rule, the trustee[38] is nominated to serve in that capacity by the debtor in a voluntary assignment or by the petitioning creditor in an involuntary bankruptcy. The Canadian system might be perceived as giving rise to conflicts of interest since, by advertising their services and encouraging debtors to consult them, trustees may leave the impression that, even after their appointment as a trustee in the case, they will continue to act exclusively in the debtor's interests whereas the Act may actually require them to act antithetically to the

---

[31] BIA, ss 5–10.

[32] BIA, s 12.

[33] BIA, ss 49, 49(4), 161.

[34] For an excellent empirical study of the trustee's role, see IDC Ramsay, 'Market Imperatives, Professional Discretion and the Role of Intermediaries in Consumer Bankruptcy: a Comparative Study of the Canadian Trustee in Bankruptcy' (2000) 74 *American Bankruptcy Law Journal* 399.

[35] BIA, s 13. A substantial number of trustees are former official receivers.

[36] Some large firms of trustees with many offices are estimated to spend over CAN$100,000 annually on advertising. Other trustees spend very little and rely primarily on word of mouth recommendations. A directive of the Superintendent (OSB Directive No 30R, issued 4 January 1991 and reissued 23 July 1993) makes a modest attempt to regulate some aspects of trustees' advertising though not the amount of advertising or the media in which it may be carried. Note too that BIA, s 202(1)(f) makes it an offence for any person directly or indirectly to solicit or canvass any person to make an assignment or a proposal under the Act or to petition for a receiving order. The prohibition may be vulnerable to attack as an unconstitutional infringement on freedom of expression under s 2(b) of the Canadian Charter of Rights and Freedoms.

[37] In a large population centre, such as Toronto, a single office may process several hundred consumer bankruptcies a year. Several large firms of trustees also operate across Canada.

[38] Up to now most of the trustees have been male.

debtor's interests.[39] Nevertheless, despite the importance of the issue, it has so far attracted little public attention.[40]

Legally, the trustee is also accountable to the estate's creditors. In practice, most unsecured creditors take little interest in the administration of the estate since they know that ordinarily very little will be left of the estate after the claims of secured creditors and preferred creditors, and the trustee's fees and disbursements, have been satisfied.[41] Where the debtor's estate amounts to less than CAN$10,000 (it was CAN$5,000 before 1998), the estate may be administered summarily ('summary administration').[42] This reduces the role of creditors in the administration of the estate still further. The statistics show that 90 per cent or more of consumer bankruptcies are administered summarily.

The court structure under the Canadian bankruptcy system differs fundamentally from the US structure and the structure of other federal systems. Canada has no separate system of bankruptcy courts.[43] Instead, the superior courts in each of the provinces and territories are invested with plenary bankruptcy jurisdiction.[44] Rights of appeal lie from their decisions to the provincial or territorial courts of appeal and thence to the Supreme Court of Canada.[45] In practice, a bankruptcy judge will seldom be involved in a consumer bankruptcy and then only at the discharge stage if the discharge is opposed, as usually it is not.

5. INITIATING A CONSUMER BANKRUPTCY PROCEEDING

It is very easy for a Canadian consumer to go bankrupt[46] under the BIA. The simple qualifying requirements under Canadian law are that the consumer must be insolvent, must reside or have property in Canada, and that his or her debts amount to CAN$1,000 or more.[47] In terms of the procedural formalities, all that

[39] As, eg, in determining the debtor's income under s 68 or filing a report under s 170.1 on the debtor's conduct since the debtor's bankruptcy.

[40] The issue is briefly referred to in the PITF Report, but was discounted because most of the Task Force members could see no conflict. Prof Iain Ramsay and this author dissented. See PITF Report (n 26 above) at 99–100, and Chapter 8.3(d) below for further discussion of the issue.

[41] For the ranking of their claims, see BIA, s 136(1)(b).

[42] BIA, s 49(6). The consequences of a summary administration are spelled out in BIA, s 155.

[43] Canada has a system of federal courts encompassing the Federal Court of Canada (FCC), with a trial and appellate division, and the Supreme Court of Canada. The Supreme Court of Canada is the final appellate tribunal on questions of provincial as well as federal law. The jurisdiction of the FCC is limited to matters of federal law and does not include bankruptcy law. The reason for this anomaly is historical. The FCC was only established in 1971 and, at this late date, it would have been very unpopular politically for the federal government to transfer bankruptcy jurisdiction to the federal courts. It should also be appreciated that under Canada's constitution all superior court judges are appointed by the federal government (Constitution Act 1867, s 96). This explains why the federal government felt quite comfortable about leaving bankruptcy jurisdiction in provincial court judges' hands.

[44] BIA, s 183(1).

[45] BIA, s 183(2) and (3).

[46] By which is meant the ease of acquiring the status of a bankrupt and not the quite separate question of obtaining a discharge from the debtor's liabilities.

[47] BIA, s 49(1) and s 2, definition of 'insolvent person'.

is that is required is a written assignment—a standard document running to a couple of pages accompanied by a preliminary statement of affairs, the nomination of a trustee who has agreed to act (rarely a problem since trustees advertise widely), and 'acceptance' of the assignment by the official receiver.[48] The official receiver cannot refuse his acceptance if the documents are in order. A modest filing fee is payable but it only amounts to CAN$75 for summary administration estates and CAN$150 for regular administrations.[49] In addition, the trustee will expect the debtor to assume responsibility for the trustee's fees and expenses if the estate contains few assets. This is likely to prove a much more serious obstacle for insolvent consumers with little or no discretionary income (the great majority) and no non-exempt assets from which the fees and expenses can be met.[50]

There is no enquiry or mandatory examination after the assignment and before the appointment of the trustee, as there used to be under the British bankruptcy system, to determine the circumstances leading to the bankruptcy. However, at the time of the first interview with the debtor the trustee is required to conduct an assessment of the debtor's financial position and to explain to the debtor the various options open to the debtor to deal with the debtor's problems.[51] Nevertheless, the final decision of which route to pursue rests with the debtor. The Canadian Act has no precise counterpart to the 'abuse' provision in s 707(b) of the American Code. Section 181(1) of the Canadian Act confers a seemingly open-ended jurisdiction on the Canadian bankruptcy court to annul an assignment and this is used intermittently to set aside an assignment by a debtor who was not insolvent.[52] However, there are no reported cases of the

[48] BIA, s 49(3), (4), Bankruptcy and Insolvency General Rules ('BIA Rules') SOR/98–240, s 1, Rule 85, and Forms 22 and 23. Section 49(4) requires the Official Receiver to appoint a trustee selected, so far as possible, by reference to the most interested creditors if ascertainable at the time. The practice has long been otherwise and the assignment completed by the debtor invariably includes the name of the trustee consulted by the debtor. In recognition of this practice, the PITF Report recommends that BIA, s 49(4) be amended to provide that the Official Receiver shall appoint as trustee the person designated in the assignment. See PITF Report (n 26 above) at ch 3(VII).

[49] BIA Rules, s 132(1)(a). Before 2001, the filing fee was CAN$50. The BIA Rules contain no provision for *in forma pauperis* filing by an indigent debtor. It has not been an issue up to now.

[50] The trustees' fees and disbursements are regulated under the BIA Rules. For the applicable tariff in summary administration cases, see Rule 128. Before 1997 trustees relied heavily on income tax refunds payable to the estate to cover a substantial part of their fees, but this source was cut off by amendments to the Income Tax Act. However, the 1997 amendments have provided trustees with a new source of income to the extent that the debtor is obliged to make surplus income payments to the trustees under revised s 68 and supporting directive. Under BIA, s 136(1)(b) the trustee's fees and disbursements have first claim on the estate among the claims of preferred creditors. From the trustee's perspective, the difficulties arise where the debtor has no surplus income under the Superintendent's standards in which case the trustee may rely on the debtor's collateral promise to make good any deficiency. On the enforceability and status of such debtor promises, see *Re Berthelette* (1999) 174 DLR (4th) 577 (Manitoba CA), and JS Ziegel, 'Financing Consumer Bankruptcies, *Re Berthelette*, and Public Policy' (2000) 33 *Canadian Business Law Journal* 294. The topic attracted prolonged discussion in PITF and the Task Force ultimately decided that a fee agreement between the trustee and bankrupt without surplus income should be enforceable up to prescribed limits even after the bankrupt's discharge: PITF Report (n 26 above) ch 3(III). The author dissented from this recommendation.

[51] OSB, Policy Statement 6R, 30 April 1998.

[52] See, eg, *Re Wale* [1996] OJ No 4489, (1996) 45 CBR (3d) 15 (Ont).

discretion being exercised because the consumer could have made a viable pro-posal.[53]

This apparent pro-debtor position must not be misconstrued. It does not mean that everything is plain sailing once the debtor has made her assignment. Rather, as will be explained hereafter, as a result of the 1997 amendments to the BIA, she may face two formidable hurdles. First, if she has 'surplus' income she will be required to pay it over to the trustee.[54] Secondly, if the trustee is of the view that she could have made a viable proposal to her creditors under BIA, Part III 2 and so reports to the bankruptcy court,[55] the court may not be willing to grant her an unconditional discharge.[56]

6. SCOPE OF THE BANKRUPTCY ESTATE

(a) General Rule

Under the Canadian Act, the trustee succeeds after the debtor's assignment to all of the debtor's property unless exempted.[57] 'Property' is defined non-exhaus-tively in the Act and includes all real and personal property, present and future, and wherever located.[58] It is this comprehensive definition and its extension to after-acquired property that provides the historical explanation for what Americans see as a major deviation in Anglo-Canadian law from the fresh start policy.[59] At bottom, however, the distinction between Canadian and US law turns on the requirements of a fresh start policy and at what point in time the debtor should be entitled to an unconditional discharge from her debts.

(b) Exempt Property

Modern bankruptcy systems agree that the debtor must not be stripped of all his assets. The debtor and his family must be allowed to keep the basic necessities

---

[53] The case law is collected in LW Houlden and C Morawetz, *Bankruptcy and Insolvency Law of Canada* (3rd edn, Toronto, Carswell, 1992) D§32 ('Houlden and Morawetz'). The court also has a general jurisdiction under BIA, s 187(5) to review, rescind or vary any order made under its bank-ruptcy jurisdiction. This power does not seem to apply to an assignment since an assignment does not derive its force from a court order.

[54] BIA, s 68 as amended in 1997. The surplus income payment requirements are discussed in 2.7 below.

[55] BIA, s 170.1(2)(c).

[56] The discharge rules are discussed in 2.8 below.

[57] BIA, s 71(2).

[58] BIA, s 2(1) ('property'). See also BIA, s 67(1)(c), (d). (Property of debtor divisible among the debtor's creditors includes all property wherever situated at the date of bankruptcy or that may be acquired by or devolve on the debtor before the debtor's discharge; and includes property over which the debtor has a power of appointment that could be exercised for the debtor's own benefit.)

[59] The reason being that §§541, 522 of the US Bankruptcy Code only vest in the debtor's estate all non-exempt legal and equitable interests of the debtor in property 'as of the commencement of the case' (§541(a)(1)). There are modest exceptions.

of life and to enable the debtor to pursue his or her livelihood. Canadian law however goes farther than present US law in allowing the scope of the exemptions to be determined by provincial law.[60] This is itself a historical anomaly that was not seriously questioned until recently.[61] There is no optional list of federal exemptions in the Canadian Act as there is under §522 of the American Code. The Canadian provinces differ widely in their exemption policies, although not as widely as the American states differ among themselves. In overall impact, Alberta and Saskatchewan confer the most generous exemptions with British Columbia arguably ranking third.[62] Among the provinces, prior to amendments adopted in 2000,[63] Ontario had the dubious distinction of having the lowest exemptions.

Figure 2.1 tracks the provincial bankruptcy rates against the provincial exemptions. US authors have frequently debated the impact of high exemptions on bankruptcy rates; the better view appears to be that there is no consistent correlation between the level of exemptions and the number of bankruptcies. As Figure 2.1 shows, this also appears to be true of the Canadian provinces for the 1991–96 period. Ontario, with the then lowest provincial exemptions, had above average bankruptcy rates. Saskatchewan, with the highest exemptions, had below average bankruptcy rates.

With respect to the actual exemptions permitted under provincial or territorial law, as of 1998 the jurisdictions differed widely with respect to the aggregate value of the exemptions for individual debtors and also in the availability of particular types of exemptions.[64] All the jurisdictions recognised exemptions involving household goods and personal effects and tools of the trade. However, not all of them recognised motor vehicles as falling into an exempt category (unless the motor vehicle could be treated as a tool of trade) and not all of them perceived the debtor's equity in a homestead as deserving even of minimal protection. On the other hand, the Prairie provinces (Manitoba, Saskatchewan and Alberta) were generous in protecting the acreage and homesteads of farmer debtors. None of the Canadian jurisdictions has embraced the concept of a 'wild card' exemption entitling a debtor to an aggregate dollar figure of exemptions

---

[60] BIA, s 67(1)(b).

[61] The incorporation of provincial exemption standards in the Canadian Bankruptcy Act 1919 may have been influenced by the US Bankruptcy Act 1898, which adopted the exemptions obtaining in the debtor's state of residence at the time of bankruptcy. The PITF Report (n 26 above) at ch 2(III) recommended an optional federal exemptions list that a Canadian bankrupt would be entitled to adopt at the time of bankruptcy in preference to the provincial standards that would otherwise apply.

[62] In 1997, the aggregate exemptions available in Alberta amounted to CAN$59,000, those in Saskatchewan to CAN$62,000. See (1999) 37 *Osgooode Hall Law Journal* 205 at 258 (Appendix). In both cases, the total figure includes a large exemption for the debtor's residence. British Columbia's third place is warranted because of amendments adopted in 1998.

[63] See SO 2000, c 26, Sched A, s 8.

[64] See (1999) 37 *Osgoode Hall Law Journal* 205, 258 (Table A-1). Since then there have been significant changes in several of the jurisdictions, notably in Ontario, but the table remains accurate in indicating the disparate treatment of exemptions among the provinces and territories.

Figure 2.1: 1991–96*

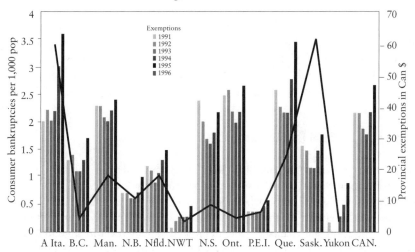

A Ita. B.C. Man. N.B. Nfld.NWT N.S. Ont. P.E.I. Que. Sask.Yukon CAN.

*Chart prepared by Victor Liu, LLB, University of Toronto (1999), under Professor Ziegel's supervision.

Notes:

(1) Vertical bars indicate consumer bankruptcies per 1,000 population for each province for the years 1991–96 (inclusive).

(2) White 'star-points' indicate the available exemptions from seizure for each province based on current exemption levels in that province. For the purposes of Figure 2.1, an assumption is made that no significant change in exemptions occurred during the 1991–96 period (inclusive).

(3) For details of actual provincial exemptions, see (1999) 37 *Osgoode Hall Law Journal* 205, 258, appendix.

(4) Source of consumer bankruptcies per 1,000 population: Bankruptcy Branch, Industry Canada.

which the debtor is free to allocate among designated real and personal property as she sees fit.[65]

[65] Apparently no study has been conducted in Canada on the impact of disparate provincial exemptions on consumer bankruptcies, but the following sample of 900 summary administration estates filed in 1998 and completed as of 8 December 2000 provides some idea of the aggregate impact of the existing exemptions:

	Median exempt value	No of estates	Median non-exempt value	No of estates
Cash	$150.00	5	$200.00	298
Furniture	$1,687.50	536	$1,000.00	15
Personal Effects	$500.00	287	$430.00	16
Life Insurance	$2,000.00	35	$600.00	58
Securities	$3,911.48	38	$800.00	61
Real Property – House	$86,000.00	50	$75,000.00	191
Real Property – Cottage	n/a	n/a	$51,000.00	2
Real Property – Land	n/a	n/a	$5,000.00	11
Automobile	$1,500.00	222	$1,775.00	302

Source: OSB Ottawa. Note that real property values refer to the estimated value at the time of bankruptcy and not to the value of the debtor's equity in the property.

The Canadian jurisdictions show remarkable unanimity in their treatment of life insurance annuities and registered pension plans—both are exempt from seizure, in and outside bankruptcy, regardless of the value of the annuity or pension plan at the time of bankruptcy.[66] These exemptions do not apply to 'registered retirement savings plans' (RRSPs),[67] a popular form of personal savings plan in Canada for self-employed individuals, partners, executives and others, but there is much pressure to give them equivalent status.[68]

(c) Optional Federal Exemptions

As previously mentioned, the PITF Report recommends the inclusion of a federal exemptions list in the BIA which a bankrupt would be free to adopt in lieu of the provincial exemptions. Debtors would have to make their election promptly following the bankruptcy. The Task Force's rationale in making the recommendation was to ensure that all bankrupts, wherever located in Canada, would have the benefit of a reasonable set of exemptions. The Task Force felt it would be premature to recommend the enactment of a mandatory schedule of exemption to the exclusion of a provincial role. The specific exemptions and exemption levels recommended in the Report are:[69]

---

[66] The availability of the exemption is a strong incentive to insolvent debtors to convert liquid assets to an insurance annuity shortly before declaring bankruptcy. This has been held to be a voidable settlement but is nevertheless protected as provincially exempt property under BIA, s 67(1)(b). See *Ramgotra (Trustee of) v North American Life Assurance Co* (1996) 132 DLR (4th) 193 (SCC).

[67] RRSPs enjoy a privileged tax treatment but can be collapsed before maturity, in which case they become fully taxable. See Income Tax Act, RSC 1985, c 1 (5th Supp) as amended, s 146.

[68] See PITF Report (n 26 above) at ch 2(II). The Report supports giving RRSPs exempt status in bankruptcy, subject to a three-year claw back of payments made into the plan before bankruptcy, and provided the plan is promptly locked in on bankruptcy. There would also be an upper limit on the eligible RRSP. See also Alberta Law Reform Institute, *Creditors' Access to Future Income Plans*, (Consultation Memorandum No 11, June 2002) (http://law.ualberta.ca/alri). The Task Force spent a considerable amount of time discussing the treatment of RRSPs in bankruptcy. However, it is important to bear in mind that only a small percentage (almost certainly less than 10%) of summary administration bankrupts have a RRSP and the median value is very modest. See OSB Ottawa (2001), *sample of 900 summary administration estates files in 1998 and completed as of 8 December 2000* (n 65 above) (35 of the bankrupts had an exempt interest in a life insurance policy or RRSP with a median value of $2,000; 58 of the bankrupts had such a non-exempt interest with a median value of $600. Under provincial law, RRSPs do not generally enjoy exempt status). An informed debtor with a substantial RRSP would ordinarily be expected to collapse the plan before going bankrupt or to opt for a consumer proposal. If the debtor chooses the latter option, there is the risk that the creditors may insist on the plan being cashed in as a condition of giving their approval to the proposal but the creditors may relent if the terms of the proposal look reasonable to them.

[69] PITF Report (n 26 above) at ch 2(III). The format of the table has been modified by the author.

(1) Apparel and household furnishings	CAN$7,500
(2) Medically prescribed aids and appliances and medicationfor use or consumption by the debtor or the debtor's family	No Limit
(3) One motor vehicle whether used for personal, trade or business purposes	CAN$3,000
(4) Tools of the trade and professional books but *not* including motor vehicles used in the trade or business	CAN$10,000
(5) Debtor's residence, defined to include a house, apartment, mobile home and house boat	CAN$5,000
(6) Real and personal property used by a debtor whose livelihood is derived from farming, fishing, forestry and other activities related to the natural resource sector of the economy. The amount of the exemption should be governed by applicable provincial/territorial law	CAN$10000–$20,000

This list is, and was intended to be, a compromise between those members of the Task Force who questioned the wisdom of federal intervention in this area and those who felt it was both justified and necessary. The group drafting the specific recommendations considered the desirability of a 'wild card' option but ultimately rejected it.

(d) Status of Secured Claims

Canadian consumer bankruptcy law is much more favourable to secured creditors than is US law. There is no automatic stay in a straight bankruptcy for the debtor's benefit against the enforcement of a security interest as there is under §362 of the US Bankruptcy Code. In Canada, the trustee can apply for a stay which, if granted, cannot exceed six months.[70] There is a similar but more expanded provision in the case of a consumer proposal under BIA, Part III 2.[71] It only has a limited effect because a secured creditor is not bound by a proposal, even if it has been accepted by the other creditors, unless the secured creditor has filed a proof of claim.[72] The BIA has no counterpart to §522(f)(1)(B) of the US

[70] BIA, s 69.3(2). Business debtors have much more significant protection under s 244 requiring a secured creditor holding a security interest in all or substantially all of the debtor's inventory, accounts receivable or other property to give the debtor 10 days' notice before enforcing the security interest. For the history of this restriction see JS Ziegel, 'Canada's Phased-In Bankruptcy Law Reform' (1996) 70 *American Bankruptcy Law Journal* 383, at 399.

[71] BIA, s 69.2(4).

[72] BIA, s 66.28(2)(b). Debtors under a BIA, Part III 1 commercial proposal are better off because secured parties can be included in a proposal without their consent. However, the proposal will not bind the secured creditors unless they approve it by the requisite majority in number and value of claims. Secured creditors in a commercial proposal are subject to an automatic stay under BIA, s 69(1) and 69.1(1) to give the debtor an opportunity either to raise the money to pay off the secured

Code allowing the debtor to avoid a non-possessory non-purchase money lien in household furniture, professional books, tools of the trade and similar items excluded from the bankrupt's estate. However, the exemption legislation in several of the Canadian provinces invalidates non-purchase money security interests in exempted property.[73]

As interpreted by the Supreme Court of Canada,[74] the BIA also recognises a security interest in the debtor's post-bankruptcy property granted by the debtor before bankruptcy if the security interest is valid under the relevant provincial law. However, this rule is subject to two exceptions. First, BIA, section 68.1 invalidates any pre-bankruptcy wage assignment or assignment of professional fees or payment for services rendered by the debtor so far as it affects post-bankruptcy entitlements. Secondly, in a controversial decision,[75] the Supreme Court also held that a security interest in after-acquired property is discharged on the debtor's discharge from bankruptcy if the property is acquired by the debtor after the discharge.

So far as rights of redemption under the Canadian legislation are concerned, in a straight bankruptcy that right is conferred on the Canadian trustee under section 128(3) of the BIA on payment of the debt or the value of the security as assessed by the secured party. However, it is not clear to what extent this right also inures for the benefit of the debtor. With respect to rights of reinstatement of the security agreement after default by the debtor, many of the provincial Personal Property Security Acts contain varying rights of reinstatement in favour of consumer debtors.[76] Presumably, these rights survive the consumer's bankruptcy, at least in the case of property excluded from the trustee's reach under section 67(1) of the Act. In the case of a consumer proposal, section 69.2(4) of the BIA also appears to confer an implicit right of reinstatement in the consumer's favour, not limited to residential real estate, in the case of security for a debt that does not become due until more than six months after the date of approval or deemed approval of the proposal. However, the right is contingent

---

claims or to allow the debtor to persuade the secured creditors that they will be better off accepting the debtor's proposal. The position under a BIA, Part III 2 proposal is ambiguous because of the provisions in ss 66.34 and 66.4(1).

[73] It has been held in Ontario that the exemptions in the Execution Act, RSO 1990, c E 24 do not apply to secured parties enforcing their security, only to creditors levying execution against the debtor's property. See *Re Vantore* (1995) 20 DLR (3d) 653 (Ont Gen Ct). The PITF Report (n 26 above) at ch 2(IV) recommends avoidance of all non-purchase security interests in exempted property intended for the personal use or consumption of the debtor or the debtor's family, including apparel, household furnishings and motor vehicles.

[74] *Holy Rosary Parish (Thorold) Credit Union Ltd v Premier Trust Co* [1965] SCR 503.

[75] *Holy Rosary Parish (Thorold) Credit Union Ltd v Bye* (1967) 61 DLR (2d) 88, as interpreted in *Re Pelyea* (1969) 11 DLR (3d) 35 (Ont CA). See further JS Ziegel, 'Post-bankruptcy Remedies of Secured Creditors: Some Comments on Prof. Buckwold's Article' (1999) 32 *Canadian Business Law Journal* 142, at 149ff *et seq*; the reply by Prof. Buckwold (2000) 33 *Canadian Business Law Journal* 128; and the rejoinder by JS Ziegel (2000) 33 *Canadian Business Law Journal* 144.

[76] For Ontario, see Ontario Personal Property Security Act (OPPSA), RSO 1990, c P 10, as amended, s 66(2).

on the court first issuing a stay of proceedings by the secured creditor. If issued, the stay cannot exceed six months.[77]

Based on the above summary, we may fairly conclude that the Canadian Act has so far paid very little attention to the needs of insolvent consumers occupying a mortgaged home, or holding a motor vehicle, essential household items and other property subject to a security interest and necessary for the debtor's livelihood or his welfare and that of his family. However, the practical position may not be as bad as the black letter law suggests it is. It appears that trustees will often co-operate in allowing the debtor's budget to include payments on secured claims for essential items, including payments on a home mortgage and vehicle, and that secured creditors will be equally amenable to such arrangements because it usually also serves their interests.[78]

7. SURPLUS INCOME PAYMENT REQUIREMENTS

(a) Current Statutory Position

Reference has already been made to the 1997 amendments to section 68 of the BIA requiring the trustee to fix the amount of the debtor's income that the debtor is required to pay to the trustee for distribution among the creditors in accordance with standards established by the Superintendent of Bankruptcy. To appreciate the practical and conceptual significance of this important change, a brief description is required of the earlier position.

The concept of requiring the debtor to pay over surplus income already appeared in the British Bankruptcy Act 1914.[79] However, the requirement was not triggered until the court made such an order on the trustee's application. In practice, it appears, trustees generally abstained from using this power but preferred to wait until the debtor made his discharge application.[80] The debtor's quest for an easy discharge order was regarded as sufficient incentive for him to turn over part of his surplus income voluntarily before the discharge hearing. If the trustee made an application for an income payment order, one of the factors required to be taken into consideration by the court were 'essential' expenditures incurred by the debtor for the maintenance of the debtor, his family and

---

[77] A further difficulty arises because it is not clear whether s 69.2(4)(b) applies where the secured party has invoked an acceleration clause, thereby taking the debt out of para (b) and bringing it under para (a) as a debt due at the date of approval. Section 66.34(1) invalidates acceleration clauses based on the consumer debtor's insolvency or the fact of a proposal having been filed. However, given the history and origins of the section, it is likely that it was only meant to apply to executory contracts and not to security agreements.

[78] However, it is not clear to what extent these sensible practices can be continued having regard to the surplus income payment requirements under revised s 68 and the OSB's cost of living standards under that section. See 2.7 below.

[79] BIA, s 51. See further *Report of the Review Committee on Insolvency Law and Practice* ('Cork Report') (Cmnd 8558, London, June 1982), ss 591–98.

[80] *Ibid.*

dependants. This formula still appears in the current British Insolvency Act 1986.[81]

The Canadian story is more complicated. As previously indicated, section 67(1)(c) of the BIA and its predecessors have long provided that, subject to the authorised exemptions, the debtor's present and future property belongs to the estate. However, there was considerable uncertainty whether 'property' included the debtor's income. In *Industrial Acceptance Corp v Lalonde*,[82] the Supreme Court of Canada held that it did.

The result was regarded as unsatisfactory since it meant either that the trustee could require the debtor to turn over all of the debtor's income or that the debtor was only entitled to claim the applicable exemptions under provincial non-bankruptcy law. To clarify the position, section 68 was added to the BIA in 1966[83] authorising the trustee, and requiring him to do so if required by the inspectors, to make an application to the court for an income payment order. Initially the amendment only applied to the debtor's earnings from employment but was subsequently enlarged to include other forms of remuneration. The court was given complete discretion in responding to the application 'having regard to the family responsibilities and personal situation of the debtor.' In a later decision, the Supreme Court of Canada held that section 68 constituted a complete code with respect to the trustee's power to attach a debtor's earnings.[84]

In practice, the result appears to have been very similar to the British experience—in consumer cases trustees were reluctant to exercise their powers because it was time-consuming, because the trustees were poorly paid for such efforts, and because there was no consistency in the payment orders made by courts.[85] In 1991, the Superintendent of Bankruptcy sought to bring some moral suasion to bear on trustees by issuing a directive that incorporated the Superintendent's 'Guidelines' for calculating surplus income.[86]

This is where matters stood when Working Group 1 of the Advisory Committee (BIAC) established by the federal government in 1993 to make recommendations with respect to Phase II of the revision of the BIA reviewed the position. Because of creditors' unhappiness with the current operation of the section, section 68 was completely revised to add powerful muscle to the section to make sure that future debtors paid over their surplus income and that trustees would not neglect their obligations.[87] Some sense of the importance which the

---

[81] Insolvency Act 1986, s 310; IF Fletcher, *The Law of Insolvency* (3rd edn, London, Sweet & Maxwell, 2002) 8–025–028. See also below ch 5(2)(b).

[82] [1952] 2 SCR 109.

[83] SC 1966–67, c 32, s 10.

[84] *Marzetti v Marzetti* [1994] 2 SCR 765.

[85] The pre-1998 case law is summarised in Houlden and Morawetz (n 53 above) at F§52.

[86] OSB Directive No 17R2, 10 January 1991. The directive was revised on 2 April 1993.

[87] Nevertheless, the author does not share Prof Telfer's or Prof Ramsay's views that revised s 68 has brought about a reconceptualisation of the role of discharge in bankruptcy or that a new view of debtor rehabilitation has emerged. See TGW Telfer, 'Access to the Discharge in Canadian Bankruptcy Law and the New Role of Surplus Income: An Historical Perspective' in CEF Rickett

federal officials attached to these goals may be gleaned from the sheer length of revised section 68: no less than 14 subsections, to which must be added another four printed pages in the OSB's supporting directive of 30 April 1998, as modestly amended on an annual basis to take account of changes in Statistics Canada's compilation of income requirements for low-income individuals and families (LICO).[88]

The following are the key features of section 68 and the directive. The trustee is initially responsible for determining the debtor's monthly income and the income of the members of his family, if living with the debtor, after deducting expenses reflecting the debtor's personal and family situation as well as the expenses of the family members.[89] The recognised expenses cover statutory payments for income taxes and such like and include non-discretionary expenses such as child support and spousal maintenance payments.[90]

The trustee must next determine the debtor's available surplus income by consulting the Superintendent's Standards showing the allowable living expenses for a person in the debtor's personal or family situation. These standards are based on Statistics Canada annual tables of low-income family units (LICO), a family unit being considered as falling into a low-income category when its income is substantially below other family units.[91] As of January 2002, the cost of living allowance was CAN$1,602 for a single person, CAN$2,002 for a couple, and CAN$2,490 for a family of three. The directive also provides that where the total monthly surplus income of the debtor is equal to or greater than CAN$100 and less than CAN$1,000, the debtor is required to pay 50 per cent of the surplus income as calculated under the directive. If the surplus income is CAN$1,000 or greater than CAN$1,000, the trustee must require the debtor to

---

and TGW Telfer (eds), *International Perspectives on Consumers' Access to Justice* (Cambridge University Press, forthcoming); and IDC Ramsay, 'Models of Consumer Bankruptcy: Implications for Research and Policy' (1997) 20 *Journal of Consumer Policy* 269 at 271. The writer believes that a more persuasive explanation is that revised s 68 is the creditors' and OSB's response to concerns over the rapidly expanding number of consumer bankruptcies and trustees' failure to use their surplus income collection powers effectively as urged in the Superintendent's 1991 directive. The Superintendent and the creditors may have hoped that the prospect of mandatory surplus income payments would stem the tide of bankruptcies, but this hope has not been realised.

[88] For the current directive, see OSB Directive No 11R, effective 1 November 2000.

[89] OSB Directive No 11R, s 4(1).

[90] *Ibid* at ss 6(2) and 6(3).

[91] LICOs are set according to the proportion of annual family income spent on food, shelter and clothing. A Canadian family with average income currently spends 44% of its after-tax income on food, clothing, shelter and other basic necessities. A low-income family is deemed one that spends 64% of its income this way. See further Bernard Paquet, *Low Income Cutoffs from 1992 to 2001 and Low Income Measures from 1991 to 2000* (Statistics Canada, November 2002, Cat. No. 75F0002MIE2002005). Statscan insists that LICO does not measure poverty in Canada since there is no objective way to measure poverty, nationally or internationally. In addition to the LICO tables, Statscan also publishes 'low income measures' tables identifying Canadian family units whose income is 50% of the median Canadian family unit income. Another low-income bench-mark, 'market-basket measure', related to families unable to afford a shopping basket of basic life necessities, is currently being contemplated for adoption by the Canadian government. See Margaret Philp, 'New Poverty Gauge Based on Survival' *The Globe and Mail*, 9 January 2003, A3.

pay over at least CAN$500 and may require the debtor to pay up to 75 per cent.[92] The surplus income amount may be amended by the trustee from time to time to take into account material changes that have occurred in the personal or family situation of the bankrupt.[93] The official receiver may also 'recommend' to the trustee and the bankrupt changes to the amount to be paid by the bankrupt where he is of the view that the amount is substantially not in accordance with the applicable standard.

It is important to emphasise that the directive applies a uniform standard of cost of living allowances for all debtors in the same family situation regardless of their social, economic or geographic background and location.[94] Seemingly, the trustee has no discretion in varying the debtor's living needs unless somehow it can brought under the rubric of non-discretionary expenses. If the debtor and the trustee cannot agree on the amount required to be paid by the debtor, the trustee must request mediation of the parties' dispute.[95] If mediation has not resolved the issue, the trustee may apply for a court hearing.[96] Mediation has so far been invoked very sparingly.[97] If there is a court hearing, it is not clear, however, how much discretion the bankruptcy court has in determining the amount of the debtor's surplus income. Section 68(10) of the BIA requires the court to act in accordance with the standards established in section 68(1) (ie, the standards set by the Superintendent) and 'having regard to the personal and family

---

[92] OSB Directive No 11R, s 7(2)(a)(b). In case of a family unit with more than one income, the debtor's surplus income is prorated as a percentage of the total family income. *Ibid* at s 8, and Example (family unit of one).

[93] BIA, s 68(4). There has been uncertainty with respect to the status of income earned by the bankrupt prior to bankruptcy but received by him after bankruptcy, and with respect to the treatment of non-periodic lump sum payments. The Supreme Court of Canada held in *Marzetti v Marzetti* [1994] 2 SCR 765 and in *Wallace v United Grain Growers* [1997] 3 SCR 701 that it is the characterisation of the entitlement, and not solely the date of accrual, that is material for ss 67 and 68 purposes, and these holdings have been applied by lower courts in a wider range of cases. See, eg, *Re Landry* (2000) 21 CBR (4th) 58 (Ont CA); and further, R Klotz, 'Who Gets the Bankrupt's Pre-bankruptcy Earnings?' (2000) 15 CBR (4th) 153.

So far as the treatment of lump sum payments is concerned, lower courts have generally held that it is a question for the court's discretion. See *Re Laybolt* (2001) 27 CBR (4th) 97 (Nova Scotia). The PITF Report (n 26 above) at ch 3(I) recommends clarification of BIA, ss 67–68 to address both issues.

[94] During the discussions preceding the adoption of the directive, CIPA (since renamed as the Canadian Association of Insolvency and Restructuring Professionals (CAIRP)) urged the adoption of differential scales depending on the debtor's province of residence and the size of the community of the debtor's residence, but its efforts were unsuccessful. The pre-1998 Guidelines also drew no geographical distinctions with respect to differences in the cost of living within a province and between the provinces. This silence influenced the court's decision in *Re Demyen* (1999) 4 CBR (4th) 67 (Sask QB) in rejecting the trustee's argument that the debtor should be required to hand over a larger share of his income because the cost of living in Regina, Saskatchewan, was lower than elsewhere in Canada.

[95] BIA, s 68(6).

[96] BIA, s 68(10)(b). The subsection does not confer a similar right of appeal on the bankrupt but this must be an oversight in the drafting. The subsection also does not explain when mediation is deemed not to have resolved an issue.

[97] Between 1 October 1999 and 17 July 2002, there were 130 mediations across Canada involving surplus income disputes and 125 involving bankruptcy discharge issues. (Information derived from table supplied by OSB to author, 26 July 2002.)

situation of the debtor'. These criteria seem to be the same as those incumbent on trustees. As a result, unless courts are willing to massage the quoted words beyond their intended meaning or somehow to find that the Superintendent's standards are too rigid, debtors may find that section 68 has forced them into a procrustean bed.

(b) Results of Surplus Income Payment Requirements

A substantial body of data is now available on the operation of the Canadian surplus income requirements and is partly reproduced in Table 2.1. The data are important because Canada is the only jurisdiction in the three Commonwealth countries with income contribution requirements surveyed in this study that has developed this much detail. Table 2.1 shows the overall results from the 257,116 consumer bankruptcies filed between 1 August 1998 and 31 December 2001 and indicates that 19.06 per cent of the consumer bankrupts had surplus incomes calculated in accordance with the Superintendent's directive. Further, 90.71 per cent of the consumer bankrupts made section 68 payments to their trustees at or above the prescribed levels; only 9.29 per cent of them failed to do so.

Table 2.2 shows the same results organised regionally by provinces and territories. The table shows wide variations in surplus incomes among the provinces. Surplus incomes in the Atlantic provinces, Manitoba and Saskatchewan, are up to 50 per cent and more less than the corresponding figures for Alberta, British Columbia and Ontario. British Columbia ranked highest with an average surplus income for the period under review of 25.33 per cent. Prince Edward Island came in lowest at 9.12 per cent. It seems reasonable to attribute the lower surplus incomes figures for Prince Edward Island and the other provinces to the average lower incomes obtaining in the Atlantic provinces, Manitoba and Saskatchewan.

Table 2.3 and Figure 2.2 tell yet another important story, and show the amount of surplus income required and agreed to be paid by the consumer bankrupts organised by province and territory in bands of CAN$100. They reveal that, nationally, 55.6 per cent of the payments are below CAN$200, the mean figure being CAN$240.16 and the median figure a still more modest CAN$180.00.

Despite the low average and median surplus income figures, the OSB feels that section 68 is meeting its intended purpose. This is because there are a significant number of debtors with surplus incomes and because the great majority of them have agreed to make the prescribed payments and are actually making them. The record of payments is much better than the performance of debtors opting to make a consumer proposal under BIA, Part III 2. In the latter case, the failure rate has fluctuated between 25.6 and 41.7 per cent.[98] Though

---

[98] See 2.12 below.

Table 2.1: Total Consumer Bankruptcy Population and Surplus Income Estates for
Canada and the Provinces from 1 August 1998 to 31 December 2001: Overall Results*

		Total population	Total SI estates	At or above standard	% At or above	Below standard	% below	% with SI
Canada	1998†	29,375	4,975	4,310	86.63%	665	13.37%	16.94%
	1999	73,124	14,015	12,636	90.16%	1,379	9.84%	19.17%
	2000	75,142	14,228	13,015	91.47%	1,213	8.53%	18.93%
	2001	79,475	15,796	14,502	91.81%	1,294	8.19%	19.88%
	Total	257,116	49,014	44,463	90.71%	4,551	9.29%	19.06%

*Source: OSB (Ottawa, January 2003).
† The 1998 numbers represent 1 August 998 to 31 December estates only.

Table 2.2: Total consumer bankruptcy population and surplus income estates for
Canada and the Provinces from 1 August 1998 to 31 December 2001: by province*

Province		Total population	Total SI estates	At or above standard	% At or above	Below standard	% below	% with SI
Newfoundland	1998†	396	10	10	100.00%	0	0.00%	2.53%
	1999	1,330	161	144	89.44%	17	10.56%	12.11%
	2000	1,557	192	175	91.15%	17	8.85%	12.33%
	2001	1,901	225	193	85.78%	32	14.22%	11.84%
	Total	5,184	588	522	88.78%	66	11.22%	11.34%
Nova Scotia	1998†	993	50	43	86.00%	7	14.00%	5.04%
	1999	2,650	297	271	91.25%	26	8.75%	11.21%
	2000	2,816	282	236	83.69%	46	16.31%	10.01%
	2001	3,440	385	323	83.90%	62	16.10%	11.19%
	Total	9,899	1014	873	86.09%	141	13.91%	10.24%
Prince Edward Island	1998†	68	3	3	100.00%	0	0.00%	4.41%
	1999	157	12	11	91.67%	1	8.33%	7.64%
	2000	182	15	14	93.33%	1	6.67%	8.24%
	2001	174	23	20	86.96%	31	3.04%	13.22%
	Total	581	53	48	90.57%	5	9.43%	9.12%
New Brunswick	1998†	444	17	13	76.47%	4	23.53%	3.83%
	1999	1,214	125	114	91.20%	1	18.80%	10.30%
	2000	1,393	153	130	84.97%	23	15.03%	10.98%
	2001	1,748	176	170	96.59%	6	3.41%	10.07%
	Total	4,799	471	427	90.66%	44	9.34%	9.81%
Quebec	1998†	10,193	1636	1363	83.31%	273	16.69%	16.05%
	1999	23,322	4406	3926	89.11%	480	10.89%	18.89%
	2000	23,170	4154	3801	91.50%	353	8.50%	17.93%
	2001	24,111	3988	3639	91.25%	349	8.75%	16.54%
	Total	80,796	14184	12729	89.74%	1455	10.26%	17.56%

Province		Total population	Total SI estates	At or above standard	% At or above	Below standard	% below	% with SI
Ontario	1998†	9,682	1775	1575	88.73%	200	11.27%	18.33%
	1999	23,279	4574	4168	91.12%	406	8.88%	19.65%
	2000	23,591	4734	4275	90.30%	459	9.70%	20.07%
	2001	25,919	5892	5367	91.09%	525	8.91%	22.73%
	Total	82,471	16975	15385	90.63%	1590	9.37%	20.58%
Manitoba	1998†	946	107	99	92.52%	8	7.48%	11.31%
	1999	2,475	235	230	97.87%	5	2.13%	9.49%
	2000	2,477	262	258	98.47%	4	1.53%	10.58%
	2001	2,492	468	438	93.59%	30	6.41%	18.78%
	Total	8,390	1072	1025	95.62%	47	4.38%	12.78%
Saskatchewan	1998†	595	39	35	89.74%	4	10.26%	6.55%
	1999	1,618	156	153	98.08%	3	1.92%	9.64%
	2000	1,834	162	144	88.89%	18	11.11%	8.83%
	2001	2,027	222	209	94.14%	13	5.86%	10.95%
	Total	6,074	579	541	93.44%	38	6.56%	9.53%
Alberta	1998†	3,104	584	533	91.27%	51	8.73%	18.81%
	1999	8,799	1836	1622	88.34%	214	11.66%	20.87%
	2000	8,844	2028	1897	93.54%	131	6.46%	22.93%
	2001	8,110	2044	1918	93.84%	126	6.16%	25.20%
	Total	28,857	6492	5970	91.96%	522	8.04%	22.50%
British Columbia	1998†	2,930	751	635	84.55%	116	15.45%	25.63%
	1999	8,181	2191	1979	90.32%	212	9.68%	26.78%
	2000	9,173	2234	2078	93.02%	156	6.98%	24.35%
	2001	9,489	2365	2217	93.74%	148	6.26%	24.92%
	Total	29,773	7541	6909	91.62%	632	8.38%	25.33%
North West Territories	1998†	15	2	0	0.00%	2	100.00%	13.33%
	1999	59	13	11	84.62%	2	15.38%	22.03%
	2000	64	8	6	75.00%	2	25.00%	12.50%
	2001	36	7	7	100.00%	0	0.00%	19.44%
	Total	174	30	24	80.00%	6	20.00%	17.24%
Yukon	1998†	9	1	1	100.00%	0	0.00%	11.11%
	1999	40	9	7	77.78%	2	22.22%	22.50%
	2000	41	4	1	25.00%	3	75.00%	9.76%
	2001	28	1	1	100.00%	0	0.00%	3.57%
	Total	118	15	10	66.67%	5	33.33%	12.71%

Source: OSB, (Ottawa, January 2003).
† The 1998 numbers represent 1 August 1998 to 31 December 1998 estates only.

Table 2.3: Consumer surplus income filings in 2001, estates with surplus income required and agreed to pay > 0 by province*

	Total	Less than CAN$100		CAN$100–$200		CAN$200–$300		CAN$300–$400		CAN$400–$500		CAN$500–$600	
		Total	%	Total	%	Total	%	Total	%	Total	%	Total	%
NF	1,901	11	4.9%	127	57.0%	38	17.0%	23	10.3%	8	3.6%	8	3.6%
NS	3,440	14	3.7%	212	56.5%	71	18.9%	38	10.1%	25	6.7%	8	2.1%
PEI	174	1	4.5%	11	50.0%	6	27.3%	3	13.6%	0	0.0%	1	4.5%
NB	1,748	3	1.7%	120	68.6%	28	16.0%	11	6.3%	4	2.3%	3	1.7%
QC	24,111	233	6.2%	2040	54.0%	773	20.5%	315	8.3%	180	4.8%	90	2.4%
ON	25,919	403	7.0%	2803	48.8%	1232	21.5%	568	9.9%	305	5.3%	188	3.3%
MB	2,492	44	9.5%	265	57.2%	84	18.1%	41	8.9%	10	2.2%	10	2.2%
SK	2,027	14	6.4%	118	53.6%	46	20.9%	25	11.4%	9	4.1%	4	1.8%
AB	8,110	58	2.9%	887	44.6%	456	22.9%	247	12.4%	137	6.9%	94	4.7%
BC	9,489	100	4.3%	1041	44.8%	600	25.8%	253	10.9%	138	5.9%	77	3.3%
NWT	36	0	0.0%	1	14.3%	2	28.6%	3	42.9%	0	0.0%	0	0.0%
YK	28	0	0.0%	1	100.0%	0	0.0%	0	0.0%	0	0.0%	0	0.0%
Canada	79,475	881	5.8%	7626	49.8%	3336	21.8%	1527	10.0%	816	5.3%	483	3.2%

	Total	CAN$600–$700		CAN$700–$800		CAN$800–$900		CAN$900–$1000		Greater than CAN$1000	
		Total	%	Total	%	Total	%	Total	%	Total	%
NF	1,901	4	1.8%	3	1.3%	0	0.0%	1	0.4%	0	0.0%
NS	3,440	4	1.1%	0	0.0%	3	0.8%	0	0.0%	0	0.0%
PEI	174	0	0.0%	0	0.0%	0	0.0%	0	0.0%	0	0.0%
NB	1,748	5	2.9%	1	0.6%	0	0.0%	0	0.0%	0	0.0%
QC	24,111	49	1.3%	30	0.8%	23	0.6%	10	0.3%	32	0.8%
ON	25,919	91	1.6%	62	1.1%	37	0.6%	20	0.3%	33	0.6%
MB	2,492	3	0.6%	5	1.1%	0	0.0%	0	0.0%	1	0.2%
SK	2,027	3	1.4%	0	0.0%	1	0.5%	0	0.0%	0	0.0%
AB	8,110	37	1.9%	23	1.2%	14	0.7%	13	0.7%	22	1.1%
BC	9,489	52	2.2%	20	0.9%	15	0.6%	6	0.3%	22	0.9%
NWT	36	1	14.3%	0	0.0%	0	0.0%	0	0.0%	0	0.0%
YK	28	0	0.0%	0	0.0%	0	0.0%	0	0.0%	0	0.0%
Canada	79,475	249	1.6%	144	0.9%	93	0.6%	50	0.3%	110	0.7%

Source: OSB, (Ottawa, January 2003).

Figure 2.2: Individual consumer surplus income filings in 2001 by
CAN$100 bands for all of Canada*

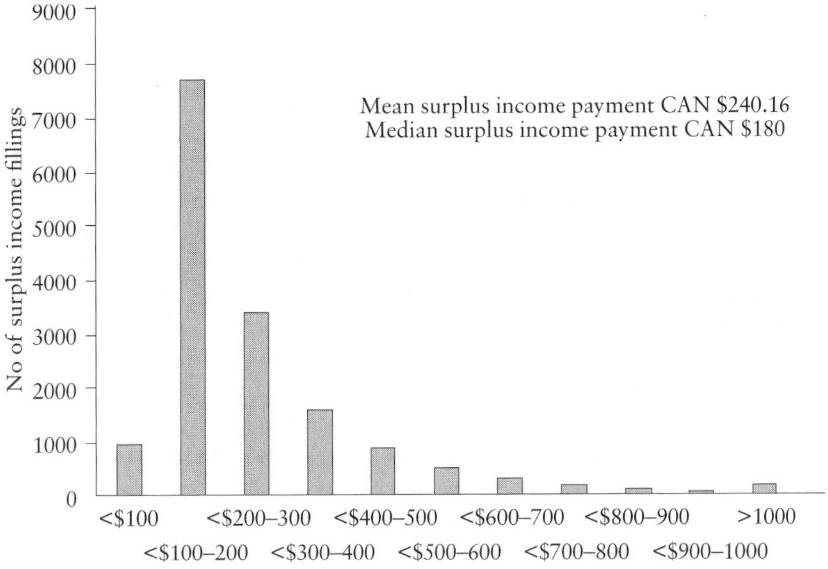

Mean surplus income payment CAN $240.16
Median surplus income payment CAN $180

Source: OSB (Ottawa, January 2003).
Note: the title of the chart has been adjusted slightly by the author.

this is conjectural, the superior performance of surplus income bankrupts may be due to a number of factors. One is the short period—nine months for most bankrupts—for which debtors must maintain their payments compared with the average length of three years for consumer proposals. Another factor is that the amount of surplus income payments is objectively defined in the Superintendent's directive and cannot be adjusted by the bankrupt to meet his individual wishes or circumstances. In a consumer proposal, on the other hand, debtors may take an unrealistic view of their future capacity to pay in order to ensure that creditors will not reject their proposals.

It is also safe to assume that Canadian creditors continue strongly to support the surplus income regime despite the evidence that they actually derive little direct pecuniary benefit from it.[99] They may feel that it sends an important

---

[99] One set of figures shows that surplus income received by the estate from files with surplus incomes in a sample of 900 summary administration files only amounted to an average of CAN$103.13 or 3.6% of total receipts or 0.4% as a percentage of the receipts from all 900 files: OSB Ottawa, *Study of Receipts and Disbursements. Sample of 900 Summary Administration Estates. Preliminary Results* (2001) 16. Median receipts from all sources for all 900 files amounted to CAN $1,795.13; the average was CAN $2, 460.84; 64.9% of the disbursements went to pay trustees' fees. Dividends paid to creditors amounted to 17.3% of the disbursements or CAN $310.56 per file of median receipts of CAN $1,795.13. *Ibid.*

message to debtors that bankruptcy does not provide a painless exit and that it encourages over-indebted consumers with higher surplus incomes to opt for a consumer proposal in place of a straight bankruptcy.

(c) Comparison with Schwartz/Anderson and Ramsay Findings

It is helpful to compare the section 68 results with the empirical findings in the studies by Schwartz and Anderson (1998),[100] and by Iain Ramsay (1996).[101] In the Schwartz/Anderson study, the overall median net monthly income of the debtors from all sources at the time of the debtors' meeting with the trustee was CAN$1,400, or CAN$16,800 if projected on an annual basis.[102] By way of comparison, in 1995 the Statistics Canada low-income cut-off (LICO) for a single adult living in a large urban area was CAN$16,874; for a family of four it was CAN$31,753.[103] Only about 37 per cent had a monthly income that was greater than their monthly expenses and the amounts were usually quite small. The 70th percentile was CAN$49 per month.[104] Prof Swartz concludes that relatively few debtors—'perhaps 10 or 15 percent'[105]—had significant amounts of surplus income, and that estimate does not take into account any special circumstances relevant to those debtors.

Prof Ramsay's sample was restricted to debtors who had filed for bankruptcy in the Toronto Bankruptcy District. The income figures might therefore be expected to be different from those in the Schwartz/Anderson sample, which was national in scope. His sample showed a median monthly net household income of CAN$1,700 or CAN$20,400 if projected over a whole year.[106] The latter figure compares with the median 1994 after-tax income of the general Ontario population of CAN$34,561. With respect to surplus income, less than one-third of the sample had surplus income of any kind at the time of declaring bankruptcy. Of the 332 debtors who had a surplus monthly income, the median was CAN$105.77 debtors, and just over 6 per cent of the total sample, had a surplus income of over CAN$300.[107]

The Schwartz/Anderson and Ramsay findings are consistent with the section 68 surplus income results reported by the OSB. However, the data must be seen in context. They do not show that the debtors were abusing the system and could have paid off their debts without going into bankruptcy. In the

---

[100] S Schwartz and L Anderson, *An Empirical Study of Canadians Seeking Personal Bankruptcy Protection* (Ottawa, Industry Canada, 1998).

[101] IDC Ramsay, 'Individual Bankruptcy: Preliminary Findings of a Socio-Legal Analysis' (1999) 37 *Osgoode Hall Law Journal* 15.

[102] S Schwartz, 'Symposium' (1999) 37 *Osgoode Hall Law Journal* 83, at 96.

[103] *Ibid*.

[104] The 80th and 90th percentiles were CAN$139 and CAN$259 respectively. *Ibid*.

[105] *Ibid*.

[106] Ramsay (n 101 above) at 15, 33.

[107] *Ibid* at 35.

Schwartz/Anderson sample, the median value of total liabilities was CAN\$26,016 compared with median assets of CAN\$3,000.[108] In Prof Ramsay's sample, 'consumer debtors' had median liabilities of CAN\$32,649[109] but a majority of the bankrupts (60.8 per cent) had assets valued at less than CAN\$5,000; about 37 per cent of them had assets valued at less than the provincial exemption from seizure of household effects of CAN\$2,000.[110] If we ignore the debtors' largely nominal value assets and concentrate on their surplus income, even if one assumes net monthly surplus income averaging CAN\$200, it would have taken the debtors in the two samples 10 to 15 years to pay off debtors' median liabilities (assuming no change in their personal circumstances during the payment period).

(d) Extension of the Nine Months' Period

The PITF Report[111] recommends that, on the trustee's recommendation, the nine months' basic surplus income payment period be extended by another 12 months. The criteria used to determine the number and amounts of additional payments will be established by the Superintendent's directive and will apparently allow trustees a limited amount of discretion in special cases in which the extra payments would create 'severe hardship' for the bankrupts.

The Report's rationale for this important recommendation is as follows. As part of his section 170 report accompanying the bankrupt's deemed discharge application under section 168.1 of the BIA, the trustee is required to include a recommendation as to whether or not the bankrupt should be discharged subject to conditions, having regard to the bankrupt's conduct and ability to make payments.[112] In practice, it seems, trustees only recommend an extended period of payments by the bankrupt in substantially less than 7 per cent of discharge applications.[113] Nevertheless, trustees felt they were being targeted by debtors seeking assurances that the trustees would not recommend extended periods of surplus payments if their services were retained. The trustees hoped that the injection of a strong objective element into the extended payment requirement would relieve them from this pressure. The PITF Report does not indicate how much surplus income would justify an extended order, the impact an extended order will have on the bankrupt's willingness to maintain the payments, and the relationship between extended orders and consumer proposals. These issues are

---

[108] Schwartz (n 102 above) at 103.

[109] Ramsay (n 101 above) at 52, Table 10.

[110] Ramsay (n 101 above) at 46, Table 7 and accompanying text. Ontario's exemption for household effects was raised in 2000 to CAN\$5,000.

[111] At ch 3(IV).

[112] BIA, s 170.1(1).

[113] It is less than 7% because 7% represents the approximate total percentage of all objections to discharge raised by trustees. Many, if not most of the objections, involve unpaid trustees' fees and the bankrupt's failure to complete the counselling sessions.

not theoretical since there is ample evidence, in Canada and elsewhere, that there is a strong correlation between failure rates and the duration of a surplus payment requirement or consumer proposal.[114]

8. THE CANADIAN DISCHARGE SYSTEM

We come now to what is the single most important difference between the Canadian and US insolvency systems—the way in which the two countries approach the debtor's right to be discharged from further payment of her debts after the initiation of bankruptcy proceedings. The Canadian developments will be dealt with in this section; the US position and the current Congressional proposals to change it will be discussed in Chapter 3 below.

As previously explained, the discharge provisions in the 1919 Canadian Bankruptcy Act were largely copied from the provisions in the British Bankruptcy Act 1914 Act, which in turn were based on the Bankruptcy Act 1883. The US fresh start model was rejected because of its laxity, which one critic described as a 'sort of constant jubilee'.[115] The essential features of the 1919 Act were the following. The debtor could apply for a discharge at any time.[116] When he did, the court had complete discretion in dealing with the application unless the debtor had committed an offence or had otherwise misconducted himself, or if the realisable assets were worth less than 50 cents in the dollar. If these restrictions did not apply, the court could grant or refuse the discharge, suspend the discharge or make a conditional discharge order linked to the debtor's future earnings or the debtor's income or after-acquired property.[117] The court had to refuse the application or suspend it for two years if the debtor had committed a bankruptcy offence.[118]

The 1949 Act[119] introduced an important procedural change in deeming the bankrupt to have made a discharge application no earlier than three months after the bankruptcy order and no later than 12 months. In the case of a first time individual bankrupt, the 1992 amendments[120] simplified the procedure still further in deeming the application to be made nine months from the date of the bankruptcy order unless the debtor had waived this entitlement.

From the beginning, a discharge application was accompanied by a report from the trustee about the debtor's conduct and the factors leading to the debtor's bankruptcy. The 1997 amendments retained this requirement and tightened it substantially.[121] The trustee is now also required to report (a) on

---

[114] See ch 2.12 below and Chapter 3 below.
[115] L Duncan, *The Law and Practice of Bankruptcy in* Canada (Carswell, 1922) 38.
[116] Bankruptcy Act 1919, ss 58–59.
[117] *Ibid,* s 58(4).
[118] *Ibid.*
[119] SC 1949, c 7, s 127.
[120] SC 1992, c 27, s 61(1), adding s 168.1(1)(f) to the parent Act.
[121] SC 1997 c 12, ss 100–101. See now BIA, ss 170–170.1.

whether the debtor had made the required surplus income payments, (b) whether the debtor could have made a viable proposal, and (c) to provide the court with the trustee's own recommendations. In setting up this seemingly complex discharge structure, the federal Parliament was obviously striving to strike a balance between enabling a 'poor and unfortunate' Canadian debtor to make a fresh start and sending a strong signal to debtors that debts could not be sloughed off easily regardless of the debtor's financial circumstances, past conduct and capacity to make future payments. Nevertheless, on paper at least, the provisions were, and remain, heavily creditor-oriented and retain a nineteenth century anti-discharge bias.

The actual practice has been very different and tells a markedly different story about the universe of over-committed debtors seeking relief from the burden of debt. For many years, between 80–90 per cent of discharge applications involved no-asset cases and an absolute or automatic discharge was granted in the great majority of cases. For example, in 1998, out of a total of 83,431 discharge applications, 79,999 (96 per cent) involved summary estates and 3,432 regular estates.[122] Of the combined cases, 60,178 (72.1 per cent) resulted in an automatic discharge; 17,736 (21 per cent) were given an absolute discharge and 5,480 (6.5 per cent) a suspended discharge. Only 14 received a conditional discharge (0.0016 per cent) and only four applications[123] were refused. By way of comparison, Prof. Ramsay reports[124] the following results from 1,118 discharge applications in his sample of 1994 bankrupts: 85.4 per cent were unopposed; of those who opposed the application, 5.7 per cent were creditors, 8.6 per cent were trustees, and 0.3 per cent came from the Superintendent of Bankruptcy. Apparently, most of the trustees' opposition related to non-payment of the trustee's fee and expenses or the debtor's failure to complete the mandatory counselling sessions. Commercial creditors rarely file an opposition to the application. For example, a search of *Quicklaw* entries for the 1992–98 period produced a list of 104 reported oppositions, of which all but 20 related to non-payment of student loans.[125]

9. OPPOSED APPLICATIONS

Before the 1997 amendments, it seems that, in the relatively few creditor oppositions that came before them, Canadian courts made a conscientious effort to

---

[122] Roundtable on Recent Consumer Bankruptcy Developments, *Materials for Distribution, 21 July 1999* (Faculty of Law, University of Toronto, Convenor: JS Ziegel) 6 (hereafter Roundtable Materials).

[123] The table refers to 'Hearing refused', which the writer interprets to mean 'Application refused'.

[124] Ramsay (n 101 above) at 69.

[125] *Quicklaw* is a leading Canadian electronic database for Canadian judgments. Undoubtedly, there were more than 104 oppositions. *Quicklaw* generally only reports cases in which a written judgment has been rendered.

distinguish between different types of debt: consumer debts versus commercial debts, tort claims versus contractual debts, debts owing to government agencies versus private sector debts (to cite some of the distinctions) as well as to the debtor's conduct and culpability if any. The courts often also reaffirmed the need to balance the public interest with the debtor's need to rehabilitate herself and to start a new economic life.[126] Nevertheless, the results varied greatly and the courts were not bound by any statutory standards. It is this feature of the pre-1997 position that most concerned Canadian creditors and that has attracted the criticism of US observers of the Commonwealth discharge system.

It is unclear how far the 1997 amendments have changed the scope of the court's discretion in dealing with discharge applications, and in particular how far a judge is free to discount the trustee's report that the debtor was in breach of section 68 of the BIA or that the debtor could have made a viable proposal. If the trustee's report is conclusive on these issues, how far does it tie the hands of the court in disposing of the discharge application? On the strength of sections 172(2) and 173(1)(m) and (n),[127] it seems clear that the court cannot grant an unqualified discharge even if the court believes this to be the best solution. The court must either dismiss the application or, more realistically, make a conditional order. If the court opts for a conditional order requiring future payments by the debtor, is the court bound to apply the Superintendent's standards? Section 172(2) does not so provide. However, if the court is free to ignore the standards, this may establish a double standard of liability for debtors: one governed by section 68 before the discharge application and the other by whatever conditional order the court deems appropriate in the circumstances. A Canadian appellate court still has to rule on these important constructional issues.

10. NON-DISCHARGEABLE DEBTS

(a) General Overview

All of the common law jurisdictions exclude various types of liability from the reach of a discharge order; this has been true of the Canadian legislation from

---

[126] For a leading case setting forth a list of the criteria, see *McAfee v Westmore* (1988) 23 BCLR 273 (CA).

[127] These provisions read as follows:

s 172(2) The court shall on proof of any of the facts mentioned in section 173:

    (*a*) refuse the discharge of a bankrupt;

    (*b*) suspend the discharge for such period as the court thinks proper; or

    (*c*) require the bankrupt, as a condition of his discharge, to perform such acts, pay such moneys, consent to such judgments or comply with such other terms as the court may direct.

s 173(1) The facts referred to in section 172 are: . . .

    (m) the bankrupt has failed to comply with a requirement to pay imposed under section 68;

    (n) the bankrupt, if the bankrupt could have made a viable proposal, chose bankruptcy rather than a proposal to creditors as the means to resolve the indebtedness;

the beginning. Table 2.4 shows the current list of Canadian exclusions[128] in a comparative setting. The Canadian list is only half the length of the US list but not as short as the Australian or British lists. The rationales for the exclusions vary and have not received much discussion in Canada. The first exclusion in the BIA (fine or penalty in criminal proceedings) presumably is intended to maintain the integrity of the criminal justice system. The second exclusion, a damage award for intentional bodily harm or sexual assault, is apparently grounded in a belief that protection of the victims in such cases outweighs the bankrupt's claim to a fresh start. A similar sentiment seems to underlie the sixth exclusion involving a debt or liability arising from false representations. However, this exclusion can be manipulated (as it has been in the past) by unscrupulous creditors and used as a collection device even though the debtor has received a discharge.

(b) Student Loans[129]

Particularly troubling is the final and most recent exclusion, which was only added in 1998. The value of student loans by federal and provincial governments tripled between 1990 and 1995 from CAN$768.5 million to CAN$2,131.5 million.[130] Student loans also figured prominently in the liability of debtors in the Schwartz/Anderson survey. The authors found that 25.3 per cent of potential bankrupts had student loans and that among young people (32 per cent of the sample were under 30) the percentage was 45 per cent.[131] For 28 per cent of the young people, student loans represented 50% or more of the overall debt.

Before 1997, student loans did not feature at all in the Canadian list of non-dischargeable debts. However, there was mounting governmental concern over the number of student borrowers seeking bankruptcy relief and section 178(1)(g) was added as part of the 1997 package of amendments.[132] Subsection 1(g) provided that a discharge was not available in respect of a federally or provincially sponsored student loan before the expiration of two years after the student ceased to be a full or part-time student. Even where the two year requirement had been met, the student was only entitled to have the debt discharged if the court was satisfied (a) that the debtor had acted in good faith in dealing with his loan liabilities, and (b) that the debtor had and would continue to experience such financial difficulties that the debtor would be unable to repay the loan.

---

[128] BIA, s 178 as amended. The PITF Report (n 26 above) at ch 3(X) recommends some modest amendments to the section.

[129] For a detailed discussion of this issue, see S Schwartz, 'The Dark Side of Student Loans' (1999) 37 *Osgoode Hall Law Journal* 307.

[130] Schwartz (n 102 above) at 109, Table 7.

[131] *Ibid* at 117.

[132] SC 1997, c 12, s 105(2).

Table 2.4: Comparative table of non-dischargeable debts in bankruptcy*

Canada	Australia	England and Wales	United States
BIA s 178 as am.	**Bankruptcy Act, s 153(2); (2A)**	**Insolvency Act 1986, s 281(3)–(6)**	**Bankruptcy Code 1978 as am., § 523**
(1) Any fine, penalty or restitution order imposed in respect of offence.	(1) A debt on a recognisance or bail bond in criminal proceedings.	(1) Debt arising out of fraudulent conduct.	(1) Income, property, employment or excise debts for varying periods.
(2) Damage award for intentional bodily harm or sexual assault.	(2) Liability to make contributions to trustee from bankrupt's income.	(2) Criminal fines, but not penalties for public revenue offences.	(2) Debt relating to fraudulent conduct.
(3) Debt or liability for alimony.	(3) Debt incurred through fraud or fraudulent breach of trust.	(3) Liability for personal (injuries, damages for negligence, nuisance, or breach of a statutory, contractual or other duty, except as otherwise directed by court.	(3) Creditors not disclosed by debtor.
(4) Debt or liability for support or maintenance order or agreement for support of spouse or child.	(4) Liability under maintenance agreement or maintenance order, but court may grant relief from arrears in payment.	(4) Debt arising under order in family or domestic proceedings.	(4) Debt for fraud while acting in a fiduciary capacity, or for embezzlement or larceny.
(5) Debt or liability for fraudulent conduct while acting in a fiduciary capacity.	(5) Debt owed for pecuniary penalty order.	(5) Other bankruptcy debts as prescribed by regulation.	(5) Debt owed for alimony, maintenance or support of spouse or child pursuant to agreement or order.
(6) Debt or liability for obtaining property by false pretences or fraudulent misrepresentation.			(6) Debt for wilful and malicious injury to entity or property of entity.
(7) Liability to creditor for debt not disclosed to trustee to extent of creditor's entitlement to a dividend.			(7) Debt for fine, penalty or forfeiture to governmental unit relating to tax (other than under (1) above or imposed for transaction within three years).

Canada	Australia	England and Wales	United States
(8) Debt for governmental loan or guarantee made for educational purposes. No discharge before 10 years after bankrupt ceased to be full- or part-time student.			(8) Debt incurred for educational purposes, except for debt more or in cases of hardship.
			(9) Debt for death or personal injury caused by the debtor's operation of a motor vehicle while intoxicated.
			(10) Debt listed by the debtor in a prior bankruptcy case in which the debtor waived discharge, or was denied a discharge.
			(11) Debt owed to a financial institution due to fraudulent act while acting in a fiduciary capacity.
			(12) Debt for malicious or reckless failure by debtor to fulfil commitment to maintain capital of federal depository institution.
			(13) Debt for payment of restitution order under title 18.
			(14) Debt incurred to pay tax to the United States that would be non-dischargeable pursuant to (1).
			(15) Debt not of the kind described in (5) that is incurred by the debtor in the course of a divorce or separation unless non-discharge will cause hardship to debtor.

Table 2.4 (cont.):

Canada	Australia	England and Wales	United States
			(16) Debt for a fee or assessment to a membership association for co-operative housing and condominiums.
			(17) Debt for a fee imposed by a court to cover court costs. Debt owed under (18) state law to a state or municipality that is in the nature of support and isenforceable under the US Social Security Act.

* This table was prepared in 1998 under the author's supervision by Martha Hundert, then a University of Toronto law student and now an associate with McCarthy Tétrault in Toronto. (The author has made some clarificatory changes to the table.)

The federal government obviously had second thoughts about the adequacy of this solution. Without prior warning, the government introduced a further amendment to section 178 as part of the 1998 budget resolution increasing the period in section 178(1)(g) from two years to 10 years.[133] This radical change in bankruptcy policy provoked much criticism from student groups, the Canadian Bar Association, and many trustees on the grounds of its harshness for students unable to find suitable jobs on graduation, and has also led to constitutional challenges under the Canadian Charter of Rights and Freedoms.[134] The student concerns found a responsive chord with the Personal Insolvency Task Force and its report recommends[135] allowing student debtors to apply for a discharge of the student loan five years after completion of the study programme and even earlier with the court's permission, in cases of hardship.

[133] SC 1998, c 21, s 103. To offset the impact of the amendment on student debtors, the 1998 federal budget introduced a new and very large scholarship programme (the Millennium Scholarship Fund) and provided various relief measures under the Canada Student Loans Program for students experiencing difficulties in making payments.

[134] *Roundtable Materials* (n 122 above) at 7.

[135] PITF Report (n 26 above) at ch 2(I). The basis of the Charter challenge is that the 1998 amendment is discriminatory and therefore violates s 15 of the Charter. See Canadian Federation of Students (CFS) Bankruptcy Charter Challenge (http://www.cfs-fcee.ca/new_campaigns/bankruptcy.shtml) (last accessed 12 September 2002).

11. CANADIAN ALTERNATIVES TO STRAIGHT BANKRUPTCY

An insolvent Canadian consumer seeking relief from her indebtedness other than through bankruptcy[136] has the following options. She may elect to seek a statutory consolidation of her debts under Part X of the BIA or make a proposal to her creditors under Part III 2 of the BIA.[137] The critical difference between a statutory consolidation and a proposal under Division 2 is that a consolidation order provides for no remission of any part of the debt whereas Division 2 clearly contemplates it although it is not mandatory.[138] Still another route open to Canadian debtors is to seek the assistance of a non-profit debt repayment and credit counselling service, such as the ones that have been active in Ontario for more than 30 years,[139] or of a commercial debt adjustment service. Credit counselling agencies are strongly supported by Canadian creditors. Undoubtedly they provide an important service but their overall impact on the Canadian consumer insolvency scene is modest since, apart from their counselling functions, they only act as debt pro-rating agencies; they have no power themselves to grant debt relief and do not ordinarily seek remission from any part of their clients' debts. Their job is to obtain creditors' acceptance to a payment plan over an agreed number of years.

Part X of the BIA has its genesis in orderly payment of debts legislation adopted in Manitoba during the Depression and subsequently copied in Alberta.[140] In a 1960 decision,[141] the Supreme Court of Canada held the legislation ultra vires the provinces as an encroachment on the federal government's exclusive insolvency

---

[136] Recall that in Canada a debtor who opts for a reorganisational proposal under Part III of the BIA, or a consolidation order under Part X, is not treated as a bankrupt person though the bankruptcy rules will apply where appropriate. See BIA, s 66(1).

[137] The consumer may also make a proposal under BIA, Part III 1 and must do so if her total indebtedness, excluding a mortgage debt on the consumer's principal residence, exceeds CAN$75,000: BIA, s 66.11. Until 1992, only one set of provisions were available for both commercial and consumer proposals. What is now Part III 1 was extensively revised in the 1992 BIA amendments and a new Division 2 was added to cater to consumer needs.

[138] See BIA, s 66.11, definition of 'consumer proposal' and s 2, definition of 'proposal'.

[139] The largest and oldest of the credit counselling agencies in Ontario is Credit Counselling Service of Toronto, which was established in 1965. There are now 27 non-profit credit counselling agencies in Ontario who are members of an umbrella organisation, the Ontario Association of Credit Counselling Services (OACCS). 'Credit counselling' is a misnomer since from the beginning the agencies have been equally active in running debt management programmes for the benefit of debtors and their creditors. For example, in fiscal year 1998 the OACCS opened 13,944 new counselling cases and 4,275 new debt management files. CAN$22.5 million was distributed to creditors under debt management plans: *OACCS Statistical Highlights 1998*. The debt repayment programme of the OACCS members has assumed much greater importance since the withdrawal of provincial financial support in March 1992 and the enhanced reliance of the agencies on financial contributions from creditor members of individual agencies. For further details, see the excellent research paper by Andrew C Dekany, *Consumer Debt Counselling in Canada* (Major Research Paper for Osgoode Hall Law School LLM Programme, September 1999).

[140] Quebec adopted a similar law much earlier, known as the Lacombe Law, which is still part of the Quebec Code of Civil Procedure. See Code, Book IV, arts 652–659.

[141] *Reference re Validity of the Orderly Payment of Debts Act 1959 (Alberta)* [1960] SCR 571 (Canada).

jurisdiction. This forced the federal government to introduce legislation of its own and it did so in 1965 by adding Part X to the BIA. Part X only applies to those provinces which have elected to adopt it; only six provinces have done so.[142] The total number of consolidation orders made in 1998 amounted to 1,539, or only about 2 per cent of the number of personal bankruptcies declared that year.

Division 2 of Part III was added as part of the major amendments to the BIA in 1992 to give insolvent consumer a more flexible and attractive reorganisational vehicle than Part X. The hope has been realised. The number of consumer proposals filed in 1995, 2,419,[143] was only 341 more than the number of Part X orders. It grew to 4,737 in 1997 and jumped to 13,383, or 16.8 per cent of the number of consumer bankruptcies, in 2001.[144] This is still well below the almost 30 per cent ratio of chapter 13 plans to chapter 7 filings in the United States, but a great improvement over the number in the earlier years. The increased filings are almost certainly due to the 1997 amendments to the BIA and the new surplus income payment provisions in section 68. Another probable reason is that as a result of the change in fee structure introduced in the BIA Rules in 1998,[145] trustees have a much stronger incentive to recommend a consumer proposal than they had before. However, there is also a grey side to the picture. There was a high failure rate in the first three years of the new proposal provisions: 39.3 per cent in 1993, 41.7 per cent in 1994, and 35.1 per cent in 1995.[146] The failure rate was much lower in 1997 and 1998: 25.6 per cent in 1997, 16 per cent up to 30 April 1998 and 13.7 per cent after 30 April.[147] The PITF Report[148] quotes a failure rate of 31.5 per cent, as of 20 June 2002, for proposals made between 1 May 1998 and 3 December 2000 and a failure rate of 34.1 per cent for proposals filed between 1 May 1998 and 30 April 1999.[149]

There appear to be various reasons for the lesser apparent popularity of BIA, Part III 2 proposals in Canada as compared to the popularity of chapter 13 in the United States. Part III 2 has a much lower monetary ceiling than chapter 13 and only covers aggregate debts up to a maximum of CAN$75,000, excluding debts secured by the debtor's principal residence, or as prescribed by regulation.[150] Still more important is the fact that a secured creditor cannot be included in a

---

[142] For the list, see Industry Canada, Office of the Superintendent of Bankruptcy, *Annual Statistical Summary for the 1995 Calendar Year*, 38, and cf BIA, s 242.

[143] *Ibid*, Table 4B, at 6.

[144] OSB, *Annual Statistical Report* 2001, 4–6.

[145] BIA Rules, Rule 129, applicable to proceedings commenced after 30 April 1998.

[146] Email to author from Trent Craddock of the OSB Office, 9 March 2000.

[147] *Ibid.*

[148] PITF Report (n 26 above) at ch 1, n 7.

[149] Another set of figures appears in OSB, *Study of Characteristics of Personal Insolvencies. Sample of 500 Division II Proposals filed June 1, 1998 to December 31, 1998, Preliminary Results and Comparison with Sample of 900 Summary Administration Estates Filed in 1998 and Closed as of December 8, 2000* (June 2001) Table 6 and Chart 5. As of 12 June 2001, 23.2% of the proposals were 'unsuccessfully completed' and 10.2% were 'ongoing failed', for a total of 33.4%.

[150] BIA, s 66.11. Cf US Bankruptcy Code §109(e). The PITF Report (n 26 above) at ch 3(II), recommends consumer access to BIA, Part 2 without a monetary ceiling but with a ceiling of CAN$100,000 on business debts owed by individual debtors.

proposal without the secured creditor's consent.[151] In practice, debtors appear to be able to work their way around this difficulty;[152] nevertheless, the exclusion of secured claims weakens a debtor's rehabilitational prospects. Another important difference between BIA, Part III 2 and US chapter 13 is that a Canadian proposal requires creditor consent before it can become effective.[153] On the other hand, approval of the proposal by the court is not a precondition in Canada, as it is of a plan under chapter 13 in the United States, unless in Canada the administrator or other interested party requests a court hearing.[154]

BIA, Part III 2 is also stricter than chapter 13 in dealing with breaches of the terms of an approved proposal. On application, the Canadian court may annul a proposal that is in breach as well as for other reasons, and if an annulment order is made the debtor is deemed to have made an assignment in bankruptcy.[155] Still more important, there is an automatic annulment where the debtor has been in default of monthly payments for more than three months,[156] but it does not also result in a deemed bankruptcy.[157] A Canadian judge, unlike his US colleague, has no power to grant the debtor a discharge from the debtor's remaining debts because of the hardship to the debtor in being required to continue with the proposal.[158] Even if the Canadian debtor successfully completes the terms of the proposal, he still faces the same number of non-dischargeable debts as he would in a straight bankruptcy; unlike an American debtor,[159] the Canadian debtor receives not even partial relief.

12. OPERATIONAL ASPECTS OF CONSUMER PROPOSALS AND COMPARISON WITH SUMMARY ADMINISTRATION RESULTS

In June 2001, the OSB published the preliminary results of a very valuable study of the characteristics of a sample of 500 Division 2 proposals and compared them with a sample of 900 summary administration bankruptcy cases. The study merits detailed examination but the following highlights must suffice for the purposes of this chapter. The median monthly income of consumer proposal debtors was CAN$2,437 (median annual income CAN$29,444) compared with

---

[151] BIA, s 66.28(2)(b).

[152] Typically by providing in the proposal that the debtor will continue to make payments to secured creditors as before. However, this approach only works if the debtor's surplus income is large enough to cover monthly payments to both secured and unsecured creditors.

[153] The creditors' consent is assumed if 25% or more of the creditors do not require a meeting and if a meeting is not asked for by the official receiver: BIA, ss 66.14(b)(iv), 66.15(2), 66.17, 66.18.

[154] BIA, s 66.22(1).

[155] BIA, s 66.3(1), (5)(a). Cf US Bankruptcy Code §1307(c) (court *may* convert a chapter 13 case to a chapter 7 case).

[156] BIA, s 66.31(1).

[157] Houlden and Morawetz (n 53 above) at E§35.12.

[158] US Bankruptcy Code §1328(b). It seems that in practice US courts are reluctant to grant this relief.

[159] US Code §1328(a) and cf *In re Kourtakis*, 75 BR 183 (Bankr ED Mich 1987); E Warren and JL Westbrook, *The Law of Debtors and Creditors* (4th edn, Little, Brown & Co, 2001) 426–27.

CAN$1,710 (annual income CAN$20,520) for the bankrupt individuals.[160] There was a similar difference in the average value of assets held by the two cohorts: CAN$54,079.45 in the case of proposals and CAN$29,815.62 for the bankrupts.[161] This difference was equally reflected in the value of types of assets (houses, autos, life insurance policies/RRSP plans etc) held by the cohorts and the frequency with which an item appears among the insolvent's assets. There was very little difference between the mean liabilities of the two groups (consumer proposals, CAN$69,076.67; summary administration cases, CAN$68,641) but there was over a 40 per cent difference between their median liabilities (CAN$46,057 and CAN$32,673 respectively).[162] In terms of the types of liabilities, there is an arresting inversion. Average unsecured liabilities are a third higher for the summary administration bankrupts (CAN$44,277) as compared with the consumer proposal debtors (CAN$31,024.74), but secured liabilities of the latter group are 50 per cent higher than for the bankrupts (CAN$38,343.95 and CAN$24,364 respectively).[163] In short, the study corroborates the intuition that consumers with higher incomes and more assets to protect will gravitate towards proposals whereas asset and income poor consumers will choose bankruptcy. A final point of comparison is also worth making: it is based on this study and on another OSB study involving surplus income payments.[164] These show median monthly payments of CAN$290.00 in case of consumer proposals and CAN$180.16 for surplus income payments.

13. REAFFIRMATION AGREEMENTS

Unlike in the United States, the question of when an agreement between a debtor and the debtor's creditors reaffirming the debtor's obligations discharged by the bankruptcy should be recognised, and the kind of safeguards necessary for the debtor's protection, have received very little attention in Canada. The topic is not even mentioned in the BIA and was not discussed as part of the deliberations leading to the 1992 and 1997 amendments to the Canadian Act. In fairness to the Working Group responsible for the 1997 amendments, it must be added that reaffirmation agreements do not enjoy a high profile in Canada and have attracted very little academic attention. Also, very little appears to be known about how widely reaffirmation agreements are relied on by Canadian creditors

---

[160] See n 149 above, at Tables 15–16.

[161] *Ibid* at Tables 19–20.

[162] *Ibid* at Table 31.

[163] *Ibid* at Tables 21–22. Presumably, secured liabilities of the consumer proposal debtors are much higher because home ownership is more common and because the home mortgages are for higher amounts. Secured amounts owing on autos are also likely to be significantly higher because the autos were bought new or are more expensive models.

[164] See OSB Industry Canada, *5 Year Review Issues, Personal Bankruptcies, Breakdown by Personal Surplus Income Code By Division Office, PSRA/6 Year Review*.

to undo the 'mischief' caused by a debtor's discharge from bankruptcy.[165] However, it would be a mistake to conclude that reaffirmation agreements are not used in Canada. The case law clearly shows the contrary.[166] Reaffirmation agreements are governed in Canada by general contract principles. This means that while a debtor's bare promise after discharge to pay a pre-bankruptcy debt will be unenforceable,[167] the promise will be enforceable if it is supported by new consideration, such as a creditor's promise to renew a line of credit or to make a new loan.[168] The position is the same with respect to the debtor's reaffirmation of her personal obligations under a secured loan. However, much uncertainty remains with respect to whether a debtor remaining in possession of collateral after a discharge and continuing to make payments to the secured party will be construed as a reaffirmation of the security agreement.[169]

To its credit, the Personal Insolvency Task Force attempted to come to grips with the reaffirmation challenges,[170] though it remains to be seen whether the Canadian Parliament can be persuaded to endorse the Task Force's complex proposals. The key recommendations are the following:

(a) the line of cases holding that retention of the collateral by the debtor after commencement of bankruptcy proceedings and accompanied by continued payments of the debts amounts to reaffirmation of the security agreement should be overruled;

(b) reaffirmation agreements in respect of unsecured transactions should be prohibited in all circumstances;

(c) reaffirmation agreements in respect of secured transactions should be prohibited except to the extent permitted by the BIA as described in the recommendations; and

(d) it should be an offence under the BIA for a creditor having knowledge of the bankrupt's discharge from bankruptcy to accept payment of any indebtedness released upon the bankrupt's discharge except in certain circumstances

---

[165] The author made enquiries with various trustees and only one had had first hand experience with a reaffirmation agreement. The others had heard vague rumours about this or that creditor trying to use reaffirmation agreements but the stories were very insubstantial.

[166] See the annotations in Houlden and Morawetz (n 53 above) H24.6, at 6-125/127.

[167] *Heather & Son v Webb* (1876) 2 CPD 1 (England); *Trans-Canada Credit Corp v Wolfe* (1994) 28 CBR (3d) 237 (Manitoba). The position is the same in England: IF Fletcher, *The Law of Insolvency* (3rd edn, Sweet and Maxwell 2002) 11–023.

[168] *Jakeman v Cook* (1875) LR 4 (Ex Div) 26.

[169] Houlden and Morawetz (n 53 above) at H24. Some Canadian courts have implied a reaffirmation or novation agreement in such circumstances. See, eg, *Seaborne Acceptance Corp v Moen* (1986) 62 CBR (NS) 143 (BCCA), criticised in Houlden and Morawetz (n 53 above) H24 at 6-126 and by Buckwold in (1999) 31 *Canadian Business Law Journal* 335. The decision can probably be justified on the ground that the lessor in that case was never notified of the debtor's bankruptcy. See JS Ziegel, 'Comment' (1999) 32 *Canadian Business Law Journal* 142. The BIA has no provision requiring the debtor or the debtor's trustee to advise the secured creditor of the estate's intentions with respect to collateral in the estate's possession after bankruptcy. The assumption seems to be that the initiative rests with the secured creditor since the secured creditor is entitled to demand release of the collateral unless the trustee elects to redeem the property. See BIA, ss 69.3(2), 128(3).

[170] PITF Report (n 26 above) at ch 2(V).

permitted by the BIA (and described in the recommendations) and any impermissible payments should be recoverable from the creditor.

Canada was the first common law jurisdiction to introduce mandatory credit counselling as part of the consumer bankruptcy process. The requirement was first introduced as part of the 1992 amendments to the BIA[171] and was extended in the 1997 amendments to consumer proposals.[172] Failure to comply with the requirement deprives the debtor of the right to an automatic discharge.[173] In addition to the counselling, which only takes place after the assignment or filing of a proposal, the trustee or administrator of a proposal must also complete an assessment of the debtor *before* the assignment or proposal.[174] The assessment requirement arises from an OSB directive and not from the Act. Nevertheless, it is an essential component of the counselling process since the trustee or administrator is obliged to review the debtor's income, assets and liabilities and to advise the debtor of the various options open to him to address his financial problems.[175] The debtor must also be told about the surplus income payment requirements under section 68 if a straight bankruptcy is his choice[176] and, if a proposal is under consideration, the trustee/administrator must satisfy herself that the debtor is in a position to make a viable proposal. A difficulty about the assessment requirement is that the trustee/administrator may not be perceived to be wholly disinterested since the size of her fees will depend on the nature of the debtor's choice.

So far as the statutory counselling is concerned, it has two stages.[177] The first stage must be conducted 10–60 days after the assignment or filing of the proposal; the second stage cannot occur before 30 days following the end of the first session and cannot be later than 120 days after the effective date of the bankruptcy or filing of the consumer proposal.[178] The first counselling session is quite benign and is designed to instruct the debtor in proper money management, spending and shopping habits and obtaining and using credit.[179] The second counselling session is much more controversial and apparently envisages the counsellor playing the combined role of social worker and psychologist to determine whether there are non-budgetary reasons for the debtor's financial problems.[180] Not surprisingly, many trustees feel uncomfortable filling this role.

---

[171] See now BIA, s 157.1 and OSB Directive No 1R2, 21 December 1994.

[172] BIA, s 66.13(2)(b).

[173] BIA, s 168.1(f).

[174] OSB Directive No 6R, 30 April 1998, s 8.

[175] *Ibid* at s 13.

[176] *Ibid* at s 11(f).

[177] See generally, CA Curnock, 'Insolvency Counselling: Innovation Based on the Fourteenth Century' (1999) 37 *Osgoode Hall Law Journal* 387.

[178] OSB Directive No 1R2, 24 December 1994, s 6.

[179] *Ibid* at s 7(1).

[180] *Ibid* at s 8 and Curnock (n 177 above).

Credit counselling has very much become the flavour of the month in all jurisdictions grappling with the problems of over-committed debtors.[181] Nevertheless, the lasting value of counselling provided after the damage has been done still has to be proven.[182] There is broad consensus that ideally budgetary management courses should be included in high school curricula but the prospects of this happening on a widespread basis appear slim. Educational authorities in Canada complain that the high school calendar is already too crowded.

---

[181] The current and prospective positions in the other jurisdictions reviewed in this study are discussed hereafter. The role of credit (debtor) counselling services in Canada has previously been mentioned, at 2.10 above, and is comprehensively discussed in Dekany (n 139 above).

[182] When interviewed, bankrupt debtors usually support it enthusiastically while trustees are more sceptical. See JS Ziegel (1996) 27 *Canadian Business Law Journal* 108, at 115, reporting on the results of *Re-Engineering Consumer Bankruptcy and Insolvency Systems: A National Assessment*, a questionnaire distributed by the OSB in 1994. In the summer of 2001, the OSB also arranged for distribution of a questionnaire to a new generation of bankrupts and debtors who had made a proposal, but the results were not available as of August 2002. Prof Ramsay views credit counselling sympathetically as part of the bankruptcy process, not so much because of its educational value as for the opportunity it provides debtors to share their concerns and anxieties with a sympathetic third party. See IDC Ramsay, 'Mandatory Bankruptcy Counselling: The Canadian Experience' (2002) 7 *Fordham Journal of Corporate & Financial Law* 525. For the US approach to credit counselling and debtor education as part of the bankruptcy process, see Chapter 3.9 below.

3

United States

GIVEN THE GREAT disparities in population and gross domestic product between the two neighbours,[1] it may seem strange to suggest that Canada and the United States have anything to learn from each other in the consumer insolvency area. The suggestion may seem even more far-fetched bearing in mind the much shorter history of Canada's bankruptcy law and the fact that it still bears the strong imprint of the British legacy, whereas the dominant ethos in the US insolvency system is the fresh start policy for individual debtors. However, this difference may narrow perceptibly if one of the many bankruptcy Bills introduced in the Congress over the past seven years is actually enacted into law.[2] In practical results, the two systems are often closer to each other than a simple reading of the rules may suggest.

Even allowing for the above differences, Canada and the United States share common features in the following critical areas. In both countries, there has been a rapid growth in the number of consumer bankruptcies since the early 1980s and this has been matched by an equally rapid escalation in the volume of personal debt and of personal debt as a ratio of net disposable income. Recent empirical investigations[3] also show close similarities in the profile of debtors going bankrupt and the causes of bankruptcy. In both countries, the great majority of bankrupt debtors are asset poor and deeply in debt, and their insolvency is often precipitated by major changes in lifestyle, such as loss of a job or other change in personal status. Single parents are a growing factor in both countries as are self-employed debtors in Canada. There are also some economic differences that bear further investigation: median and average incomes of US bankrupts appear to be substantially higher than those of Canadian bankrupts. Among the types of debt, before the 1998 amendment to the BIA, student loans appear to have played a more prominent role in Canada

---

[1] Canada's population is 31 million, that of the United States 281 million: United Nations Statistical Office, *Population and Vital Statistics Report* (New York, 2002). Canada's GDP in 2001 was CAN$1,092 billion compared to US$10,208 billion for the United States. See Statistics Canada, CANSIM II, Table 380-0001, No 13-001-XIB; and US Department of Commerce, Bureau of Economic Analysis, National Accounts Data.

[2] See s 3.5 below.

[3] See TA Sullivan, E Warren and JL Westbrook, 'Consumer Debtors Ten Years Later: A Financial Comparison of Consumer Bankrupts 1981–1991' (1994) 68 *American Bankruptcy Law Journal* 121; JL Westbrook, 'Comparative Empiricism' (1999) 37 *Osgoode Hall Law Journal* 143; and JS Ziegel, Book Review, 'A Canadian Perspective' (2001) 79 *Texas Law Review* 1241.

than in the United States. On the other hand, medical and medically related debts are a major factor in US consumer bankruptcies, unlike Canada where they occupy a low profile.[4]

Since this study is primarily concerned with a comparison of insolvency systems, the following overview will focus on the key features of the US consumer bankruptcy regime in order to highlight the similarities and differences between it and the Canadian regime.

2. CONSTITUTIONAL STRUCTURE AND HISTORICAL EVOLUTION

As in Canada's case, the US Constitution empowers the federal government to legislate in the bankruptcy area. However, on paper the US government's constitutional jurisdiction is not as extensive as that of the Canadian government. Article 1, section 8, clause 4 of the US Constitution only authorises Congress to establish 'uniform laws on the subject of Bankruptcies throughout the United States'. This would seem to leave much more scope for a concurrent role by the states than is true of the provinces in Canada. However, the practical difference seems to be much smaller given a strong federal pre-emption doctrine in the United States and a generous concurrency doctrine in Canada although unevenly applied by the Canadian Supreme Court in the bankruptcy area.[5] One important difference between the constitutional provisions is that US courts have not restricted the federal bankruptcy power to insolvent persons[6]—a requirement that up to now has always been treated as a sine qua non of the exercise of the federal jurisdiction in Canada.[7]

(a) Pre-1898 Developments

In the United States, debt problems were already a familiar phenomenon in the colonial states and many of the states had insolvency relief legislation of various

---

[4] Sullivan, Warren and Westbrook report that in 1987 more than 9 million US families spent more than 20% of their income on medical care, that medical problems were an important part of more than a quarter of US bankruptcies in 1998, and that one-fifth of the households in the authors' sample of debtors listed medically related problems as a reason for the bankruptcy filing. See TA Sullivan, E Warren and JL Westbrook, *The Fragile Middle Class: Americans in Debt* (New Haven, Yale University Press, 2000) 141. By way of contrast, in Canada, Schwartz and Anderson found that medical and dental problems only accounted for 1.5% of the total number of debts among their debtors. JS Ziegel, Book Review (n 3 above) at 1250. For a more recent analyses of the Canadian bankruptcy factors see Craig Campbell, *Increased Rate of Consumer Bankruptcy in Canada: Socioeconomic Influences (1977–1997)* (Ottawa, Corporate Law and Policy Directorate, Industry Canada, January 2002).

[5] See Chapter 2.1 above.

[6] CJ Tabb, *The Law of Bankruptcy* (Foundation Press, 1997) 46.

[7] JS Ziegel, *A Comparison of Canadian and United States Commercial Bankruptcy Law: A Study* (Industry Canada, 2002) 143–44.

types before the founding of the American Union in 1789.[8] The states found it necessary to maintain their interest for most of the nineteenth century because of the long travail to reach agreement on a national bankruptcy Act that would survive for more than a few years. The first federal Bankruptcy Act was only adopted in 1800 and only lasted two years. Two more Acts were adopted in 1841 and 1867 with similarly disappointing results.[9] It was only with the adoption of the 1898 Act that rival factions—mercantile and industrial interests in the north-east versus agricultural interests in the south and the newly settled territories in the far west—were able to accommodate their conflicting interests on a long term basis.[10]

The 1898 Act also established the basic principles of twentieth century US bankruptcy law, one of which was the adoption of the fresh start doctrine for individual bankrupts.[11] It does not appear that the implications of the doctrine were much debated before passage of the law. Rather, as one US scholar describes it:

> There is no single fact or event that explains why the United States made such a radical change in its discharge laws. Instead, several factors, including federalism, the expanding western frontier, and the development of adequate alternative debt collection devices under state law, combined to produce this result.[12]

(b) 1898–1978

In the consumer area, many minor amendments to the Bankruptcy Act were adopted in the first 37 years of its life but the first major change only appeared in the Chandler Act of 1938.[13] This introduced a new chapter, Chapter XIII, designed to give wage-earners a compositional alternative to going into straight bankruptcy. In 1970, Congress established a National Bankruptcy Commission with the mandate to conduct a comprehensive review of the 1898 Act and to submit proposals for a completely revised Act. The Commission's report was

---

[8] See PJ Coleman, *Debtors and Creditors in America* (Madison, State Historical Society of Wisconsin, 1974).

[9] The 1841 Act lasted three years, the 1867 Act 11 years. See DA Skeel, Jr, *Debt's Dominion: A History of Bankruptcy Law in America* (Princeton University Press, 2001) ch 1.

[10] See DA Skeel, Jr, 'The Genius of the 1898 Bankruptcy Act' (1998/99) 15 *Bankruptcy Development Journal* 321; and CJ Tabb, 'A Century of Regress or Progress? A Political History of Bankruptcy Legislation in 1898 and 1998' (1999) 15 *Bankruptcy Development Journal* 343. Prof Skeel gives a much more nuanced account of the events leading up to the adoption of the 1898 Act that emphasises the importance of individual politicians and lawyers as well as ideologies. He also credits the rising US bankruptcy bar with a significant role.

[11] Provisions for a voluntary bankruptcy system followed by the discharge of remaining debts already appeared in the short-lived Act of 1841 and, according to Coleman (n 8 above) at 287–88), were used by nearly 34,000 petitioners and almost US$400 million was written off, an average of more than US$11,000 a case.

[12] DG Boshkoff, 'Limited, Conditional, and Suspended Discharges in Anglo-American Bankruptcy Proceedings' (1982) 131 *University of Pennsylvania Law Review* 69, at 105.

[13] 52 US Stat 840 (1938).

published in 1973[14] and, after extensive hearings in both chambers, Congress approved the Bankruptcy Reform Act of 1978.[15] So far as consumer insolvencies were concerned, the Commission's Report affirmed its strong support for the fresh start principle and was opposed to its dilution. Congress heeded this advice.[16] The 1978 Act also included a revised chapter 13 for wage-earner plans which was more consumer-friendly than its 1938 predecessor.[17] Bankruptcy legislation has continued to figure prominently on Congress' agenda since then. Three of the post-1978 developments are particularly relevant and are discussed below.

(c) Bankruptcy Amendments and Federal Judgeship Act of 1984[18]

This amending Act is important from the consumer insolvency perspective because it marked the first successful breach by the credit industry lobby in the fresh start doctrine. The industry had persuaded Congress that large numbers of consumers were abusing their rights of access to chapter 7. Congress responded by adding §707(b) to the Code.[19] This allows the bankruptcy court on its own motion or on motion by the US trustee (but importantly not on the request or suggestion of any other party in interest) to dismiss a petition by a consumer debtor on the ground that the granting of relief (ie, discharge of the petitioner's unpaid debts) would be a substantial abuse. However, the industry won a largely symbolic victory. Congress intentionally refrained from defining 'abuse' and courts have given it sharply different meanings.[20] Secondly, a creditor is not permitted to bring its own motion but must rely on the haphazard prospect of the court or the US trustee feeling sufficiently aroused by the facts of a case to be willing to set the machinery in motion themselves.

(d) National Bankruptcy Review Commission

The National Bankruptcy Review Commission (NBRC) was established as part of the Bankruptcy Reform Act of 1994 but its terms of reference were much

---

[14] *Report of the Commission on the Bankruptcy Laws of the United States*, HR DOC No 93-137 (1973).

[15] Pub L No 95-598, US Code Title 11 (the Act is also frequently referred to as the Bankruptcy Code and that practice is followed in this study); Tabb (n 10 above) at 37–39.

[16] For the details, see Skeel (n 10 above) at ch 5. It seems in fact that the retention of the fresh start principle provoked little debate.

[17] The 1938 chapter is correctly referred to as 'Chapter XIII', its 1978 successor as 'chapter 13'.

[18] 98 US Stat 333 (1984).

[19] 11 USC §707(b) reads: 'After notice and a hearing, the court, on its own motion or on a motion by the United States trustee, but not at the request or suggestion of any party in interest, may dismiss a case filed by an individual debtor under this chapter whose debts are primarily consumer debts if it finds that the granting of relief would be a substantial abuse of the provisions of this chapter. There shall be a presumption in favour of granting the relief requested by the debtor.'

[20] See Tabb (n 10 above) at §2.14.

more circumscribed than those of its predecessor of 1973. Congress made it clear that it was 'generally satisfied with the basic framework' of the current law and that the Commission should focus on 'reviewing, improving, and updating the Code in ways which do not disturb the fundamental tenets of current law.'[21] It is doubtful that the Congressional members quite anticipated the adroit way in which the Commission would use its restricted mandate to beat off demands for means testing from the credit industry and its supporters.

The Commission reported on 20 October 1997. The Commission's 1028-page Report included 142 recommendations covering the full spectrum of commercial and consumer bankruptcies. The Commission reported that it had spent more time on consumer bankruptcies than on any other area of its enquiry and that its constant goal had been to strive for balance in the bankruptcy system and not to placate any particular constituency.[22] There was broad consensus among the nine commissioners on most of the recommendations but they were sharply divided on the key issue whether means testing should be introduced so as to restrict the number of chapter 7 filings. The majority of the Commission rejected it on the following grounds: because such a radical proposal was outside their remit, because they felt it was unwarranted and would impose heavy administrative costs, and because they were philosophically opposed to it.[23] Among the dissenting commissioners, the Honourable Edith Hollan Jones, a judge on the Fifth Circuit Court of Appeals, argued vociferously and tenaciously in favour of rolling back what she perceived to be the tide of abusive filings.[24]

The consumer bankruptcy recommendations in the NBRC Report included the following:

(1) establishment of a national filing system, heightened requirements for accurate information in schedules accompanying petitions and creation of opportunities for all chapters 7 and 13 debtors to participate in financial education programmes;[25]
(2) repeal of §522(b)(1) and (2) allowing states to opt out of the federal exemptions and changes to the existing federal exemptions;[26]
(3) reaffirmation agreements should only be allowed in respect of secured claims and for allowed part of secured claim but excluding attorney's fees and other expenses;[27]

---

[21] Report of the National Bankruptcy Review Commission, *Bankruptcy: The Next Twenty Years, Final Report* (20 October 1997) 50–51 (hereafter NBRC Report).

[22] *Ibid* at vi–vii.

[23] *Ibid* at 90–91.

[24] Apart from her dissents in the Commission's Report, Judge Jones' views are also expounded at length in EH Jones and TJ Zywicki, 'It's Time for Means Testing' (1999) *Brigham Young University Law Review* 177.

[25] NBRC Report (n 21 above) at recommendations 1.1.1, 1.1.2, 1.1.5.

[26] *Ibid* at recommendations 1.2.1–1.2.3.

[27] *Ibid* at recommendation 1.3.1.

(4) secured creditors' rights in chapter 7 would be clarified and security interests in personal and household goods valued at less than US$500 should be
disallowed;[28]

(5) with respect to most non-dischargeable debts, credit card debts that did not
exceed the debtor's credit limits should be dischargeable unless they were
incurred within 30 days before the order for relief.[29]

(6) §523(a)(8) should be repealed and student loan debts should be dischargeable.

(7) with respect to chapter 13 repayment plans, (a) payments on unsecured
debts should be determined by guidelines based on a graduated percentage
of the debtor's income, (b) the Code should permit conversion of a chapter
13 case to chapter 7 unless the debtor has been granted a chapter 7 discharge
within the preceding six years, (c) §362 should be amended to deny the automatic stay to repeat filers, and (d) the 'super-discharge' provisions in §1328
should be left intact;[30]

(9) debtors who choose chapter 13 repayment plans should be treated differently from chapter 7 debtors in consumer credit reports, and debtors who
complete a voluntary education programme should have the fact recorded
in such reports;[31]

(10) trustees should be encouraged to establish credit rehabilitation programmes to enable chapter 7 discharged debtors to obtain better and
cheaper access to credit.[32]

(e) Congressional Bills 1997–2002

The US credit industry obviously had few illusions about where the wind was
blowing among the Commissioners. Even before the Commission released its
report, the industry launched a powerful and well financed campaign for the
adoption of a Bill that would reflect its views of the changes that were needed.[33]
Bills introduced in the House of Representatives and the Senate in the 105th
Congress in 1997 and 1998 were passed by large majorities but, as previously
indicated, fell victim to the Congressional time-table, and none was enacted.
The credit industry renewed its pressure with undiminished intensity in the 96th
Congress. HR 833[34] was approved by the House of Representatives, again by a
large majority, in April 1999; S 625,[35] which closely tracked HR 833, was

---

[28] NBRC Report (n 21 above) at recommendation 1.3.4.
[29] *Ibid* at recommendation 1.4.1.
[30] *Ibid* at recommendations 1.5.4, 1.5.5, 1.5.7.
[31] *Ibid* at recommendations 1.5.8, 1.5.9.
[32] *Ibid* at recommendation 1.5.9.
[33] For details of the industry's campaign and the battles in Congress, see among the voluminous
literature J Braucher, 'Options in Consumer Bankruptcy: An American Perspective' (1999) 37
Osgoode Hall Law Journal 155 and E Warren, 'The Changing Politics of American Bankruptcy
Reform' (1999) 37 *Osgoode Hall Law Journal* 189.
[34] Bankruptcy Reform Act 1999, HR 833, 106th Congress, 1st Session.
[35] Bankruptcy Reform Act 1999, S 625, 106th Congress, 1st Session.

approved by the Senate Judiciary Committee in May 1999 and by the full Senate on 2 February 2000. A jointly approved Senate and House of Representatives Bill, HR 2145, was forwarded to President Clinton for his approval on 7 December 2000, but was pocket vetoed by him before he left office. Two new bills, HR 333 and S 420,[36] substantially reproducing the ethos of HR 2145, were reintroduced in the 107th Congress at the beginning of 2001. They were respectively approved by the House of Representatives and Senate in the spring and summer of 2001 and a joint conference committee was expected to be established to resolve differences between the two bills. However, the tragic evidence of 11 September 2001 brought the negotiations to a halt and the conference committee was not struck until the spring of 2002. The committee quickly became deadlocked, not over consumer bankruptcy provisions but over an amendment that would deny discharge from bankruptcy to individuals who had been successfully sued or fined for interfering with abortion clinics and those who worked in them.[37] The conference committee reported having reached agreement on the outstanding issues on 26 July 2002 but the agreement was criticised by pro-life Republicans and the bill was withdrawn by its sponsors from further consideration until after the summer recess.[38] The conference committee did not reach agreement before the Congressional elections in November 2002, and the bills died. However, Congressman F James Sensenbrenner introduced a new bill, HR 975, the Bankruptcy Abuse Prevention and Consumer Protection Act of 2003, on 27 February 2003, and the bill was approved by the House of Representatives on March 2003. HR 975 is identical in most respects to the bankruptcy reform bill considered by the Congress in the 107th Congress.[38a]

All these Bills are or were very long and complex. All cover much more than consumer bankruptcy issues although changing the pro-debtor ethos of chapters 7 and 13 is a primary goal of the Bills' sponsors. It is these aspects of the Bills that have attracted intense opposition from consumer bankruptcy scholars, consumer organisations, and members of the consumer bankruptcy bar, and have provoked much critical comment form the media. If a sufficiently close version of either HR 333 or S 420 is enacted, the focus of US consumer bankruptcy law will be changed fundamentally and perhaps permanently.[39] The fresh start policy will be reversed with the introduction of a mandatory means test. It is important to appreciate, however, that the conceptual approach adopted in these Bills is different from the route chosen in the 1997 Canadian amendments.

[36] Bankruptcy Reform Act 2001, S 420, 107th Congress, 1st Session.

[37] J Braucher, 'Means Testing Consumer Bankruptcy: The Problem of Means' (2002) 7 *Fordham Journal of Corporate and Financial Law* 407. See also 'Bankruptcy Talks Collapse on Abortion Issue' *New York Times*, 10 May 2002; and American Bankruptcy Institute, 'Bankruptcy Bill Conference Reaches Critical Stage' *Legislative Highlights* (http://www.abiworld.org/legis/highlights/02junleghi.html) (June 2002).

[38] ABI World Newsletter 26–29 July 2002 (www.abiworld.org/headlines).

[38a] American Bankruptcy College, *LegInfo* email newsletter, 28 February 2003 and 28 June 2003.

[39] CJ Tabb, 'The Death of Consumer Bankruptcy in the United States?' (2001) 18 *Bankruptcy Development Journal* 1.

The current Congressional Bills provide that if the debtor satisfies a complex means test,[40] the court must dismiss the chapter 7 petition or, if the debtor agrees, convert the proceedings to a chapter 13 case.[41] If the debtor opts for a chapter 13 plan, another means test will be applied[42] to ensure that the debtor makes realistic payments from the debtor's surplus income.

HR 333 and S 420 therefore maintain the appearance that the fresh start policy is being retained but that it will be restricted to those who 'really' need it. Other debtors will be limited to the chapter 13 route. Other important changes in the Congressional bills include:

(1) use of pre-petition screening and determination by accredited not-for-profit counselling agencies to determine (a) the debtor's financial status, and (b) whether agreement can be reached outside the Code on a repayment plan;[43]
(2) development of financial management and training curriculum and materials for programmes of debtor education[44];
(3) the scope of non-dischargeable debts is expanded[45];
(4) requirements for trustees to satisfy themselves that the debtor is eligible to file a chapter 7 petition where such a petition is filed[46]; and
(5) major changes in chapter 13 to eliminate perceived abuses and to ensure that the debtor makes realistic payment proposals based on the statutory standards.[47]

One much debated change that appeared in HR 833, but was subsequently dropped, involved the imposition of a US$250,000 homestead ceiling on state based exemptions.[48] However, S 420 retains a provision[49] extending the time a debtor must live in the state to be able to invoke its exemptions.

The NBRC recommendations and the provisions in the current Congressional Bills will receive further attention under the appropriate headings in the following summary of the principal features of the existing Code.

3. JUDICIAL AND ADMINISTRATIVE STRUCTURES

The United States has a separate system of bankruptcy courts staffed with full time judges although constitutionally the bankruptcy judges are only adjuncts of the

---

[40] See 3.5 below.
[41] S 420 (n 36 above) at §102(a), amending 11 USC §707.
[42] S 420 (n 36 above) at §102(h).
[43] *Ibid* at §106.
[44] *Ibid* at §105. Earlier Bills would also have obliged bankrupt debtors to enrol in an accredited programme as a condition of the debtor's discharge from bankruptcy.
[45] *Ibid* at §314.
[46] *Ibid* at §102(a)(4)(C).
[47] *Ibid* at §§102(b), 309, 318.
[48] However, this was a Greek gift to creditors since states would have been free to opt out of the exemption.
[49] S 420 (n 36 above) at §307.

federal district court.[50] In the normal course of events, it appears, the judges do not become much involved in chapter 7 consumer petitions unless there is an objection to the otherwise automatic discharge.[51] However, the court's approval is necessary for a chapter 13 repayment plan and, since the Bankruptcy Code confers no judicial powers on a registrar (as is the case under the Canadian BIA), all interlocutory applications must be heard by a bankruptcy judge. It seems safe to conclude therefore that the specialisation of US bankruptcy judges and their daily involvements gives them a better feel for the complexities of consumer bankruptcy than is enjoyed by Canadian superior court judges. US scholars have also frequently commented on the pivotal role which bankruptcy judges play in shaping the bankruptcy cultures in their districts and in determining whether bankruptcy attorneys recommend a chapter 7 or chapter 13 filing to their clients.[52]

At the administrative level, the US counterpart to the OSB in Canada and the official receivers are the US trustees and the Executive Office for United States Trustees (EOUST), which is located in Washington, DC, and is a subdivision of the Department of Justice. The US trustees are responsible for the administrative aspects of the Bankruptcy Code in much the same way as the OSB and his officials are in Canada.[53] Unlike the OSB, EOUST has no power to issue directives with statutory force and plays no role in the drafting of bankruptcy regulations.[54] However, the regional US trustees are responsible for the appointment of private sector 'panel trustees' for chapter 7 purposes and of 'standing' trustees to administer chapter 13 plans.[55] All trustees must meet eligibility requirements but there is no formal licensing system. The compensation of panel trustees is determined by the bankruptcy judge subject to an upper ceiling based on the value of the estate.[56] Since the great majority of consumer filings under chapter 7 involve no-asset cases, it appears that the trustee must often settle for a prescribed share (US\$60 at the present time) of the fee paid by the debtor at the time of the filing.[57] Chapter 13 standing trustees are paid a percentage of the amount paid by the debtor under the plan and enjoy a much higher status and earn much more than panel trustees. In some localities standing trustees also exert considerable influence on attorney's recommendations to debtors whether to file for bankruptcy under chapter 7 or chapter 13.[58]

---

[50] The reasons for this unusual position are complex and arise out of the Senate's unwillingness during discussions on the 1978 Code to confer Art III status on bankruptcy judges. For the details see Tabb (n 6 above) at §1.19.

[51] 11 USC §§341, 727.

[52] See, eg, J Braucher, 'Lawyers and Consumer Bankruptcy: One Code, Many Cultures' (1993) 67 *American Bankruptcy Law Journal* 501; and TA Sullivan, E Warren and JL Westbrook, 'The Persistence of Local Legal Culture: Twenty Years of Evidence from the Federal Bankruptcy Courts' (1994) 17 *Harvard Journal of Law and Public Policy* 801.

[53] See Tabb (n 6 above) at §1.20.

[54] These fall within the purview of the US Judicial Conference.

[55] 28 USC §586(a) and (b).

[56] 11 USC §§326, 330.

[57] 11 USC §330(b)(1).

[58] See Braucher (n 52 above) at 556–61.

Initiating a voluntary bankruptcy under chapter 7 is even easier than is the filing of an assignment under the BIA in Canada. This is because the US Code does not require a minimum amount of debt and does not require proof of the petitioner's insolvency.[59] However, these are not important practical differences. More significant is the fact that the petition is not required to designate a trustee to administer the prospective estate. Rather, the filing of the petition under §301 triggers an automatic order for relief, including the appointment of an interim trustee by the US trustee from among the panel trustees in the district.[60] This means that if the debtor wants professional advice before filing he must consult an attorney,[61] although there is nothing to stop the debtor from making a *pro se* filing and such filings are said to have increased significantly in recent years.[62] Para-legals to assist the debtor in preparing the documents are also active in this area.[63] What is conceptually significant is the fact that the US system avoids the conflict of interest that arises in Canada when a future trustee advises an over-committed debtor on the best course of action for the debtor to follow, prepares the assignment or consumer proposal if either of those steps is decided upon, and then acts as assignee of the estate or administrator of the proposal with corresponding obligations to the court and the creditors. Contrary to what might be expected, the deployment of two professionals in chapter 7 (an attorney or other professional to advise the debtor and prepare the petition and accompanying schedules, and the panel trustee actually to administer the estate) does not saddle the debtor with two sets of costs since the debtor is not responsible for the panel trustee's fees and expenses.[64]

The US$200 'filing' fee in a voluntary case[65] is substantially higher than the current CAN$75 filing fee for a summary estate in Canada but presumably is not so high as to discourage petitions by even very low-income consumers. Also the US$200 fee covers the administration fee payable to the panel trustee. The court

[59] 11 USC §§301, 101(13) (definition of 'debtor').

[60] 11 USC §701(a)(1).

[61] Bankruptcy attorneys advertise their services widely and appear to be used in the great majority of bankruptcy filings. In the case of indigents, some attorneys (not necessarily bankruptcy specialists) will provide their services pro bono and bankruptcy assistance clinics, financed from various sources, have also been established in major US cities such as Boston and Philadelphia.

[62] Edward M Flynn, EOUST research analyst, estimates that about 10% of chapter 7 petitions are filed pro se. He also points out that there are great regional variations in the number of pro se filings; eg, they are very common in California, particularly in the Los Angeles area, but are fairly uncommon in other parts of the United States. Many pro se debtors also use a bankruptcy petition preparer service who may charge US$150 or so and are not supposed to offer any legal guidance to the debtor. An increasing number of the petition preparers are Internet-based: email message to author, 15 January 2003.

[63] They have aroused the ire of Congress because of alleged abuses. See, eg, S 420 (n 36 above) at §221. See also n 62 above and note that bankruptcy petition preparers are already regulated in §110 of the Code.

[64] However, in chapter 7 cases part of the filing fee is ear-marked for the case trustee. See n 65 below. In chapter 13 cases the standing trustee receives a percentage of the debtor's payments made by the debtor under the plan.

[65] The fee actually represents the aggregate of: US$155 filing fee, US$30 administrative fee for 'noticing' the bankruptcy, and a US$15 trustee surcharge. The US$200 is distributed as follows: US$60 goes to the chapter 7 case trustee, US$82.50 to the US bankruptcy court, US$42.50 to the US trustee, and US$15 to the US Treasury: email messages to author from Edward M Flynn, 7 February 2000 and 15 January 2003.

cannot waive payment of the fee but it can be paid by instalments.[66] After the petition has been filed, the US trustee is obliged to convene and preside at a meeting of creditors, which the debtor is also obliged to attend, and to advise the debtor, inter alia, of the potential consequences of seeking a discharge in bankruptcy, including the effect of a bankruptcy on the debtor's credit history, and the debtor's ability to file a petition under a different chapter of title 11.[67] At this juncture, the creditors are also free to elect their own trustee but, as in Canada, rarely exercise the right although it seems that one or more of them often attend the meeting. Presumably the opportunity to question the debtor and lay the groundwork for a non-dischargeable debt,[68] or, very infrequently, to oppose a discharge under §727, provides the incentive for them to do so. Apparently reaffirmation agreements are also often negotiated at the meeting.[69]

4. EXEMPTIONS AND TREATMENT OF SECURED CREDITORS

(a) Exemptions

In Canada, until recently, the topic of exemptions attracted very little policy discussion, the assumption being that since section 67(1)(b) of the BIA has relegated determination of the applicable exemptions to the province of the debtor's residence, there was nothing left to discuss. In the United States, on the other hand, the issue has been highly controversial for many years and received close attention in the NBRC Report.

The first two US Bankruptcy Acts in the nineteenth century contained federally determined exemptions for the debtor's benefit.[70] This was changed in the 1867 Act to give the debtor the combined benefit of the federal exemptions as well as the exemptions allowed under the law of the debtor's state of residence.[71] It was further changed in the 1897 Act by restricting the debtor's entitlements to the state exemptions.[72] Even in the nineteenth century this formula led to widely disparate results because the state exemptions differed greatly in types and amounts. The differences continued to mount as the years

---

[66] Federal Rules of Bankruptcy Procedure §1006. The US Supreme Court has held that the requirement of a filing fee does not violate a debtor's constitutional rights: *United States v Kras* 409 US 434 (1973). Congress has also introduced a pilot programme for *in forma pauperis* filing in a few selected districts. See Tabb (n 6 above) at 119; and Federal Judicial Center, *Implementing and Evaluating the Chapter 7 Filing Fee Waiver Program*, Report of the Committee on the Administration of the Bankruptcy System of the Judicial Conference of the United States (Federal Judicial Center, 1998). The recent and current Congressional Bills previously referred to also confer power on bankruptcy courts to grant relief from filing fees to debtors.

[67] 11 USC §341(d). Presumably this is one of many instances where local culture exerts its influence in determining the debtor's choice of chapter filing.

[68] See 11 USC §523.

[69] Reaffirmation agreements are discussed in 3.8 below.

[70] Tabb (n 6 above) §9.2 at 643.

[71] Bankruptcy Act 1867, Ch 176, §14.

[72] Bankruptcy Act 1898, §6.

progressed. Particularly offensive to the critics was the fact that several states—currently Florida, Iowa, Kansas, South Dakota and Texas[73]—gave unlimited homestead exemptions, thereby turning them into debtors' havens and bringing the bankruptcy system into disrepute.[74] Other critics were even more concerned about the very low and inadequate exemptions afforded in many other states. Attempts were made to challenge the constitutionality of the federal government's delegation of the exemptions power to the states but these proved to be (and have so far remained) unsuccessful.[75]

The whole issue was comprehensively addressed in the 1973 Bankruptcy Commission Report.[76] The Commission recommended imposing a uniform set of federal exemptions of real and personal property for all debtors and presented a modern and well conceived list of exemptions based on the Uniform Exemptions Act drafted by the states'-sponsored National Conference of Commissioners on Uniform State Laws (NCCUSL). The National Conference of Bankruptcy Judges (NCBJ) took a different tack and recommended that debtors be permitted to elect between the state exemptions and the proposed federal exemptions. The House of Representatives supported the NCBJ position while the Senate favoured retention of the status quo. A compromise was agreed on giving debtors the option of choosing between the state exemptions and non-bankruptcy federal exemptions, and the new federal bankruptcy exemptions, unless the debtor's state had opted out of the federal exemptions.[77] It is not clear what Congress expected to happen. In any event, 35 states have opted out of §521(b), thus frustrating the prospect of any significant reduction in the disparate exemption claims made by insolvent debtors.

The exemptions imbroglio is revisited in the NBRC Report. The Commission was strongly of the view that the existing position is inconsistent with a coherent federal bankruptcy policy, unfair to creditors and debtors, and greatly complicates administration of the Bankruptcy Code.[78] The Commission therefore reaffirmed the earlier position of the 1973 Bankruptcy Commission recommending a uniform set of exemptions for all bankrupt debtors. The NBRC Report does, however, make one important concession to state interests by permitting a debtor to opt for the state homestead exemption if the exemption is not less than US$20,000 and not more than US$100,000.[79]

Judging by the current crop of Congressional Bills, the Commission's recommendations appear only to have had a limited impact. HR 833, as passed by the

---

[73] NBRC Report (n 21 above) at 299.

[74] Adding fuel to the controversy was the unresolved problem whether federal courts should, or could, police planned pre-bankruptcy conversion of non-exempt assets to exempt assets. See NBRC Report (n 21 above) at 123–24.

[75] Tabb (n 6 above) ch 1.9, at 47. The leading case is *Hanover National Bank v Moyses* (1902) 186 US 181.

[76] NBRC Report (n 21 above) at 119.

[77] 11 USC §522(b)(1).

[78] NBRC Report (n 21 above) at 121–22.

[79] *Ibid* at recommendation 1.2.2.

House of Representatives, imposed a US$250,000 homestead ceiling but allowed the states to opt out of the restriction. The Bill extended the time debtors must live in the state to be able to invoke its exemptions and reduced the exemptions if the debtor had converted assets with intent to hinder, delay or defraud the debtor's creditors.[80] S 625 did not have an exemption ceiling. S 945 and S 1301, as adopted by the Senate in 1998, capped state homestead exemptions for bankruptcy purposes at US$100,000. S 420 increased the ceiling to US$125,000, but any limitation continued to prove unacceptable to politicians from states with unlimited homestead exemptions. As a result, in April 2002, the conference committee that was convened to resolve the differences between S 420 and HR 333 removed the US$125,000 homestead cap from S 420 but retained it for some debtors such as convicted felons or those with debts under federal or state securities law, and also denied use of a homestead exemption by a debtor who had not resided in the state for at least 40 months.[81]

(b) Secured Claims

With respect to secured claims, the US rules are substantially more accommodating in protecting the debtor's interests than is the BIA, though the US rules are complex and fall far short of creating a debtor's paradise. To summarise:

(1) Secured creditors are precluded by the automatic stay in §362(a) from repossessing or otherwise enforcing their security interest without the court's leave. However, secured creditors are entitled to 'adequate protection' against a decline in value of the collateral during the period of suspension of the secured creditor's right.

(2) Subject to the automatic stay rule, the basic principle is one of recognition of security interests validly created and perfected under pre-bankruptcy law. At the time of bankruptcy, therefore, the individual debtor must elect[82] whether to redeem or surrender the collateral or to reaffirm the security agreement by negotiating new terms with the secured party.

(3) If the debtor opts to redeem (an unlikely event since the debtor will rarely have the cash), she will have to pay the full balance, not just the allowed value of the collateral.[83]

---

[80] This summary and the later summaries in this chapter are based on National Bankruptcy Conference, *Comparison of Significant Consumer Bankruptcy Provisions of HR 833 as passed by the House and S 945 as introduced* (1999) 2; and Braucher (n 37 above) at 432–34, n 113. The author is indebted to Prof Melissa Jacoby of Temple University Law School for providing him with a copy of the *Comparison* and analyses by other commentators of the 2001 Bills.

[81] Braucher (n 37 above) at 432–33, n 113.

[82] 11 USC §521.

[83] 11 USC §506(d), as interpreted in *Dewsnup v Timm* 502 US 410 (1992), a leading but controversial decision. See the discussion in Tabb (n 6 above) at 559 *et seq.*

There are two important exceptions to these principles:

(a) the debtor's right under §522(f)(1)(B) to avoid a non-possessory non-purchase money security interest in described and exempted personal property when held primarily for personal, family or household use, or constituting implements, professional books and tools of the trade, and professionally prescribed health aids for the debtor or the debtor's dependants; and

(b) the debtor's right under §722 to redeem personal property exempted under §522 by paying the secured party's allowed claim in respect of the collateral.[84]

Neither of these two exceptions applies to security interests in real property nor to motor vehicles and many other essential items in daily use above the exempted levels. If the debtor wishes to stretch out the payments, cure any default or reduce the lien to its current market value for the purposes of redemption,[85] she will have to file a plan under chapter 13 and meet that chapter's conditions. However, in the interests of protecting the flow of investments for the residential market, even chapter 13 does not permit modification of secured claims in real property that is the debtor's principal residence.[86]

So far as future changes in these rules are concerned, the NBRC recommendations and the current and recent Congressional Bills move in opposite ideological directions. The NBRC recommendations would in effect disallow purchase money security interests in exempt personal or household property for less than US$500[87] on the ground that vendors do not genuinely rely on such low cost items as security and because their principal value lies in forcing debtors to pay up in bankruptcy. The current congressional Bills, on the other hand, prohibit strip-downs of under-secured debt in chapter 13,[88] authorise creditors to seize collateral if the debtor does not redeem the property or affirm the debt,[89] and provide secured creditors and lessors with relief from the automatic stay where the debtor has failed to surrender collateral or is in breach of the lease,[90] and impose restrictions on conversion of chapter 13 plans to chapter 7.[91]

---

[84] An allowed claim in respect of a secured debt is a secured claim to the extent of the value of the creditor's interest in the collateral at the time of the claim. See 11 USC §506(a). That value will often be much less than the debt itself, thus giving the debtor a strong incentive to redeem the collateral if the debtor can raise the cash with which to do it.

[85] Commonly referred to in the US literature as 'lien stripping'.

[86] 11 USC §1322(b)(2).

[87] NBRC Report (n 21 above) at recommendation 1.3.4.

[88] eg, S 420 (n 36 above) at § 306.

[89] *Ibid* at §§304, 305.

[90] *Ibid* at §§305, 311.

[91] *Ibid* at §309.

5. MEANS TESTING AND US DISCHARGE POLICY:
CURRENT REGIME AND FUTURE PROSPECTS

(a) The Battle of Numbers and Philosophies

Applied literally, the fresh start policy means that once a debtor has filed a proper petition, surrendered his non-exempt property and otherwise complied with the procedural requirements, he should be entitled to a discharge from the balance of his debts. However, even the United States has never given such literal meaning to the policy and has always imposed some restrictions and exceptions. Both have grown over the years with the result, as Prof Whitford has noted, that it would be more accurate to describe it as a 'stale start' policy.[92]

This is because under chapter 7 a consumer's right to go bankrupt and obtain a clean discharge under §727(a)[93] is subject to four important exceptions: (1) the 'abuse' doctrine in §707(b),[94] (2) the long list of liabilities excluded from discharge in §523, (3) where the debtor has been guilty of misconduct in the period prior to bankruptcy or during bankruptcy, or has been granted a discharge in a case commenced within six years before the filing of the current petition,[95] and (4) where the debtor has entered into a reaffirmation agreement.[96]

Each of the exceptions has its own history and rationale. The §707(b) exception, as we have seen,[97] was added in 1984 at the behest of the credit industry which was already then concerned about the escalating number of consumer bankruptcies. The fact that the section does not define what amounts to an abusive filing and that the courts have not been able to agree about it, does not detract from the fact that conceptually the exception represents an important dilution of the fresh start doctrine. To determine what amounts to abuse, one must first define the purpose and proper scope of the fresh start policy. The traditional answer has been that the object is to assist 'the honest but poor and unfortunate debtor' to re-establish himself socially and economically as a productive member of the community.[98] However, this explanation does not tell us what is so objectionable about conditioning the debtor's discharge to paying off a percentage of his debts where he is in a position to do so.

The rationale for the long list of non-dischargeable debts in §523 of the Code (a list more than twice as long as the Canadian list and much longer than the

---

[92] WC Whitford, 'Changing Definitions of Fresh Start in U.S. Bankruptcy Law' (1997) 20 *Journal of Consumer Policy* 179.

[93] 11 USC §727(a): 'The court shall grant the debtor a discharge, unless . . . .'

[94] 11 USC §707(b). For the text of §707(b) see n 19 above.

[95] See 11 USC §727(a)(1)–(9).

[96] See 11 USC §§ 524(c), 727(a)(10).

[97] See 3.2(c) above.

[98] The *locus classicus* is the US Supreme Court's oft cited judgment in *Local Loan Co v Hunt* (1934) 292 US 234, 244, in which the court described the bankruptcy discharge as designed to give 'the honest but unfortunate debtor . . . a new opportunity in life and a clear field for future effort, unhampered by the pressure and discouragement of preexisting debt.'

British list)[99] rests on a variety of public policies, some more persuasive than others, each of which is regarded as sufficiently important in respect of that debt or obligation to trump the debtor's search for a fresh start. The denial of a discharge based on the debtor's pre-bankruptcy or intra-bankruptcy misconduct or lack of co-operation, as prescribed in §727(a), is presumably grounded in the belief that strong sanctions are required to deter such transgressions, although other jurisdictions are content to leave their courts considerable discretion in determining an appropriate penalty for such misconduct. The impulse for the denial of a discharge where the debtor has obtained a discharge within the preceding six years[100] is obviously based on a desire to avoid abuse of the bankruptcy process. What is noteworthy is the rigidity of the exclusion in §727(a)(8) and (9). The US court is given no discretion regardless of the particular circumstances. This is in contrast to the Canadian position[101] where a previous bankruptcy merely precludes the court from granting the debtor an unconditional discharge.[102]

(b) Grounds of Opposition to Discretionary Discharges and Means Testing

This cursory examination then shows that there are many exceptions to the fresh start policy in US bankruptcy law. It also raises the question why some US observers are very critical of the Commonwealth style of discretionary discharges (assuming this is still a fair description of the British and Canadian systems) and why there is so much opposition to a statutorily sanctioned system of means testing. Why are some exceptions more acceptable than others and, still more pertinently, is there an intrinsic quality to the fresh start policy that should entitle every petitioner to a clean slate regardless of the circumstances? Why should a bankrupt be required to surrender his non-exempt existing assets for the benefit of his creditors but not be expected to pay down the debts from future surplus income? The answer to these questions appears to rest in the following contentions or explanations which have been culled from a variety of sources[103]:

---

[99] Chapter 2.10, Table 2.4 above.

[100] 11 USC §727(a)(8), (9).

[101] BIA, ss 172(2), 173(1)(j).

[102] Note that BIA, s 173(1)(j) applies to any previous bankruptcy or proposal made by the debtor however distant in time. However, since the Canadian court has a very broad discretion under s 172(2), it could discount the earlier bankruptcy or proposal by suspending the discharge for only a token period where it felt that there was no causal connection between the earlier event and the current discharge application.

[103] See generally M Howard, 'A Theory of Discharge in Consumer Bankruptcy' (1987) 48 *Ohio State Law Journal* 1047; CJ Tabb, 'The Scope of the Fresh Start in Bankruptcy: Collateral Conversions and the Dischargeability Debate' (1990) 59 *George Washington Law Review* 56, at 89–103, and the more specific sources cited hereafter.

(1) that to impound a consumer bankrupt's future income would violate the Thirteenth Amendment to the US Constitution against involuntary servitude;

(2) that a coercive payment regime will provoke the consumer's resistance and encourage the consumer to change jobs or otherwise become less productive, and perhaps to disappear completely;

(3) that it is much better to secure the debtor's consent to a voluntary payment system by giving the debtor incentives that are not available in a straight bankruptcy than to coerce him to make involuntary payments;

(4) that the British style income payment and discretionary discharge system is based on the historical role of the British insolvency legislation as a creditors' debt collection instrument: this was not true (it is argued) of the US National Bankruptcy Act of 1898 because pre-bankruptcy debt collection rules generally fall under state jurisdiction;[104]

(5) that a British style income payment and discretionary discharge system is intrusive, paternalistic and subjective since no two debtors and their families have the same needs and face the same circumstances;[105]

(6) that to attempt to engraft a means test on what is already a very complex and overburdened US consumer bankruptcy system would be the straw that breaks the camel's back;[106]

(7) that since the bulk of consumer bankruptcy debts today consist of consumer credit liabilities, it is more efficient to oblige the credit industry to internalise its losses or to tighten its credit granting standards if creditors believe their losses are too high than to expect consumers to resist the impulse for instant gratification encouraged by the ready availability of consumer credit;[107]

(8) that there is no evidence of large scale abuses in the existing bankruptcy system and that the overwhelming percentage of those seeking chapter 7 bankruptcy protection are hopelessly insolvent and would not be able to pay off their indebtedness in any reasonable time frame even if means testing and a mandatory chapter 13 regime were to be introduced.[108]

The author has commented elsewhere[109] on these defences of the status quo but three of the arguments warrant further discussion. This is because they have figured prominently in the opposition to the means testing and other creditor-oriented provisions in the recent and current Congressional Bills, and

---

[104] See Boshkoff (n 12 above) at 103 *et seq*.

[105] *Ibid* at 120–23. J Braucher, 'Lawyers and Consumer Bankruptcy: One Code, Many Cultures' (1993) 67 *American Bankruptcy Law Journal* 501, at 583 (eloquently expressing similar sentiments without allusion to the British style provisions), cited in E Warren, 'A Principled Approach to Consumer Bankruptcy' (1997) 71 *American Bankruptcy Law Journal* 483, at 505.

[106] Warren (n 105 above) at 505–6. The metaphor is the author's, not Prof Warren's.

[107] TH Jackson, *The Logic and Limits of Bankruptcy Law* (Harvard University Press, 1986) ch 10, at 234–36.

[108] TA Sullivan, E Warren and JL Westbrook, 'Consumer Bankruptcy in the United States: A Study of Alleged Abuse and of Local Legal Cultures' (1997) 20 *Journal of Consumer Policy* 223.

[109] JS Ziegel, 'The Philosophy and Design of Contemporary Consumer Bankruptcy Systems: A Canada-United States Comparison' (1999) 37 *Osgoode Hall Law Journal* 205, at 245–48.

are also relevant in the Canadian context. The first issue is whether the US consumer bankruptcy figures show filings by a large number of consumers with surplus income who could afford to make substantial payments on their debts. The second is whether the cost of applying a means test of the complexity envisioned in the Congressional Bills would exceed potential benefits and whether debtors with surplus income should be denied access to chapter 7 altogether and be forced either to file under a revised and restrictive chapter 13 or to forego bankruptcy relief altogether. The third issue is whether the traditional US fresh start policy can be justified on insurance or behavioural principles whether or not a debtor has surplus income determined on some acceptable basis.

(c) Is Means Testing in Fact Needed?

This study has previously noted[110] the Schwartz/Anderson finding, corroborating the earlier findings in the Brighton/Connidis study,[111] that very few of the potential bankrupts in their sample had significant amounts of surplus income.[112] In the United States, Sullivan, Warren and Westbrook reported similar findings in their 1981 study of a large cross-section of American consumer bankrupts[113] and reaffirmed those findings in an analysis of a sample of bankrupts a decade later.[114] These findings contradicted an earlier industry sponsored study by the Credit Research Center at Purdue University, published in 1982,[115] which claimed that about 20 per cent of the bankrupts in the sample of files examined by the researchers had surplus incomes from which they could have paid off part of their debts.

The battle of statistics was resumed with the introduction of the Congressional Bills and the critics' complaint that the means testing provisions in the Bills were aimed at non-existent targets. Four new studies were published. Two of the studies were sponsored by the credit card industry (Ernst & Young Studies 1 and 2),[116] one by the American Bankruptcy Institute (Culhane and

---

[110] Chapter 2.7(c) above.

[111] JW Brighton and JA Connidis, *Consumer Bankrupts in Canada*, Ottawa: *Consumer and Corporate Affairs Canada* (1982).

[112] However, these findings must now be compared with post-1997 Canadian experience under the BIA, s 68 surplus income payment requirements, chapter 2.7(b) above.

[113] TA Sullivan, E Warren and JL Westbrook, *As We Forgive Our Debtors: Bankruptcy and Consumer Credit in America* (OUP, 1989) ch 12.

[114] TA Sullivan, E Warren and JL Westbrook, 'Consumer Debtors Ten Years Later: A Financial Comparison of Consumer Bankrupts 1981–1991' (1994) 68 *American Bankruptcy Law Journal* 121.

[115] Credit Research Center, Krannert School of Management, *Consumers' Right to Bankruptcy: Origins and Effects*, monograph No 23 (Purdue University, 1982). For a vigorous critique of the methodology used in this study and earlier industry sponsored studies, see E Warren, 'The Market for Data: the Changing Role of Social Sciences in Changing the Law' [2002] *Wisconsin Law Review* 1.

[116] Ernst & Young, 'Chapter 7 Bankruptcy Petitioners' Ability to Repay: The National Perspective, 1997' (March 1998) and Ernst & Young, 'Chapter 7 Bankruptcy Petitioners' Repayment Ability under HR 833: The National Perspective' (March 1999). Apparently there were other credit industry sponsored studies as well, which were not included in the GAO appraisal referred to in n 119 below.

White Study),[117] and a fourth was initiated by two researchers in EOUST (Bermant and Flynn Study).[118] The studies were based wholly or in part on the criteria used in the Congressional Bills to determine debtors' repayment capacities. The studies reached different conclusions. The March 1998 Ernst & Young Study and the January 1999 Study by Bermant and Flynn estimated the number of 'can pay' debtors in their samples at 15 per cent; the second (March 1999) Study by Ernst & Young reported a figure of 10 per cent while the Culhane and White Study came in with the lowest estimate at 3.6 per cent. At the request of the US Senate Judiciary Committee, the US General Accounting Office (GAO) studied the results and concluded[119] that the differences were mainly due to differences in the researchers' methodologies, assumptions about debtors' expenses, and interpretation of the Congressional Bills used by the researchers in their studies. It would be presumptuous for a non-US observer to mediate these conflicting results. It would be equally inappropriate to use the Canadian surplus income figures for comparative purposes because they are based on an entirely different set of criteria.

(d) The Cost of Means Testing

US critics of the Congressional Bills have also charged that the cost of mean testing over a million petitioners a year would be prohibitive[120] and wholly disproportionate to any likely benefits for creditors. This author is not aware of reported studies comprehensively investigating this aspect of means testing. The means testing requirements are much more stringent under the Congressional Bills than under section 68 of the BIA and involve many more steps.[121] The cost could average out at US$100 per debtor or, say, US$100 million a year for 1 million bankrupts.[122] Assuming 10 per cent of the 1 million debtors (100,000) taking the means test opt for chapter 13, the cost of administering the payments

---

[117] MB Culhane and MM White, 'Taking the New Consumer Bankruptcy Model for a Test Drive: Means-Testing Real Chapter 7 Debtors' (1999) VII *American Bankruptcy Institute Law Review* 27.

[118] G Bermant and E Flynn, EOUST, *Incomes, Debts, and Repayment Capacities of Recently Discharged Chapter 7 Debtors* (January 1999).

[119] USGAO, Report to Congressional Requestors, *Personal Bankruptcy: Analysis of Four Reports on Chapter 7 Debtors' Ability to Pay* (Washington, June 1999) 3 (hereafter GAO Report).

[120] See, eg, Braucher, (n 37 above).

[121] For the details see 3.5 below.

[122] The current number of consumer bankruptcies is in the vicinity of 1.5 million, including chapter 13 filers. For the purpose of this estimate, it is assumed that about one-third of the bankrupts, the traditional ratio, will continue to file under chapter 13 without subjecting themselves to a means test. According to Prof Warren, the GAO scored just one segment of Bill HR 833 for estimated costs. It concluded that, unlike the current system requiring about half the cost of administering the bankruptcy system to be covered by general tax revenues, implementation of the means test would impose (presumably additional) costs of US$333 million over 2000–04, while it would decrease the government fee receipts by US$4 million: Warren, 'What is a Women's Issue? Bankruptcy, Commercial Law, and Other Gender-Neutral Topics' (2002) 25 *Harvard Women's Law Journal* 19, at 54, n 116, citing CBO, *Cost Estimate HR 833 Bankruptcy Reform Act of 1999* (5 May 1999).

by debtors and making remittances to creditors for up to five years could amount to another US$3 billion.[123] These potential costs should be measured against the Reports' estimates of the amount of unsecured non-priority debt (such as credit card debt) that the 'can pay' debtors could potentially repay over five years. They range from US$1 billion to about US$4 billion[124] although industry estimates are much higher.[125] It is important to emphasise, however, that criticism of the Congressional Bills is not restricted to the costs and complexity of the means test requirements. It is equally directed to the futility of forcing debtors into chapter 13 if they fail to qualify for chapter 7 or be denied bankruptcy relief altogether. The current structure of chapter 13 is examined hereafter.[126] Suffice it to say here that in the view of many US observers, the chapter is not meeting its original purpose. The national failure rate is between 60 to 70 per cent.[127] The reason is said to be that too many attorneys and bankruptcy judges are encouraging use of the chapter by consumers with inadequate discretionary incomes. The critics allege that the Congressional Bills will make things worse, not better. This result will ensue because of (in their view) the coercive effects of the means testing requirements coupled with much stricter chapter 13 provisions. The overall effect therefore of the new legislation will be detrimental at both ends of the spectrum: at one end, insolvent debtors will not wish to run the gauntlet of the means testing requirements and will be left to fend off their creditors as best they can. At the other end of the spectrum, debtors will attempt to meet chapter 13's new exacting requirements but be no more successful than the current cohort of chapter 13 debtors.

(e) Internalising Losses, Insurance Principles, and More

Over the years, a small number of economists and other scholars (mainly US)[128] have examined US discharge policy and other aspects of the consumer bankruptcy system from an economic perspective. At one end of the spectrum, these analysts have enquired whether current discharge rules can be justified on insurance and similar risk allocation principles. At the other end of the spectrum, the critics have argued that the existing rules encourage opportunistic behaviour by

---

[123] For the existing legal and administrative costs under chapter 13, see 3.7 below.

[124] GAO Report (n 119 above) at 2.

[125] Warren (n 122 above) at 47, n 94, cites industry advertisements (echoed by members of Congress) claiming that the record number of personal bankruptcies 'cost American families $400 a year.' Given 100 million American families, this would translate into the staggering sum of US$40 billion!

[126] See 3.7 below.

[127] The NBRC Report (n 21 above) cites a completion rate of only 32 per cent. For similar findings by US scholars see Braucher (n 37 above) at 409, n 9.

[128] See among others Symposium, 'The Economics of Bankruptcy Reform' (1977) 41(4) *Law and Contemporary Problems* 1; JC Weistart, 'The Costs of Bankruptcy' (1977) 41(4) *Law and Contemporary Problems* 107; TH Jackson, *The Logic and Limits of Bankruptcy* (Harvard University Press, 1986) chs 10 and 11; RA Posner, *Economic Analysis of Law* (5th edn, 1998) 442–43.

debtors who are not asset or income poor and that the rules should therefore be changed to avoid such abuses. Although these seem to be contradictory approaches, properly understood, it is believed that they can be reconciled.

The rationalisation of the fresh start policy as a form of social insurance or risk allocation proceeds from the proposition that consumers cannot reasonably provide for or anticipate basic changes in their financial fortunes resulting from such events as job loss or change of employment, serious illness or accidents, family deaths or marital break-ups. Creditors, it is argued, are in a much better position to absorb these risks, first, because they can diversify them over a large number of borrowers and, secondly, because their statistical records will tell them the magnitude of such risks and what allowance they should make for them in calculating the cost of the credit.[129] It is obvious that such internalisation must take place now, even in the absence of a fresh start rule, because creditors have no other choice in the vast majority of bankruptcies involving asset and income poor consumers. The internalisation approach is all the more attractive because of the ready availability of large amounts of credit to consumers in the contemporary North American environment, the heavy selling of goods and services on credit, the frequency of 'no down payment' and deferred payment offers, and the general inducement to spend now and pay later.

Prof Jackson has offered[130] other rationalisations to support a discharge result, based on psychological findings that are also helpful in explaining risk allocation and insurance theories in the consumer bankruptcy context. He points out there is strong evidence that the power of impulsive behaviour in many consumers is such that when presented with the choice of present gratification or future enhanced benefits, consumers will often prefer the former over the latter. Faced with this dilemma, it is argued, if individuals cannot adequately control their impulses they may welcome the assistance of a socially imposed rule. A statutory cooling off period, minimum down payments, maximum maturity periods and regulation of interest rates are examples of possible controls. Several of them have been used in the past, though often for other reasons. However, restrictions on the extension and cost of credit are very unpopular with lenders and have been progressively dismantled to the point where little remains of them. Given the absence of other suitable options, Prof Jackson argues, a legal rule discouraging the extension of excessive credit through the fresh start rule will achieve the same result by forcing creditors to better police the borrowers or to run the risk of the borrower becoming bankrupt without repaying his debts. Also, considering that we are seeking to protect the consumer against the consequences of impulsive behaviour it would be equally

---

[129] As Prof Weston notes in 'Some Economic Fundamentals for an Analysis of Bankruptcy' in Symposium (n 128 above) 47, at 56–59, given the improved techniques for credit scoring and credit assessment with computer technology, the costs of doing so have become much reduced and the predictions much more accurate. He was writing 20 years ago and it is safe to assume that the technology has become much cheaper in the interval and the feasibility of accurate scoring still better.

[130] TH Jackson, *The Logic and Limits of Bankruptcy Law* (1986) ch 10, 232 *et seq*.

inappropriate to allow the consumer to waive ex ante the benefits of the discharge rule.

The second phenomenon invoked by Prof Jackson[131] to justify a fresh start policy rests on evidence that individuals appear to make choices by processing information that consistently under-estimates future risks ('cognitive dissonance'). In the context of the use of credit, he argues, these factors, may lead individuals to under-estimate the risks that over-spending may impose on their future well-being and that of their families. He believes it would be too difficult for consumers to make their own correction for these known biases, and therefore concludes that these incomplete heuristics provide a second normative justification for a socially imposed rule of a non-waivable fresh start.

Attractive as these arguments are, there are limitations to basing the discharge of debts on risk allocation and social insurance grounds and it is important for us to understand what they are. In invoking risk allocation models, authors often analogise to the rules in contract law excusing a party from further performance of his obligation because of a supervening event. There is much controversy in Anglo-Canadian and US law over the doctrinal basis of this rule—whether it is based on the parties' imputed agreement or some broader ground of public policy. What is not in doubt, however, is that in practice courts on both sides of the border have shown themselves very reluctant to excuse performance because changing circumstances have made it much more expensive for a party to meet its contractual obligations than may have been anticipated. What this means is that the contract analogy must either be abandoned in the bankruptcy discharge context or be substantially remodelled to serve its intended purpose.[132] But doing so raises a new set of questions and in particular this question: when should the law deem the creditor to have completely waived his claim to further payment? Insolvency per se would obviously not be sufficient from an economic (or social) perspective if the debtor has surplus income and could continue to make at least some payments.

One encounters similar difficulties in seeking to spell out the terms of an imputed insurance policy, whether arising by operation of bankruptcy law or because of the credit contract between the parties. No insurance policy is open-ended and insurers have long learned to protect themselves against moral hazard risks and risks arising by adverse selection.[133] In the credit area, moral hazards would be created by such events as the debtor running up large debts on a credit card in contemplation of the debtor's bankruptcy or borrowing a large sum of money to discharge a secured debt against exempt property. Adverse selection would occur if the debtor failed to disclose his bankruptcy within the past six years or other personal characteristic affecting his suitability as a borrower. We may be sure that an informed creditor-cum-insurer would be

---

[131] TH Jackson, *The Logic and Limits of Bankruptcy Law* (1986) ch 10, 232 *et seq* at 234–36, 237.

[132] Cf R Hillman, 'Contract Excuse and Bankruptcy Discharge' (1990) 43 *Stanford Law Review* 99.

[133] Cf R Cooter and T Ulen, *Law and Economics* (Scott, Foresman & Co, 1997) app at 65–66; and RA Posner, *Economic Analysis of Law* (5th edn, Aspen Publishers, Inc, 1998) 442–43.

alert to protect itself against these and similar risks and would object strenuously to any legislatively imposed insurance policy (via a discharge rule) that denied it the right to do so or did not write such exemptions into the law itself.

Still more important is the question whether the creditor as insurer should be required to forego payment of the balance of the debt after bankruptcy even if the debtor has a bright income future—the same question that arises in determining risk allocation under a change of circumstances doctrine. The answer presumably will be the same. In short, whether we invoke insurance principles or risk allocation theories, we are forced to confront the same issues as have faced Commonwealth legislators. This is to determine whether a bankrupt should be entitled to an absolute discharge in all cases or whether the court should have a range of options. Of course, it may be argued, as the critics have argued, that the costs of administering a means testing system may be so high, both economically and socially, that it is better to let some percentage of debtors off the hook than to risk jeopardising the whole discharge system.

The limited liability so readily available to shareholders of incorporated companies throughout the common law world is an analogy that is also often invoked to justify a clean and unqualified discharge rule. However, the analogy proves too much. In the case of close corporations, lenders often contract around limited liability by requiring personal guarantees from the directors or principal shareholders of the company. There is also much dissatisfaction among creditors with the limited liability rule for close corporations because it lends itself to easy abuse. As a result, Commonwealth courts and legislatures have shown an increasing willingness to impose personal liability on directors in a variety of circumstances, including particularly those cases where the company continues to trade when the directors know or ought to know that the company will not be able to meet its liabilities.[134]

(f) Professor Michelle White's Concerns[135]

Prof Michelle White of Michigan University has addressed[136] similar concerns but from a very different perspective. The focus of her inquiries has been not

---

[134] See JS Ziegel, 'Creditors as Corporate Stakeholders: The Quiet Revolution—An Anglo-Canadian Perspective' (1993) 43 *University of Toronto Law Journal* 511 and, for an update on Canadian, particularly Ontario, case law developments, WD Gray, 'Creditors, Losers under CBCA Reform but Winners in Judge-Made Corporate Law' (*Canadian Business Law Journal, forthcoming*).

[135] In examining Prof White's writings in this area, the author has been greatly assisted by a lengthy memorandum prepared for him by Prof Saul Schwartz of Carleton University in August 1999. Because of space constraints, only limited use is made of the memorandum in what follows. In any event, Prof Schwartz should not be held responsible for any inadequacies in the account given in the text.

[136] See in particular MJ White, 'Personal Bankruptcy under the 1978 Bankruptcy Code: An Economic Analysis' (1987) 63 *Indiana Law Journal* 1; MJ White, 'Economic versus Sociological Approaches to Legal Research: the Case of Bankruptcy' (1991) 25 *Law and Society Review* 685; and MJ White, 'Why it Pays to File for Bankruptcy: a Critical Look at the Incentives Under the US Personal Bankruptcy Law and a Proposal for Change' (1998) 65 *University of Chicago Law Review* 685.

to rationalise the existing US fresh start rule. Rather, it has been to show that current US bankruptcy rules easily lend themselves to abuse and that, as rational maximisers of their welfare, US debtors can be expected to exploit the rules to their advantage unless the rules are changed. In an article published in 1987,[137] she used the disparate state exemption rules to show how a calculating debtor could use them to his advantage in determining (a) whether he would benefit by petitioning for his bankruptcy, and (b) if the answer was yes, whether he should proceed via chapter 7 or chapter 13. She supported her conclusions with a narrow empirical base. In a 1998 article in the University of Chicago Law Review, Prof White returned to the same themes but on a more expanded basis using data from the US Survey of Consumer Finances to determine the proportion of respondents who would benefit financially from declaring bankruptcy under various assumptions concerning their access to property exemptions. She concluded that between 10 and 25 per cent of the respondents would benefit financially from declaring bankruptcy although the median benefits would be quite small. Using the same data set she then recalculated the net financial benefit of declaring bankruptcy assuming the respondents engaged in various kinds of strategic behaviour such as converting all non-exempt assets into exempt assets. Assuming the most widespread strategic behaviour, her conclusion was that the proportion of respondents who would benefit financially ranged from 20 to 60 per cent, although again the median benefits remained very modest.

In order to deter such opportunistic conduct, Prof White proposed two possible bankruptcy reforms, Reform I and Reform II. Both reforms would require debtors to repay unsecured debts from future income that is above the greater of US$7,500 or 90 per cent of gross income. The difference between Reforms I and II is in the level of asset exemptions allowed. Reform I would allow exemptions similar to those in force as of 1994 while Reform II would replace all state and federal asset exemptions with a single US$30,000 exemption that would apply to all assets, including home and personal property. Using this simulation, she concluded[138] that her proposed reforms would 'reduce the overall proportion of households that benefit financially from bankruptcy, but would accomplish this mainly by reducing the proportion of high ability to pay households that have an incentive to file.'

Prof White's approach is open to a variety of criticisms. Among the most important objections are that her analyses are not based on the profiles of actual bankrupts and do not take into account non-economic factors. She also fails to explain why, if debtors are rational actors and wealth maximisers, the statistics do not disclose a much higher percentage of bankrupts with high incomes and assets than is the case. Her approach is in stark contrast to the sociologically

---

[137] *Ibid.* ('Personal Bankruptcy under the 1978 Bankruptcy Code'.)
[138] *Ibid.* ('Why It Pays to File for Bankruptcy'), at 716.

oriented position adopted by Sullivan, Warren and Westbrook[139] who, on the basis of their empirical research, conclude that consumer insolvencies are a complex phenomenon driven by a multiplicity of factors, none of which can explain the results by itself. These authors do, however, attach much importance to local cultural factors.

Given the fact that the Canadian discharge rules have from the beginning been very different from the US rules and are even more so since the 1997 BIA amendments, it is idle to speculate what results would have emerged from a White type analysis in a Canadian context. It would be fair to state however that her philosophy would have resonated well with the proponents of the 1997 amendments. It is even clearer that it permeates many aspects of the current Congressional Bills.

(g) Means Testing Under S 420

The means testing provisions in the Congressional Bills and the consequences of the court finding the petitioner to have surplus income are very different from those introduced in the 1997 Canadian legislation, and it is necessary to explain the proposed US provisions. The provisions in S 420, the Bankruptcy Reform Act 2002, incorporating HR 333 with amendments and approved by the Senate on 17 July 2001, will be used as representative of the general run of recent Congressional proposals.[140]

An earlier version of the draft legislation would have excused debtors below the national median income from the need to submit to detailed means testing. However, this provision was deleted in 1998. S 420, required all debtors to undergo means testing. The median income test only comes into play *at the end* of the process to determine whether creditors, in addition to judges and trustees, can bring abuse challenges and also to determine who is subject to a presumed abuse challenge.[141] Debtors therefore face potentially two abuse challenges under §707: (a) a claim based on presumed abuse combining an income means test and a median income test, and (b) a non-presumptive abuse test with different standards depending on whether the challenge is raised by the court or trustee, or by a creditor. In either event, if abuse is found, the chapter 7 petition must be dismissed but the debtor will be allowed to convert the proceedings to chapter 13 as an alternative to dismissal.

---

[139] TA Sullivan, E Warren and JL Westbrook, *As We Forgive Our Debtors: Bankruptcy and Consumer Credit in America* (Oxford University Press, 1989) chs 12 and 13; and TA Sullivan, E Warren and JL Westbrook, 'Law, Models, and Real People: Choice of Chapter in Personal Bankruptcy' (1988) 13 *Law and Social Inquiry* 661.

[140] The following description borrows heavily from Braucher (n 37 above) at 433 *et seq*, and also makes use of the summary of the earlier Bills in E Wedoff, ABI, *Updated Analysis* (1 November 1999) 4–6 with respect to the fate of S 420 and HR 333 and the introduction of new HR 975 in February 2003, see above n 38a and accompanying text.

[141] S 420 (n 36 above) at §102(a)(6) and (7).

Under S 420, every debtor would have to file an itemised statement of monthly net income. Failure to do so will result in automatic dismissal of the case.[142] Abuse will be presumed if current monthly income, after allowing for specified expenses, multiplied by 60 is the lesser of (a) 25 per cent of unsecured claims or US$6,000, whichever is greater, or (b) US$10,000.[143] Current monthly income will be based on an average of the debtor's income over the last six months and, in a joint case, of the spouse's income. The permissible expenses include[144]:

(1) expenses under Internal Revenue Service (IRS) national and local standards for housing, transportation, food and clothing;

(2) actual expenses in categories listed by the IRS standards as 'other necessary expenses';

(3) an additional 5 per cent of the IRS food and clothing standards if reasonable and necessary;

(4) actual reasonable and necessary expense for an elderly or disabled household member;

(5) 'actual' administrative expenses of a hypothetical chapter 13 debtor;

(6) actual reasonable and necessary private school expenses up to US$1,500 per year per child;

(7) actual reasonable and necessary expenses for home energy costs in excess of IRS local standards;

(8) monthly secured debt payments, defined as amounts due to secured debtors for 60 months after the petition date, plus additional amounts necessary to retain a residence, motor vehicle or other necessary property in a chapter 13 filing; and

(9) priority debt payments,[145] such as child support and tax obligations, again divided by 60 months for the calculation.

Where the debtor's net current monthly income, after allowing for the permissible heads of deductions, is US$100 or more,[146] the debtor would only be able to defeat a §707(b) dismissal motion by demonstrating 'special circumstances' requiring additional expenses or adjustment of currently monthly income sufficient to reduce the net balance to less than US$100. Even where the §707(b) presumption was rebutted, on motion the court could still be required to consider whether the debtor filed the petition in bad faith and whether the totality of the circumstances demonstrated abuse.

The debtor's schedules of current income and expenses (currently required to be filed under the Federal Rules of Bankruptcy) would be required to include a

---

[142] S 420 (n 36 above) at §§102, 315(b), 316.

[143] *Ibid* at §102(a)(2)(B)(iv).

[144] Braucher (n 37 above) at 435–37. The author is indebted to Prof Braucher for allowing him to paraphrase her excellent summary.

[145] Priority debts are defined in 11 USC §507.

[146] The US$100 is derived from the fact that, multiplied by 60, it yields US$6,000, one of the tests applied under S 420 §102(a)(2)(B)(iv).

statement of current monthly income, together with a list of the authorised deductions. The trustee would be obliged to review these materials and, within 10 days after the statutory meeting of creditors, file a statement with the court indicating whether the debtor's schedules gave rise to a presumption of abuse. If the presumption applied and the debtor's income was at least equal to a defined national median income, the trustee would be obliged to file either a motion under §707(b) or a statement why such a motion was not being filed.[147]

The debtor's attorney will also be at risk if the attorney files a false or misleading petition and supporting schedules and documents, and is found to have acted negligently or recklessly. In such circumstances, the court on motion could award damages against the attorney, which could include both reimbursement of the trustee's expenses and a civil penalty.[148]

As will be noted from the above very condensed description, the means test under S 420 differs in structure and consequences from the BIA position in Canada in the following respects:

(1) Under S 420, in determining the debtor's surplus income, the debtor is allowed to deduct attorney's fees, and amounts owing under secured debts and priority obligations as well as the prescribed living expenses. In this respect, the proposed US bench-marks are more generous than the Canadian ones.

(2) Apparently, it would be much more difficult for the debtor to prove special circumstances under S 420 justifying the deduction of higher expenses than is arguably possible in Canada under the broader discretion given the trustee under the Superintendent's standards.

(3) Once the net amount of surplus income has been calculated, if it is US$100 or more, it will trigger the prescribed consequences. In contrast, under the Canadian regime, the debtor is only required to surrender one-half of the surplus income.

(4) The purposes of the means testing also differs. The primary purpose of the means test under S 420 is to deny the debtor access to chapter 7 if surplus income is shown; it will serve a secondary purpose in determining the amount of 'disposable income' under existing §1325(b)(1)(B) if the debtor

---

[147] S 420 (n 36 above) at §102(c).

[148] *Ibid* at §102, adding 11 USC §707(b)(4)(C). Under existing Bankruptcy Rule §9011(b) an attorney filing a petition or other documents in court is already deemed to certify, inter alia, that, to the best of the attorney's knowledge, information and belief, 'formed after an inquiry reasonable under the circumstances' the allegations and other factual contentions have evidentiary support. Under the amended provisions an attorney's signature of a petition, pleading or written motion constitutes certification that the attorney has:

  (i) performed a reasonable investigation into the circumstances that gave rise to the petition, pleading, or written motion; and

  (ii) determined that the petition, pleading, or written motion:

    (I) is well grounded in fact; and

    (II) is warranted by existing law or a good faith argument for the extension, modification, or reversal of existing law and does not constitute an abuse under paragraph (1).

elects to convert to chapter 13 or if he by-passes chapter 7 altogether. 'Disposable income' will now mean 'current monthly income' as determined under S 420 §102.[149] Under the BIA regime, the situation is reversed. If surplus income is found, the debtor will be required to pay it over in a straight bankruptcy proceeding but apparently retains considerable flexibility in determining how much of his income he will turn over in a consumer proposal.

Overall, the Canadian provisions are much more user friendly, much simpler, and much less bureaucratic.

6. NON-DISCHARGEABLE DEBTS

(a) Current Position and NBRC Recommendations

§523 of the Bankruptcy Code lists the exceptions to a discharge obtained by a debtor under §727 and the discharge granted by the court from an uncompleted chapter 13 plan.[150] Depending on how one counts them, there at least 18 types of dischargeable debts and liabilities and, as previously shown,[151] the United States has the dubious distinction of having the largest number of non-dischargeable debts by a wide margin—more than twice as many in the BIA and almost four times as many as under the Australian and British legislation. It seems that many US pressure groups see the exclusions as a necessary trade off for the generous fresh start policy[152] and, not surprisingly, it is even more difficult to find a common denominator for the US exclusions than it is in the case of the Canadian exclusions.

The US exclusions cover a wide range of taxes involving income, property, employment or excise debts, various types of fraudulent or otherwise tortious conduct, domestic alimony, maintenance and support obligations, unpaid student loans, and such miscellanea as debt for a fee or assessment becoming due and payable after the order for relief to a membership association for co-operative housing and condominiums[153] and debts for a fee imposed by a court to cover court costs.[154]

Many of the exclusions appear to have little practical importance in low-income consumer bankruptcies. The NBRC was, however, concerned about the

---

[149] S 420 (n 36 above) at §102(b)(c).

[150] See 11 USC §1328(b),(c).

[151] See chapter 2.10 above at Table 2.4.

[152] It is not the only reason. Other public policy reasons also play a role, particularly with respect to the non-dischargeability of alimony and family maintenance arrears, unpaid taxes and student loans, compensation for criminal injuries, and restitution for goods and services obtained fraudulently.

[153] 11 USC §523(a)(16).

[154] 11 USC §523(a)(17).

frequency with which credit card companies invoked the false representations exception to discharge under §523(a)(2)(A) with a view to holding debtors liable for credit card debts incurred shortly before bankruptcy,[155] and about disagreement among the bankruptcy courts concerning the interpretation of the provisions and when it was appropriate to imply false representations by the debtor when using the credit card. The Commission favoured adopting a 30-day 'bright line' test as a compromise solution to catch debtors incurring pre-bankruptcy credit card debts without an illegal intent.[156]

(b) Dischargeability of Student Loans

The Commission was equally concerned about the non-dischargeability of student loans under §523(a)(8) and recommended the repeal of the provision[157]— another of the Commission's recommendations that has not been followed.

Before the 1970s, student loans were not treated differently from other debts for discharge purposes but since then their dischargeability has been increasingly restricted. The current Code makes student loans non-dischargeable under all chapters of the Code for seven years after the beginning of the repayment period of the loan unless the student bankrupt can show 'undue hardship.' However, the exception has been narrowly construed by the courts,[158] whose judgments seemed to reflect a widely held sentiment that debtors should be held to a higher standard with respect to non-commercial loans designed to improve the debtor's future earning capabilities. As in Canada's case, these strictures ignored the fact that students were often persuaded to borrow the money for ill-conceived vocational courses offered by commercial establishments and that the students became bankrupt precisely because they were not successful in securing well paying jobs.[159] As the Commission notes, guaranteed student loans would be unnecessary if they did not involve substantial risks, again an observation that seems to be equally apposite for Canada.

The Report also notes[160] the interesting fact that although student loans were dischargeable without restriction under chapter 13 plans prior to the 1994 amendments, there was little evidence of chapter 13 being used for this purpose.

---

[155] The NBRC Report (n 21 above) at 192, cites one industry report claiming that Visa members were currently challenging dischargeable debts in 99% of credit card bankruptcy cases. Note that 11 USC §523(a)(2)(C) also creates presumptions of non-dischargeability in favour of credit card companies for the purpose of proving a false representation under para (B) for debts relating to 'luxury goods or services' owed to a single creditor and aggregating more than US$1,150 or cash advances under an open-ended credit plan made to the debtor, in both cases within 60 days of the initiation of bankruptcy proceedings.

[156] *Ibid* at 194–95.

[157] NBRC Report (n 21 above) at recommendation 1.4.5 *et seq.*

[158] *Ibid* at 207–8.

[159] *Ibid* at 215, citing GAO analysis of defaulting student borrowers.

[160] *Ibid* at 210–11.

The effect of the 1994 amendment[161] was to put the dischargeability of student loans on the same plane for both chapter 7 and chapter 13 purposes and, not surprisingly, US courts have been even-handed in applying the hardship test equally narrowly in both situations.[162]

(c) Current Bills

As already intimated, the recent and current Congressional bills do not implement the NBRC recommendations. The trend in fact is the other way. For example, both HR 833 and S 625 expanded, though to different degrees, the presumption of fraud in the case of 'luxury goods' and cash advances secured by the debtor shortly before bankruptcy.[163] There are some procedural changes in debts incurred to pay non-dischargeable debts, which are also made non-dischargeable,[164] and some expansion of taxes and other debts, including credit card debts, made non-dischargeable in chapter 13.[165]

7. ALTERNATIVES TO STRAIGHT BANKRUPTCY: CHAPTER 13 PLANS

(a) 1938 Origins, 1978 Revisions and 1994 Amendments

Chapter 13 had its origins in the Chandler Act of 1938 and was influenced by earlier wage-earner plans introduced at the state level, notably Alabama. However, it departed from them by adding the 'unique powers' of bankruptcy law as, for example, by granting the debtor a discharge from the balance of the debts not covered under the terms of the plan. The 1938 legislation was very extensively revised in the 1978 Bankruptcy Code. This also greatly increased the ambit of chapter 13 by making it available to all individuals with regular income and increased the debt levels up to US$250,000 for non-contingent unsecured debts and US$750,000 for secured debt.[166] These changes reflected Congress' intention that chapter 13 should function as the 'primary' rehabilitative chapter for individual consumer debtors.[167]

The basic differences between a chapter 7 and a chapter 13 bankruptcy are these. Under chapter 7 the debtor loses all his non-exempt assets (including most of his secured assets unless he is in a position to redeem them or enters into a

---

[161] See now 11 USC §1328(a)(2).

[162] NBRC Report (n 21 above) at 213–14.

[163] S 420 (n 36 above) at §310, and cf HR 833 (n 34 above) at §133, S 625 (n 35 above) at §310.

[164] S 625 (n 35 above) at §314(a), HR 833 (n 34 above) §146, and S 420 (n 36 above) at §314(a).

[165] S 625 (n 35 above) at §§314(b), 704; HR 833 (n 34 above) at §§127, 807; and S 420 (n 36 above) at §314(b).

[166] 11 USC §109(e).

[167] Tabb (n 6 above) at 895, citing HR Rep No 595, 95th Congress, 1st Session 118 (1977).

reaffirmation agreement) but obtains the benefit of an immediate discharge from all dischargeable debts. Under chapter 13, on the other hand, the debtor retains his assets, including importantly his secured assets, but must make payments for three to five years in accordance with a court approved plan. In one sense, chapter 13 has been substantially successful in achieving its designers' goals since for a decade or more it has accounted for about one-third of all consumer bankruptcy proceedings. In another sense, chapter 13 has been a failure since in about two-thirds of the cases no plan is ever filed or, if filed, is not completed successfully.[168] The complaint has also frequently been made that many debtors use chapter 13 simply to keep secured creditors at bay or because they have been ill-advisedly encouraged to invoke the chapter although their personal circumstances did not justify it.[169]

Broadly speaking, chapter 13 and Part III 2 of the BIA have similar goals but the means by which they achieve them differ significantly. Chapter 13 is also much more detailed and technical than BIA, Part III 2 and has given rise to much more litigation than its Canadian counterpart. Some important differences between the two regimes have already been noted. The following notes are designed to amplify these differences and to explain the workings of chapter 13 in greater detail.

Like chapter 7, a chapter 13 proceeding is initiated by the filing of the debtor's petition,[170] which also results in an automatic stay of proceedings against the debtor under §362 by secured as well as unsecured creditors. The filing of the petition also triggers the appointment of a trustee, who is usually the standing trustee for that bankruptcy division appointed by the US trustee. As under chapter 7 (but unlike the Canadian position), the debtor has no input into the selection of the trustee. Once appointed, the trustee has many of the same duties and responsibilities as the trustee in straight bankruptcy proceedings.[171] One important exception to the trustee's role is that the debtor enjoys the rights and powers of a trustee under §363 of the Code with respect to the sale, use or lease of the debtor's property.[172]

§ 1322 spells out in considerable detail the mandatory and permissible contents of a chapter 13 plan. Thus the plan must provide for the submission of all or part of so much of the debtor's future income to the supervision or control of the trustee as is necessary for the execution of the plan. It must also provide for full payment of §507 priority claims and provide equal treatment for all claims in a class if the plan provides for several classes of creditors.[173] The plan may, inter alia, modify the rights of secured creditors (other than in respect of a security interest in real property constituting the debtor's principal residence)[174] by

---

[168] See the important analytical literature cited in Braucher (n 37 above) at 409, nn 9–10.
[169] NBRC Report (n 21 above) at 233–34.
[170] 11 USC §301.
[171] 11 USC §1302(b). Part III 2 of the BIA has no counterpart to this provision.
[172] 11 USC §1303.
[173] 11 USC §1322(a).
[174] 11 USC §1322(b)(2),

providing for the curing or waiving of any default and, even in the case of such real property liens, may provide for the curing of any default within a reasonable time and maintenance of payments on which the last payment is due after the date on which the final payment under the plan is due.[175] The plan may also provide for the assumption, rejection or assignment of an executory claim or unexpired lease not previously rejected under §365.[176] A plan's maximum period can run for three years unless otherwise ordered by the court, in which case it may last up to five years.[177]

A basic difference between chapter 13 and the consumer proposal provisions in the BIA resides in the disposition of a plan. Under Part III 2 of the BIA, the future of a plan rests with the creditors who must support it by the requisite majorities. Under the US Code, confirmation of a plan is the court's responsibility although the court does not have an unfettered discretion. §1325 provides that the court shall confirm the plan if, inter alia, the plan is proposed in good faith, unsecured creditors will receive not less than they would in a liquidation of assets under chapter 7 (the 'best value' test) and if, in the case of secured claims:

(a)   the holder of such claims has accepted the plan;
(b)   the plan entitles the secured party to retain its security and the value of the property to be distributed under the plan is not less than the allowed amount of such claim; or
(c)   the debtor surrenders the secured property.[178]

In addition, the debtor must also satisfy the court that she will be able to meet all payments under the plan and be able otherwise to comply with the plan.[179]

The debtor encounters further hurdles if the trustee or holders of unsecured claims object to the plan. In that case, the court cannot approve the plan unless the value of any property to be distributed is not less than the amount of the claim or unless the plan provides that all of the debtor's 'disposable income' for the next three years is to be committed to payments under the plan.[180] 'Disposable income' is defined as meaning, where the debtor is not engaged in business, income received by the debtor which is not reasonably necessary for the maintenance or support of the debtor or the debtor's dependants.[181]

---

[175]   11 USC §1322(b)(2),(5).

[176]   The Canadian BIA has no counterpart to §365 and the status of realty leases in bankruptcy is governed by provincial law. See BIA, s 146. BIA, s 65.2 deals with disclaimers of realty leases in commercial proposals under BIA, Part III 1, but this has no counterpart in BIA, Part III 2. Subject to these exceptions, the debtor's or trustee's entitlement to assume, reject or assign executory contracts will be governed by common law principles.

[177]   11 USC §1322(d).

[178]   11 USC §1325(a)(5). Note carefully that these conditions are framed in the alternative and that the second option permits a strip down of the lien to the allowed value of the claim. The value of a secured claim is determined under 11 USC §506(a).

[179]   11 USC §1325(a)(6).

[180]   11 USC §1325(b).

[181]   11 USC §1325(b)(2).

Bankruptcy judges have varied widely in their interpretation of the income test[182] and the subjective character of the test has attracted much adverse comment.

If a plan is approved by the court, it binds every creditor whether or not the creditor's claim is provided for in the plan and even though a creditor has objected to the plan. Unless the plan provides otherwise or the court makes a different order, the property covered by the plan vests in the debtor and vests in him free and clear of any claim or interest of any creditor provided for by the plan.[183]

In theory at least, an important attraction for debtors are the favourable discharge provisions in §1328 of the Code.[184] On completion of the plan payments, the debtor is entitled to a discharge from *all* debts provided for in the plan with the exception of five types of debt.[185] These are important exclusions; nevertheless, they are a great improvement on the 18 categories excluded from a chapter 7 discharge under §523 and are conceptually superior to the Canadian consumer proposal provisions, which offer no relief at all from otherwise non-dischargeable debts.

A different regime applies where the debtor seeks a discharge without having completed the plan payments.[186] The court can accede to the debtor's request if three conditions are satisfied: (i) non-completion of the plan was 'due to circumstances for which the debtor should not be held accountable'; (ii) the value of any property distributed under the plan is not less than the amount that would have been distributed in a chapter 7 liquidation; and (iii) modification of the plan under §1329 is not practicable. It seems that in practice US courts have been reluctant to find that the first condition was satisfied. Even if all three conditions are met, what the debtor ends up with is a result substantially less favourable than a discharge from a completed plan. This is because in a discharge under §1328(b) the debtor is still saddled with the full range of non-dischargeable debts under §523(a),[187] thereby seemingly leaving the debtor no better off than he would have been in a straight liquidation under chapter 7.

---

[182] 'Some courts confirm plans paying zero percent to unsecured creditors. Other courts condition confirmation on payment of high percentages of unsecured debt.' NBRC Report (n 21 above) at 235.

[183] 11 USC §1327.

[184] Commonly referred to as 'superdischarge provisions.'

[185] The five categories are: liabilities arising after the last plan payment; family support obligations; student loans, liabilities for personal injuries or death caused by the debtor when driving while impaired; and restitution orders or fines imposed on the debtor following a conviction: 11 USC §1328(a). Importantly, the exclusions do not extend to money, property or services allegedly secured by the debtor by fraudulent means unless there has been a conviction and restitution order. Cf the position in a chapter 7 discharge where no conviction is required: 11 USC §523(a)(2).

[186] 11 USC §1328(b).

[187] 11 USC §1328(c).

(b) NBRC Report and Recommendations[188]

Some of the Commission's concerns with the existing operation of chapter 13 have already been noted: the high non-completion rate of plans and misguided attempts to steer debtors into the chapter when they are not suited for it. The Commission was also concerned with other important facets of the operation of chapter 13 and made recommendations to address these problems. The issues and the Commission's recommendations[189] are summarised below.

(1) *Disparate treatment of disposable income requirement and uneven treatment of unsecured debtors.* The Report notes the courts' widely varying interpretation and scrutiny of the 'disposable income' requirement in §1325(b) and the disparate treatment of unsecured creditors under confirmed plans. Thus, some plans involved negligible or no pay-outs to unsecured creditors while others allow maximum pay-outs to non-dischargeable debts.[190] Some courts have developed guidelines requiring a minimum percentage of pay-outs to unsecured creditors from disposable income but the Commission criticises this standardised approach as being too rigid. The Report recommends instead[191] that debtors be required to pay a graduated percentage of their adjusted gross income, thereby recognising the fact that higher income debtors can afford to pay a higher fraction of their disposable incomes than lower income earners. Although this is not stated explicitly, presumably the Commission also intended the disposable income payments to be distributed evenly among unsecured creditors.

(2) *Consequences of incomplete payment plans.* The Commission was concerned that the current chapter 13 makes no provision for automatic conversion of failed plans to a chapter 7 bankruptcy. Debtors must request the conversion and since many debtors are unaware of the option they do not exercise it.[192] To address this problem, the Commission recommended the adoption of a default rule leading to automatic conversion to chapter 7 proceedings.

(3) *Multiple filings and abusive use of chapter 13.* It appears that a substantial number of debtors make serial filings under chapter 13 in order to avoid eviction by landlords or foreclosure of homes and repossession of motor vehicles.[193] The Commission found the evidence of abuses to be inconclusive and

---

[188]   NBRC Report (n 21 above) at 233 *et seq.*

[189]   *Ibid* at recommendation 1.5.4 *et seq.*

[190]   *Ibid* at 235.

[191]   *Ibid* at 268.

[192]   *Ibid* at 275. The Report notes that in the period 1980–88, dismissal was the most common disposition of failed chapter 13 cases: 49% were dismissed and only 14% were converted to chapter 7.

[193]   *Ibid* at 278–79. Another source of abuse involved debtors who file chapter 7 cases to be relieved of dischargeable debts and personal liability followed by a chapter 13 filing to restructure secured and non-dischargeable debts (so called 'chapter 20' cases). The US Supreme Court has upheld the legality of this two-case approach. *Ibid* at 364.

was not persuaded that the solution adopted by some courts—barring access to chapter 13—was warranted. In the Commission's view,[194] a better solution was to deny the debtor an automatic § 362 stay if two or more chapter 13 petitions had been filed within the preceding six years and if the individual has been a debtor in a bankruptcy case within the preceding 180 days. This would ensure that serial filings were not being made simply to stall landlords and secured creditors.

(4) *Retention of 'super-discharge' feature under §1328(a).*[195] The Commission did not accept the criticisms that non-dischargeable debts should not be treated differently in chapter 13 than under chapter 7. The Commission believed the disparate treatment was consistent with the purposes of chapter 13 and that if the debtor was not relieved of non-dischargeable debts after making payments for three to five years the debtor would often be worse off at the end of the repayment period than he was at the beginning. In the Commission's view, the super-discharge feature also encourages chapter 13 payments because it avoids objections that some creditors might otherwise be able to raise against an ordinary discharge under §523(a)(2) (allegations of fraudulent conduct by debtor).

(c) HR 833, S 625 and S 420 Provisions[196]

As previously noted, the NBRC recommendations had little impact on the Congressional Bills. Almost without exception, the HR 833, S 625, and S 420 chapter 13 provisions are creditor-driven and are designed to curb perceived debtor abuses as is shown by the following summary.

(1) *Lien-stripping and cram-down in chapter 13.* S 625 prohibited cram-down of any transaction completed within the preceding five years where the creditor held a security interest in an automobile or six months in relation to any other property. The prohibition covered both purchase and non-purchase money security interests.[197] The HR 833 provisions were slightly less draconian.[198] S 420 applies a three-year period for motor vehicles and a one-year period for other things of value.[199]

(2) *Super-discharges and non-dischargeable debts.* S 625 added taxes and various other debts, including some types of credit card debt, to the list of

---

[194] *Ibid* at 281–82.

[195] *Ibid* at recommendation 1.5.7.

[196] So far as Bills HR 833 and S 625 are concerned, the following summary is based on ABI, *Summary of Key Areas of Disagreement: S 625/HR 833 Conference* (15 February 2000) 6 *et seq*; and ABI, *Comparison of Consumer Bankruptcy Provisions in Various Versions of Legislation* (8 February 2000).

[197] S 625 (n 35 above) at §306.

[198] HR 833 (n 34 above) at §122.

[199] S 420 (n 36 above) at §306

non-dischargeable debts in §1328(a) of the Code.[200] The HR 833 provisions were substantially the same but slightly worse with respect to non-dischargeable taxes. S 420 apparently restricts the non-dischargeability of taxes to those involving fraudulent conduct.[201]

(3) *Tax returns.* S 625 and HR 833 required the debtor to file tax returns for the last six years as part of the chapter 13 documentation, arguably even where the existing law did not require a tax return from the debtor. S 420 requires automatic filing of a copy of the tax return for the latest taxable period, and also requires the debtor to file a copy of the return for the preceding three years at the request of the judge, the US trustee or any party in interest.[202]

(4) *Mobile homes.* S 625 and S 420 prohibited the cram-down of mobile home liens, whether in respect of purchase money or non-purchase money loans.[203]

(5) *Repeat filings and filings after prior discharge.* S 625 and HR 833 contained a variety of provisions designed to curb these perceived abuses, as also does S 420.[204]

(6) *Plan requirements.* S 625 required a five year repayment plan from debtors whose cases were converted from chapter 7 to chapter 13 or where a chapter 7 petition was dismissed under §707(b).[205] HR 833 contained a similar requirement but required payments to be based on the debtor's income above the median national average.[206] S 420's requirements are similar to those in HR 833.[207]

8. REAFFIRMATION AGREEMENTS

Reaffirmation agreements (RAs) signed by debtors in favour of creditors during bankruptcy proceedings or following the debtor's discharge from bankruptcy have long been common in the United States, and have been the subject of much critical discussion.[208] Prior to the Bankruptcy Reform Act of 1978, federal law

---

[200] S 625 (n 35 above) at §716.

[201] HR 833 (n 34 above) at §315(c)(2)(A) and (f); S 420 §707.

[202] *Ibid* at §315(c)(2)(A) and (f).

[203] S 625 (n 35 above) at §306(a) and (c); HR 833 (n 34 above) at §102, 302(e).

[204] S 625 (n 35 above) at §302, HR 833 (n 34 above) at §117 (restrictions on automatic stay); S 625 (n 35 above) at §312, HR 833 (n 34 above) at §137 (no discharge in chapter 13 cases within five years of prior case); S 420 (n 36 above) at §§303, 309, 311.

[205] S 625 (n 35 above) at §318.

[206] HR 833 (n 35 above) at §606.

[207] S 420 (n 34 above) at §318.

[208] The NBRC reported that reaffirmation agreements were 'at center stage' throughout the Commission's hearings and debates: NBRC Report (n 21 above) at 146. For a leading empirical study of reaffirmation practices, see MB Culhane and MM White, 'Debt After Discharge: An Empirical Study of Reaffirmation' (1999) 73 *American Bankruptcy Law Journal* 709.

did not regulate the use of RAs. Nevertheless, the National Bankruptcy Commission, whose report was presented to Congress in 1973, was so alarmed about the abuses frequently accompanying RAs that it wished to outlaw them altogether.[209] This was not politically acceptable and Congress settled on a compromise solution[210] involving judicial approval of such agreements as a condition of their validity. At the same time, the 1978 Act also added strong provisions[211] voiding any judgment obtained in respect of a discharged debt and imposing an injunction on the commencement or continuation of an action or the use of any other means to collect a discharged debt from the debtor or the debtor's property. The 1978 provisions were amended in 1984, and again in 1994, to make it clear[212] that a court hearing and judicial approval were not necessary where the RA filed in court was accompanied by a declaration or affidavit by the debtor's attorney stating that the agreement was a fully informed and voluntary agreement, that it did not impose undue hardship on the debtor or his dependants, and that the attorney had fully advised the debtor of the legal effect and consequences of the agreement.

(a) NBRC Recommendations

The NBRC, reporting in 1997, was of the view that the 1978 reaffirmation amendments had not achieved their goals and expressed concern that by all accounts RAs continue to grow in number and scope.[213] The Commission was also disturbed that some attorneys sign affidavits without satisfying themselves that the RA will not cause the debtor undue hardship, and was even more disturbed by the disclosure that Sears and other large retail stores were by-passing the statutory requirements altogether and continuing to collect payments on discharged debts.[214] The Commission's original inclination (like that of its 1973 predecessor) was to ban RAs altogether. It subsequently modified its position to allow reaffirmation agreements for secured debt and limited to the value of the collateral and excluding any additional amounts for attorneys' fees, collection costs and such like.[215]

---

[209] NBRC Report (n 21 above) at 148–49.

[210] See 11 USC §524(c).

[211] See now 11 USC §524(a).

[212] See now 11 USC §524(c)(3).

[213] The NBRC Report (n 21 above) notes (at 152) that, according to a 1996 *Visa* study, 52% of debtors reported reaffirming one or more debts with the majority of reaffirmations involving secured debt, particularly secured debt relating to motor vehicles.

[214] *Ibid* at 162–63. Sears was subsequently prosecuted and agreed to return the monies it had collected.

[215] *Ibid* at 160. For some reason, unlike the Commission's other recommendations, this one does not appear in bold type and as a separate paragraph.

(b) Position Under Current Bills

Once again, the Commission's recommendations made no impact on Congress. HR 833 did not directly erode the current reaffirmation provisions. However, it did so indirectly by precluding the use of class actions against creditors (such as the one brought against Sears) who ignored the Code's requirements. S 625 had no new reaffirmation provisions although there was the threat of a regressive Reed-Sessions amendment to §204 of the Bill that would have seriously undermined the disclosure requirements in §524(c) of the Code.[216] S 420 would require the General Accounting Office to conduct a study of the reaffirmation process under the Code to determine the overall treatment of consumers within the context of that process, and to report back to Congress on the results of the study together with legislative recommendations to address any abusive or coercive tactics found in the reaffirmation process.[217]

9. CREDIT COUNSELLING AS PART OF THE BANKRUPTCY PROCESS[218]

The United States has had creditor-inspired non-profit facilities since the 1960s for the counselling of over-committed debtors and the establishment of repayment plans. Until now, these extra-curial efforts have received no official status under the federal bankruptcy legislation but the position could change significantly as a result of the following provisions in S 420:

(1) *First,* a consumer debtor will not be allowed to file a bankruptcy case unless the debtor has received credit counselling from an approved non-profit budget and counselling agency within 180 days of the filing an individual or group briefing (including a briefing conducted by telephone or on the Internet) that outlined the opportunities for available credit counselling and assisted the debtor in performing a related budget analysis.[219] The counselling requirement does not apply to a debtor who resides in a district where the approved credit counselling agencies are not reasonably able to provide adequate services to additional debtors seeking credit counselling to comply with the Act's requirements. The debtor may also be excused if he can satisfy the court of 'exigent circumstances' meriting waiver of the counselling requirements and that he unsuccessfully sought credit counselling services during the five-day period following the request.[220]

---

[216] ABI, *Comparison* (n 196 above) at 7, labelled the amendment as a 'step back from current law.'

[217] S 420 (n 36 above) at §205.

[218] See also, AC Dekany, *Debt Counselling in Canada* (unpublished LLM thesis, 1999) 28–33; E Wedoff, *Updated Analysis* (1 November 1999) 51–52; and ABI, *Comparison* (n 196 above).

[219] S 420 (n 36 above) at §§106(a), 111. Cf HR 833 (n 34 above) at §302(a), S 625 (n 35 above) §105.

[220] S 420 (n 36 above) at §106(3).

(2) *Secondly,* once the requisite facilities have been established, chapter 7 or chapter 13 debtors will be denied a discharge from their debts if they have failed to complete an instructional course of personal financial management from an approved agency.[221] To determine the feasibility of the new requirement, a pilot educational programme for debtors' financial management will be tested in six judicial districts over an 18 months' period and evaluated for its effectiveness.

(3) *Third,* with a view to encouraging debt repayment arrangements outside bankruptcy, the claims of unsecured creditors may be reduced by up to 20 per cent if the debtor can show that she offered an alternative repayment schedule through an approved credit counselling agency, that the offer provided for payment of at least 60 per cent of the debt over the repayment period or an extension thereof, that no part of the debt was non-dischargeable, and that the creditor had unreasonably refused to consider the offer.[222]

(4) *Fourthly,* with a view to curbing abuses by profit-oriented debt relief agencies, the Bills envisage the establishment of regulations to govern such agencies' conduct.[223] The regulations would also penalise the agencies (1) for failing to provide promised services, (2) providing negligent counselling to debtors or making false statements in bankruptcy filings, (3) misrepresenting services to be provided to debtors, and (4) encouraging the incurring of debt by debtors for bankruptcy-related services.

These proposed legislative initiatives have not escaped criticisms. They would impose substantial added workloads and responsibilities on bankruptcy judges, court clerks, the US trustees and the Federal Trade Commission, and it is not clear whether Congress would be ready to vote the required funds and to appoint the needed number of new judges. From the debtors' perspective, the Bills do not indicate who is to pay for the required counselling and financial management programmes if debtors lack the means to pay for them out of their own resources. So far as the incentive to use out of court repayment facilities are concerned, critics have noted that it will be expensive and time-consuming for a debtor to prove that a creditor unreasonably refused a repayment offer and that a debtor will usually be better off making the offer in the form of a chapter 13 plan.

It is ironic that the Bills require debtors to prove that they have consulted a consumer credit counselling agency before filing a petition. These agencies have

[221] *Ibid* at §106(b) and (c). Cf HR 833 (n 36 above) at §§104, 302(b),(c), and S 625 (n 35 above) at §104.

[222] S 420 (n 36 above) at §201(a). Cf HR 833 (n 34 above) at §109, S 625 (n 35 above) at §201.

[223] S 420 (n 36 above) at §§227, 228. Cf HR 833 (n 34 above) at §§105, 106, 526. 'Debt relief agency' is defined in S 420 §226(a)(12A) as a person providing consumer bankruptcy goods and services for reward but excludes tax exempt non-profit organisations, creditors providing debt restructuring assistance to a debtor of the creditor, depositary institutions and credit unions.

been described as being in a state of turmoil,[224] and have long been criticised by consumer activists[225] because of their lack of independence and heavy reliance on creditor financing, and their failure to advise debtors where creditors have violated relevant federal consumer credit laws or where recourse to bankruptcy would provide better relief.

As is true in Canada's case, the requirement for debtors to have attended a financial management course as a precondition to discharge raises challenging moral and pedagogical questions. The preliminary trials that have been conducted so far in the United States also indicate that motivating debtors to attend the courses regularly for an extended period and taking the instruction seriously will tax the ingenuity of the planners.[226]

---

[224] See DA Lander, 'Recent Developments in Consumer Debt Counselling Agencies' (2002) 21 *American Bankruptcy Institute Journal* 14; and DA Lander, 'Snapshot of an Industry in Turmoil: the Plight of Consumer Debt Counseling' (2000) 54 *Consumer Finance Law Quarterly Report* 330.

[225] See HB Hoffman, 'Consumer Bankruptcy Filers and Pre-Petition Consumer Credit Counseling: Is Congress Trying to Place the Fox in Charge of the Henhouse?' (1999) 54 *Business Lawyer* 1629; and RL Stehl, 'The Failings of the Credit Counseling and Debtor Education Requirements of Proposed Consumer Bankruptcy Reform Legislation of 1998' (1999) 7 *American Bankruptcy Institute Law Review* 133.

[226] See K Gross, 'Developing a Model for Assessing Financial Literacy Education: Thinking Through Multiple Lenses for Multiple Purposes' in J Niemi-Kiesilainen, IDC Ramsay and WC Whitford (eds), *Consumer Bankruptcy in a Global Perspective* (Hart Publishing, forthcoming) and S Block-Lieb, K Gross and RL Wiener, 'Lessons from the Trenches: Debtor Education in Theory and Practice' (2002) 7 *Fordham Journal of Corporate and Financial Law* 503.

4

Australia[1]

IN THE INTRODUCTION to this study it was stated that Australia's bankruptcy law was particularly suited for comparison with Canada's consumer insolvency regime because of strong similarities between the two countries—in size of populations, geographical land masses, a large ethnic component, market economies, consumption patterns and lifestyles, a parliamentary system of government and insolvency law principles derived from England. It is believed the following review bears out these expectations but also highlights some important differences that carry useful lessons for other Commonwealth jurisdictions, including Canada.

1. RAPID GROWTH IN CONSUMER BANKRUPTCIES

An appropriate starting point is to note the rapid growth in the number of personal bankruptcies that Australia, like Canada, experienced between 1987–88 and 2001–02 (see Table 4.1). The number of personal bankruptcies for the administrative year ending 30 June 1999 was 26,376 compared with 8,124 for the year 1987–88, a 225 per cent increase over a 12-year period.[2] There were 1,678 non-bankruptcy personal insolvency proceedings in 1998–99 under Parts IX and X of the Commonwealth Bankruptcy Act 1966,[3] giving a total number of 28,054

---

[1] The following sources were principally relied on for this overview: RF Mason, 'Consumer Bankruptcies: an Australian Perspective' (1999) 37 *Osgoode Hall Law Journal* 449; RF Mason and J Duns, 'Developments in Consumer Bankruptcy Law in Australia' in J Niemi-Kiesilainen, IDC Ramsay and WC Whitford (eds), *Consumer Bankruptcy in a Global Perspective* (Hart Publishing, forthcoming).); D Rose (ed), *Lewis' Australian Bankruptcy Law* (11th edn, LBC Information Services, 1999); Insolvency and Trustee Service Australia (ITSA), *Profile of Debtors 2002*; ITSA, *Annual Report by the Inspector-General in Bankruptcy on the Operation of the Bankruptcy Act* hereafter Annual Report. The author obtained much help from ITSA's senior officials in Canberra, Melbourne and Sydney and was privileged to be able to visit ITSA's offices in Sydney and Melbourne in March 1999 and to observe their operations at first hand. The author is also greatly indebted for additional information on recent developments to Prof Mason, David Bergman, Adviser, Policy and Legislation, ITSA, Canberra, and Janice Pentland, chair, Australian Financial Counselling and Credit Reform Association (AFCCRA).

[2] ITSA, *Annual Report 1998–1999*, at 8, Table 2.1. Of the 26,376 bankruptcies, 5,905 (22.4%) were business-related. *Ibid* at 9. The proportion of business-related bankruptcies declined over the 12-year period but at an uneven rate. *Ibid*. In 1998–99, 94.5% of the bankruptcies resulted from debtors' petitions and 5.5% from creditors' petitions. *Ibid*, at 8. The Australian statistics provide no definition for 'business-related' bankruptcies.

[3] Parts IX and X are Australia's counterpart to BIA, Part III 1 and III 2 in Canada. See 4.7 below.

personal insolvency proceedings for that year.[4] In 2001–02, the number of business and non-business bankruptcies totalled 24,109, of which 83.1 per cent were non-business (ie consumer) bankruptcies and 94 per cent of the bankruptcies were based on debtors' petitions.[5] The number of Parts IX and X insolvency proceedings amounted to 3,748,[6] thereby giving a total of 27,857 personal insolvencies.

In absolute numbers, the number of Australian personal bankruptcies in 1997–98 was only 29.5 per cent of the Canadian 1998 figure.[7] Also, the rate of insolvency in Australia in 1997–98 per 1,000 head of population, 1.35, compared with 2.72 for Canada.[8] However, Australia is catching up. The Commonwealth consumer insolvency rate grew from 0.50 in 1986–87 to 1.35 in 1997–98, an increase of 170 per cent compared with an increase in Canada's rate of just under 200 per cent.[9] Outstanding amounts for personal finance loans and other advances increased in Australia from AU$25,217 million in 1988 to AU$57,846 million in 1997,[10] or 129 per cent, compared with an increase in the Canadian balances of 175 per cent.[11]

Table 4.1: Business and non-business personal bankruptcies in Australia*

Year	Business	Non-business	Total
1987–88	2,259	5,865	8,124
1988–89	2,088	4,994	7,082
1989–90	2,947	5,546	8,493
1990–91	4,203	8,888	13,091
1991–92	5,387	11,493	16,880
1992–93	4,796	9,981	14,777
1993–94	4,335	9,693	14,028
1994–95	3,998	10,132	14,130
1995–96	4,773	12,589	17,362
1996–97	5,191	16,639	21,830
1997–98	4,854	19,554	24,408
1998–99	4,962	21,414	26,376
1999–2000	3,899	19,399	23,298
2000–01	4,440	19,467	23,907
2001–02	4,070	20,039	24,109

Source: RF Mason, 'Consumer Bankruptcies: An Australian Perspective' (1999) 37 *Osgoode Hall Law Journal* 449, 471, and separate table supplied by Prof Mason to the author. The 2001–02 figures are subject to verification.

[4] ITSA, *Annual Report 1998–1999*, 36, 41–42. The national bankruptcy rate was 1 bankruptcy per 682 (or 1.46 per thousand): ITSA, *Profile of Debtors 2002*, 6.
[5] ITSA, *Annual Report 2001–2002*, 5–6.
[6] *Ibid* at 3, 37, 51.
[7] OSB, *International Statistics* (June 1999) 3, 30.
[8] *Ibid* at 4, 32.
[9] *Ibid* at 4, 32.
[10] *Ibid* at 33.
[11] *Ibid* at 5.

ITSA's *Profile of Debtors 2002*[12] also provides the following key characteristics of Australian debtors who became bankrupt in the 2001–02 administrative year:[13]

(1) 24 per cent of the bankrupts were under the age of 30, 32 per cent were between the ages of 30 and 39, and 44 per cent were over 40.[14]

(2) There were more male than female bankrupts across all age groups.[15]

(3) 57 per cent of the bankrupts obtained advice on bankruptcy procedures from professional sources (ie financial counsellors, solicitors, accountants or registered trustees), with the main source being financial counsellors[16]; 24 per cent had obtained such advice from ITSA contacts.[17]

(4) Unemployment was declared by the bankrupts as the most common cause of non-business bankruptcies (39 per cent of bankrupts) compared to 21% who pointed to the excessive use of credit.[18]

(5) In the 12 months' period before bankruptcy, 27% of the bankrupts had incomes of less than AU$10,000, 61 per cent had incomes of less than AU$20,000, and 81 per cent had incomes of less than AU$30,000. The average income of the bankrupts was AU$19,430; the median income was AU$15,000.[19]

(6) The average amount of unsecured debt per bankrupt was AU$66,290, the median amount AU$18,141. In dollar amounts, banks accounted for 32 per cent of total debts and finance companies for 14 per cent. Tax claims accounted for 8 per cent and 'other' for 41 per cent.[20]

(7) 90 per cent of all bankrupts had non-divisible (ie exempt) assets of less than AU$10,000. Only 5 per cent of the bankrupts were home owners or in the process of purchasing a home at the date of bankruptcy. This figure compares with 66.2 per cent of all dwellings in Australia that are fully owned or being purchased.[21]

(8) The largest group of bankrupts (44 per cent) were single persons with no dependants. Couples with dependants were next at 22 per cent. Single parents and married persons with no dependants accounted for 17 per cent each of all bankrupts.[22]

---

[12] See n 1 above.

[13] The *Profile* contains a similar analysis of debtors who entered into debt agreements: *ibid* at 15 *et seq*.

[14] *Ibid*, at 7.

[15] *Ibid*.

[16] On the role of financial counsellors in Australia, see 4.8 below.

[17] *Profile* (n 1 above) at 8.

[18] *Ibid* at 9.

[19] *Ibid* at 11.

[20] *Ibid* at 12–13. Unsecured debt includes that part of secured debt estimated to exceed the value of the collateral.

[21] *Ibid*, at 14.

[22] *Ibid*.

2. CONSTITUTIONAL AND ADMINISTRATIVE STRUCTURE

In Australia, as in Canada, bankruptcy legislation is a central government responsibility.[23] However, the Commonwealth government's jurisdiction is restricted to non-corporate insolvencies. The first Commonwealth Bankruptcy Act was only adopted in 1924[24] and was completely revised in 1966.[25] The 1966 Act is still in force. It has been amended many times since 1966, and in important respects. The latest set of amendments were adopted in 2002[26] and were largely driven by official concerns about perceived debtor abuses of the bankruptcy system.[27]

In terms of administrative structures, there are both similarities and significant differences between the Australian and Canadian regimes. The administration of the Commonwealth Bankruptcy Act (BA) is the responsibility of the Insolvency and Trustee Service Australia (ITSA), an executive agency within the Attorney General's department. ITSA is headed by the Inspector-General, who is also responsible for supervising the work of ITSA's official receivers.[28] The official receivers (ORs) are appointed by the Secretary to the Attorney General's Department.[29] They also double as agents of the Official Trustee (OT)[30] where there is no private 'registered trustee' (RT), as is overwhelmingly the case (to the tune of 95 per cent of the time) in personal insolvency cases.[31] Private trustees are required to be registered by the Inspector-General, who issues the registrations on the recommendations of a committee.[32]

3. INITIATION OF STRAIGHT BANKRUPTCY PROCEEDINGS

There are important differences as well between the Australian and Canadian procedures for the initiation of bankruptcy proceedings, but the important

---

[23] Commonwealth Constitution, s 51(xvii).

[24] Bankruptcy Act 1924 (Cth).

[25] Bankruptcy Act 1966 (Cth).

[26] See Bankruptcy Legislation Amendment Act 2002 (Cth) (BLAA), and Bankruptcy (Estate Charges) Amendment Act 2002 (Cth). The two Bills resulting in the amendments were first introduced in 2001 but lapsed when federal elections were called on 10 November 2001. The government was returned to office and the Bills were reintroduced in the House of Representatives on 21 March 2002. The important consumer insolvency amendments appear in the BLAA.

[27] See D Williams, Attorney General, News Release, 'Bankruptcy Crackdown' (21 March 2002) and T Gallagher, 'Reforms to Bankruptcy Legislation' (2000) 10(2) *New Directions in Bankruptcy* 14.

[28] Bankruptcy Act 1966 (Cth), ss 11–12 as am.

[29] *Ibid*, s 16 as am.

[30] *Ibid*, s 18(8) as am.

[31] In the 2001–02 reporting year, 95% of the new non-business bankruptcies were administered by the OT and 5% by the RTs. Significantly the OT also handled 85% of the business bankruptcies. ITSA, *Annual Report 2001–2002*, 7.

[32] Bankruptcy Act 1966 (Cth), Pt VIII as am. See especially s 155C; *Lewis* (n 1 above) at 31–33.

point worth stressing here is that it is even easier—and certainly much cheaper—for Australian debtors to initiate bankruptcy proceedings than it is for a Canadian debtor. In Australia, the consumer can opt to file a Declaration of Intention to File a Petition before filing a petition,[33] though there is no need to file a notice of discontinuance if the consumer decides not to proceed. There is no fee for the filing of a declaration and the effect of a declaration is to stay enforcement proceedings for seven days by creditors (other than secured creditors) against the debtor personally or his property in respect of a 'frozen debt.'[34] The concept of the declaration was introduced in 1989 to 'minimize the risks of mistaken and hasty bankruptcies'[35] and to encourage the search for alternative solutions to the debtor's problems. However, it is widely recognised in Australia that the seven-day moratorium on creditors' action is too short and there have been suggestions about extending it to 30 days.[36]

So far as consumer bankruptcies are concerned, the procedure is initiated by the debtor filing a petition with the official receiver accompanied by a statement of affairs.[37] Again no filing fee is payable. The documents are often filed by mail and in any event the debtor does not need the assistance of a professional. It seems that it is quite common for welfare workers and non-profit debtors' counselling agencies to assist the debtor with advice and help in completing the forms. There is no need for the debtor to consult a registered trustee. In practice, 95 per cent of personal bankruptcies are administered by the Official Trustee, with only the remainder passing through the hands of registered trustees.[38] The petition need not aver that the debtor is insolvent or has committed an act of bankruptcy. If the documentation is in order and the debtor is not ineligible to file for bankruptcy, the official receiver must accept the petition and bankruptcy follows automatically.[39]

---

[33] Bankruptcy Act 1966 (Cth), s 54A as am; *Lewis* (n 1 above) at 91–92. In the period 1998/99, ITSA issued 469 declarations as compared with 24,109 bankruptcy orders made that year: ITSA, *Annual Report 2001–2002*, 3.

[34] Bankruptcy Act 1966 (Cth), ss 54E as am, 5. 'Frozen debt' is defined in s 5 and means a debt affected by the filing of a declaration.

[35] Mason (n 1 above) at 463.

[36] A different tack was adopted in the 2001 version of the BLAA Bill. This would have imposed a mandatory 30-day cooling-off period after presentation of the petition to allow petitioners to reconsider their decision and withdraw it if they so wish. The provision was much criticised and it was deleted from the version of the bill introduced in March 2002. See J Pentland, AFCCRA Report, *Sharkwatch* (June 2002) 4–5.

[37] Creditors, of course, are also entitled to present a petition but only 1,427 sequestration orders were made in 2001/02 amounting to 4.9% of all personal bankruptcies occurring that year: ITSA, *Annual Report 2001–2002*, x.

[38] See n 31 above.

[39] *Lewis* (n 1 above) at 90, 93–94; Bankruptcy Act 1966 (Cth), ss 57(7), 55(2), 5 (definition of petition), 57A. The BLAA, Sch 1, s 29, adding new s 55(3)(3AA), substantially changes this procedure and confers an important discretion on the official receivers to reject a petition if (a) it appears from the information in the statement of affairs (and any additional information supplied by the debtor) that, if the debtor did not become a bankrupt, the debtor would be likely (either immediately or

Just as important, if there is no registered trustee the Official Trustee is obliged to administer the estate regardless, it would seem, of the size of the estate and whether it will yield sufficient assets (by itself or together with the debtor's contributable earnings)[40] to cover the Official Trustee's expenses and allowable remuneration.[41] The Official Trustee is not allowed or entitled to enter into a fee agreement with the debtor. Since most estates administered by the Official Trustee are no-asset estates and the sums recovered as income contributions are equally modest, this means in effect that many consumer bankruptcies are subsidised in Australia in one fashion or another. However, the subsidy is not large and its existence has not stirred noticeable public controversy for reasons explained in the following email message to the author from a very experienced ITSA official:

> ITSA's procedures for 'doing' a consumer bankruptcy involve (broadly) the following:
>
> (1) Debtors' petition (DP) bankrupts complete their own DP and Statement of Affairs (S of A) forms and file them in person or by post with an ITSA Office. The bankrupt is interviewed briefly, to ensure he/she has received prescribed information about the alternatives to bankruptcy and considered those alternatives. If the DP is filed by post, no interview occurs, but a form for the debtor to complete, confirming receipt of the prescribed info, is sent to the debtor and the DP is not accepted until that form is returned.
>
> (2) When ITSA staff accept a DP, the debtor becomes a bankrupt, No assignment documentation is involved, as any divisible property vests in the Official Trustee, by operation of law, under s 58 of the Bankruptcy Act 1966.
>
> (3) Key information from the S of A is keyed by ITSA staff into OTISS (our computer database) and parts of it transferred electronically onto the publicly accessible bankruptcy register, called the National Personal Insolvency index (NPII).
>
> (4) OTISS generates notices to creditors, advising them of the bankruptcy. No special correspondence to government offices is required. In the typical consumer bankruptcy, the notice will state that there are no or few divisible assets and no dividend is expected. For that reason, the notice does not call for proofs. It does invite creditors to contact ITSA if they have information about, e.g., assets omitted from the S of A.

---

within a reasonable time) to be able to pay all the debts specified in the statement of affairs; and (b) at least one of the following applies:

    (i) it appears from the information in the statement of affairs (and any additional information supplied by the debtor) that the debtor is unwilling to pay one or more debts to a particular creditor or creditors, or is unwilling to pay creditors in general;

    (ii) before the current petition was presented, the debtor previously became a bankrupt on a debtor's petition at least three times, or at least once in the period of five years before the presentation of the current position.

[40] For the debtors' income contribution requirements, see 4.5 below.

[41] With respect to these, see Bankruptcy Act 1966 (Cth), s 163 as amended and Bankruptcy Regulations 8.12, 16.07 and Sch 10. By way of contrast, where a RT has been appointed to administer the estate, the trustee is entitled to a minimum fee of AU$1,109 and, if the estate funds are insufficient, may recover the difference from the debtor: Bankruptcy Act 1966 (Cth), s 161B as am.

(5) The notice will say whether the bankrupt appears eligible for early discharge (6 months) or normal discharge (3 years). ITSA does not notify creditors of the fact of a bankrupt's discharge. The discharge date is recorded on the NPII.'[42]

The ITSA official also explained that, at the time of the communication in 2000, ITSA only had 26 staff members (out of 240 staff members Australia-wide) who handled processed (ie, no-asset) bankruptcies and that the Inspector-General had estimated ITSA's cost per processed bankruptcy at AU$80, including ITSA's overheads. If ITSA's share of departmental corporate service overheads were added, the AU$80 would rise to about AU$100.

4. SCOPE OF ESTATE AND EXEMPTIONS

Like the Canadian BIA, the Australian Act prima facie vests all the debtor's present and future property, real and personal, in the trustee on the debtor's bankruptcy. However, as appears from the following list,[43] the Australian exemptions[44] are more flexible and, in some cases more generous, than the exemptions available to Canadian debtors under many of the provincial exemptions:

(1) property held by the bankrupt in trust for another person;
(2) the bankrupt's household property[45];
(3) property used by the bankrupt in earning income by personal exertion up to approximately AU$2,600,[46] or as increased by creditors or the court;
(4) property used by the bankrupt primarily for transportation up to a maximum of approx. AU$5,000,[47] or such greater amount as approved by creditors;
(5) prescribed interests in life or endowment assurance as well as in regulated superannuation funds or approved deposit funds;

---

[42] Email message to author from ITSA official, Canberra (16 February 2000). In a message to the author of 6 January 2003, David Bergman of ITSA (n 1 above), confirmed that the account in the text still accurately reflects ITSA's current procedures. In a further message of 29 January 2003, he also confirmed that there have been no complaints about ITSA subsidising bankruptcies and no formal suggestions that bankrupts should pay fees to cover the costs of administration. He added, 'Of course, if there are funds in the estate and the Official Trustee is administering the estate, the Commonwealth will receive fees (as would any private trustee) in priority over other creditors. As you would expect, this is not usually the case and the Commonwealth foots the bill.'

[43] See Mason (n 1 above) at 463–64. The author has slightly altered the phrasing in Prof Mason's list.

[44] Bankruptcy Act 1966 (Cth), s 116(2)

[45] Prof Mason (n 1 above) explains, at n 71, that this means household property of a kind prescribed by the regulations or exempted by creditors' resolution and that Regulation 6.03(2) provides that divisible property does not extend to household property that is reasonably necessary for the domestic use of the bankrupt's household, having regard to current social standards.

[46] The figure is subject to CPI adjustment.

[47] The figure is subject to CPI adjustment.

(6) Compensation for personal injuries or death of a member of the family, and property purchased with such protected money;
(7) Amounts paid to the bankrupt as loan assistance for rehabilitation, household or re-establishment support under various state and federal rural support statutes.

Still more significant is the fact that the exemptions apply across the Commonwealth and do not turn on the vagaries of provincial law, as is true in Canada. Equally striking is the fact that the Australian legislation provides no general exemptions for homesteads or farming property.[48]

5. INCOME CONTRIBUTION REQUIREMENTS

In Australia, the overwhelming majority of consumer bankruptcies are no-asset cases and so, there too, creditors must look to contributions from the debtor's income if they are to receive any payments. Australia adopted surplus income provisions in 1991 very similar in structure and purpose to the Canadian 1997 BIA amendments, not because of public concern that there were too many consumer bankruptcies but in reaction to former business tycoons who were perceived to live in luxury despite their bankrupt status.[49] Under Division 4B, added to Part VI of the Bankruptcy Act, a trustee must assess a bankrupt's income for a 12-month contribution assessment period. If the income exceeds the 'actual income threshold amount' ('AITA')(s 139K) applicable to the bankrupt, the bankrupt must pay a contribution to the estate. The AITA is calculated on the basis of the 'base income threshold amount' ('BITA') specified at the time of assessment in Pension Rate Calculator A of the Social Security Act 1991, and increased by a percentage according to the number of persons residing with the bankrupt and not earning income of their own.[50] The bankrupt's required contribution is 50 per cent of the difference between the assessed income and the actual income threshold amount. The definition of income under s 139L is very broad and includes the value of benefits provided to the bankrupt from non-employment sources and 'loans' by associated entities.[51]

---

[48] There is a limited exception to this rule with respect to property, the whole or substantially the whole of which is purchased with 'protected' money: Bankruptcy Act 1966 (Cth), s 116(2)(n); *Lewis* (n 1 above) at 156. Money is 'protected' money if it is either 'exempt money' (s 116(2)(d)) or 'exempt loan money in relation to that time'. In correspondence with this author Prof Mason had no obvious explanation for the absence of a homestead or farming exemption but conjectured that it might be because home ownership is not regarded as important in Australia as it is in North America. For a different perception, however, see R Brading, 'Australia Needs Chapter 13 Protection' (2002) 12(2) *ITSA New Directions* 19.

[49] For details of the Australian provisions, see Mason (n 1 above) at 466–67.

[50] *Lewis* (n 1 above) at 167; Mason and Duns (n 1 above) at 26. For a very recent discussion see L O'Neill, *The Income Contribution Scheme in Bankruptcy* (ITSA, 2002). As of 20 September 2002, the threshold amount for a person without dependants was AU\$32,614.40 per annum or approximately equal to a salary of AUS\$42,150.00 per annum: O'Neill, *ibid* at 8.

[51] *Lewis* (n 1 above) at 168; O'Neill (n 50 above) at 12 *et seq*.

The actual results from the income contribution scheme seem to be very modest. In the 2001–02 period, only 1,653 of the bankrupts (approx. 6.8 per cent of the number of bankruptcy estates being administered) were found liable to make a contribution.[52] The amounts collected from all trustees came to AU$6,874,692 and another AU$3,020,840 was outstanding at the end of the fiscal period.[53] In considering these figures, it is important to bear in mind that they are not restricted to consumer bankrupts but include contributions from bankrupts operating a business or working as professionals. This will be particularly true in the case of estates administered by registered trustees.

Debtors are entitled to appeal their assessments to the Official Receiver on grounds of hardship but the appeal is limited to one or more of the following factors[54]:

(1) the cost of ongoing medical attention and supplies required by the bankrupt or a dependant and which are to be met by the bankrupt;
(2) child day-care costs necessary to enable the bankrupt to continue working;
(3) the cost of rent for accommodation, other than for government-supplied accommodation;
(4) substantial travelling expenses to and from work;
(5) inability, through unemployment, illness or injury, of the bankrupt's spouse, or another person who resides with the bankrupt, to continue to contribute to the costs of maintaining the bankrupt's household; and
(7) other reasons as prescribed.[55]

The trustee's assessment of the bankrupt's liability to make a contribution and the amount thereof may also be reviewed by the Inspector-General. Apparently there were 20 such applications in 2001–02; 16 of the assessments were overturned and new assessments were raised.[56]

---

[52] ITSA, *Annual Report 2001–2002*, 19, Table 13. Of the total number, 1,174 of the estates were administered by the OT and 479 by RTs. It does not appear that the number of bankrupts found liable to make a contribution is confined to individuals who have been made bankrupt the same year.

[53] *Ibid.* The figures in the text have been arrived at by adding the amounts collected by the Official Trustee to those collected by registered trustees. The aggregate figure of receipts leaves a false impression and is heavily skewed by the fact that most of the estates administered by the OT are closed in the year of bankruptcy without being assessed for any contribution. Cf *ibid* at 14–15, Tables 9 and 10 (OT received 26,673 estates in 2001–02 and finalised 26,463; RTs received 2,385 estates and finalised 1,383).

[54] Bankruptcy Act 1966 (Cth), s 139T as am. The 2002 amendments to the Act, s 91, repealed s 139T and replaced it with a new provision authorising the trustee to adjudicate the bankrupt's written request for a review of the assessed contribution on the grounds of hardship. If the request is refused the bankrupt is entitled to appeal to the Inspector-General.

[55] In the 2001–02 fiscal year, there were 28 such hardship applications. There were also two applications on hand at the beginning of the year; 16 of the applications were allowed, four were refused, and seven were withdrawn; one application remained on hand as of 30 June 2002: ITSA, *Annual Report 2001–2002*, 20, Table 14.

[56] ITSA, *Annual Report 2001–2002*, 55.

Despite its good intentions, a recent study concludes[57] that the income contribution scheme suffers from serious defects due variously to the overly generous BITA permitted by the Act and the high delinquency rates in payments due from bankrupts, the costs of collection and insufficient incentives for trustees to pursue delinquent bankrupts.

6. DISCHARGE PROVISIONS AND NON-DISCHARGEABLE LIABILITIES

(a) Discharge Provisions

There are interesting similarities and contrasts with the Canadian position here as well. Under the Australian Bankruptcy Act, a bankrupt is entitled to an automatic discharge after three years[58] unless the trustee or official receiver objects,[59] in which case the discharge may be postponed for a maximum of five or eight years depending on the grounds of objection.[60] The grounds of objection, 14 altogether, are based on various forms of misconduct by the bankrupt before or during bankruptcy and include a general category labelled 'misleading conduct.'[61] Unlike in Canada, the objections are considered not by a judge but by the Inspector-General acting on his or her own initiative or at the debtor's request.[62] The debtor is also entitled to have the objections reviewed by the Administrative Appeal Tribunal.[63] There are no suspended or conditional discharges under the Australian Act—again in contrast to the Canadian position. In the 2001–02 period, there were 24 objections relative to a five year postponement and 266 objections relative to a an eight year postponement of the discharge.[64]

Before the 2002 amendments, the Australian bankrupt was also eligible to apply for an early discharge[65] where the following conditions were satisfied: (a) there was insufficient money in the estate to pay the trustee's remuneration; (b) the debtor had not entered into voidable transactions; and (c) the debtor's income during the one-year period following the application for early discharge did not exceed the actual income threshold amount. During the 2001–02 year,

---

[57] O'Neill (n 50 above) at 20 *et seq*.

[58] Bankruptcy Act 1966 (Cth), s 149(4).

[59] *Ibid*, s 149B. The trustee must file a notice of objection if he believes this is the only way to make the debtor comply with a duty he has not discharged. Bankruptcy Act 1966 (Cth), s 149B(2). Seemingly creditors have no standing to object nor is the trustee required to provide them with a report about the debtor's conduct or with other circumstances comparable to those referred to in ss 170–170.1 of the Canadian BIA.

[60] Bankruptcy Act 1966 (Cth), s 149A, as further amended in 2002.

[61] *Ibid*, ss 149D(1) and 148 (definition of 'misleading conduct').

[62] *Ibid*, s 149K.

[63] *Ibid*, s 149F.

[64] ITSA, *Annual Report 2001–2002*, Table 22. The Report does not give the number of automatic discharges.

[65] Bankruptcy Act 1966 (Cth), s 149T.

the Official Trustee received 6,168 early discharge applications and registered trustees, 174.There were also 122 applications on hand at the beginning of the year. The Official Trustee rejected 839 (13 per cent) of the applications and registered trustees rejected 79 (40 per cent). Under the pre-2002 provisions the debtor lost his eligibility for an early discharge if he had been guilty of one of eight forms of misconduct, had been a previous bankrupt, or had made an arrangement with his creditors.[66] The disqualifying conditions included the debtor's bankruptcy during the previous 10 years and the fact that the debtor's unsecured liabilities exceeded 150 per cent of the debtor's income during the year preceding the date of bankruptcy.[67]

The early discharge provisions were repealed in the 2002 amendments.[68] Various reasons were given for the repeal.[69] They included the contention that early discharge discouraged debtors from entering into formal or informal arrangements with creditors for the settlement of their debts and that many of the bankruptcies were due more to the debtor's lack of financial responsibility than to his misfortune. Somewhat inconsistently, it was also believed that some deserving debtors were excluded from access to the early discharge provisions because of the restrictive conditions attaching to the provisions and that it was desirable to treat all debtors alike.

(b) Non-Dischargeable Liabilities

There are only five types of non-dischargeable obligations under the Australian Act, a number that compares favourably with the eight under the BIA and the 18 or more under the US Bankruptcy Code.[70] The five Australian exclusions are[71]: child and spousal support obligations; ongoing liability for contributions

---

[66] *Ibid*, ss 149X–149Y.

[67] *Ibid*, ss 149X, 149Y. The debtor's failure to surrender his passport was also a disqualifying condition: s 149ZE. Apparently, this restriction was based on well-founded experience that high profile debtors were tempted to flee Australia to escape accountability!

[68] BLAA (n 26 above) Sch 1, Part 1, item 127.

[69] Mason and J Duns (n 1 above), text accompanying nn 60–65. See also ITSA, *Bankruptcy Legislation Amendment Bill 2002: Abolition of Early Discharge* (undated memorandum provided to the author by David Bergman on 30 July 2002 as an email attachment). Opinion among debtor-oriented agencies was divided. Community legal service agencies were opposed. On the other hand, the author was informed by an executive member of AFCCRA that AFCCRA did not actively oppose repeal of the early discharge provisions because its members did not feel it was of great significance to low-income debtors. AFCCRA was, however, keenly concerned about the retention of s 271(a) of the Bankruptcy Act making the bankrupt guilty of an offence if, within two years before the petition, the bankrupt materially contributed to the insolvency, or increased its extent, by any gambling or by speculations that were rash and hazardous and not connected with a trade or business: *Lewis* (n 1 above) at 309. Gambling is a problem among the clients served by AFCCRA and AFCCRA's executive argued that it was wrong to penalise such debtors, given that the states greatly benefited from gambling revenues and did little to discourage gambling.

[70] See comparative table, Chapter 2.10, Table 2.4 above.

[71] Bankruptcy Act 1966 (Cth), s 153(2); *Lewis* (n 1 above) at 248.

from income; debts incurred through fraudulent conduct; liability under a pecuniary penalty order; and a debt on a recognisance or bail bond.

7. ALTERNATIVES TO STRAIGHT BANKRUPTCY

Prior to 1996, the only alternative to a bankruptcy available to Australian consumers was an arrangement with creditors under Part X of the Bankruptcy Act. Part X was designed for commercial and professional debtors and was too expensive and complex for consumer purposes. A much simpler procedure for consumer debtors was recommended by the Australian Law Reform Commission in 1977,[72] and was implemented in the amending Bankruptcy Act of 1996 adding a new Part IX to the parent Act.[73] Part IX is intended to be 'a viable low cost alternative to bankruptcy for low-income debtors with little or no property, with few creditors, and with low levels of liability.' To be eligible for a Part IX debt agreement, the debtor must satisfy the following conditions[74]:

(1) the debtor's unsecured debts must not exceed a threshold amount (AU$61,061 in 2001);
(2) the value of the debtor's divisible property does not exceed the threshold amount;
(3) the debtor's after-tax income for the first 12 months of the proposed debt agreement period is not likely to exceed one-half of the threshold amount (AU$30,530.50 in 2001)[75];
(4) in the 10-year period preceding the proposed debt agreement the debtor has not been a bankrupt, has not been a party to a debt agreement, and has not given 'an authority' for the initiation of Part X proceedings under section 188 of the Bankruptcy Act.

The actual procedure is as follows.[76] The debtor submits a proposal and statement of affairs to the Official Trustee.[77] The proposal may involve payment by instalments, payment by lump sum, or transfer of an asset to the creditors.[78] The OT verifies the debtor's eligibility requirements and, if these have been met, forwards the proposal to the debtor's creditors. Voting is by mail or at a meeting of creditors and acceptance of the proposal requires approval by a majority in number of the creditors and 75 per cent in value before the statutory

---

[72] Australian Law Reform Commission, *Insolvency: The Regular Payment of Debts* (ALRC 6, 1977).

[73] Mason (n 1 above) at 456–57.

[74] ITSA, *Analysis of Debt Agreements* (July 2000) 1; *Lewis* (n 1 above) at 266, and BLAA, Sch 1, amending Bankruptcy Act 1966, s 185C(5).

[75] The one-half threshold amount was increased to three-quarters in the 2002 amendments.

[76] *Lewis* (n 1 above) at 267–69; Mason (n 1 above) at 461–62.

[77] Bankruptcy Act 1966 (Cth), ss 185C–185E.

[78] *Ibid*, ss 185C, 185E.

deadline.[79] Section 185M of the Bankruptcy Act allows for variation of the debt agreement, either on the debtor's initiative or at the behest of a creditor. Two other features of Part IX debt agreements that distinguish them from Canadian consumer proposals are the following. First, debt agreements are not required to be administered by a trustee. Secondly, there is no automatic termination of a debt agreement because of default in payment. Debt agreements can only be terminated by resolution of the creditors or by the court. So far as the administration of debt agreements is concerned, the debtor is apparently free to administer the agreement herself but this seems to be rare and may not occur at all. The majority of debt agreements are currently administered by a new breed of self-styled debt administrators who have sprung up since 1996. Many of them appear to have an accounting background but are not registered trustees, and importantly they operate on an inter-state basis. There is concern about their operations and the 2002 amendments empower the Inspector-General to regulate the activities of debt agreement administrators.[80]

Part IX has only been in effect since December 1996 and published results are only available for the first six years of its operation.[81] During the reporting period 2001/02, 5,647 debt agreements (23 per cent of the number of business and non-business bankruptcies in the same period) were accepted for processing by the Official Trustee, of which 3,294 (58 per cent) were also accepted by creditors and 1,852 (33 per cent) were rejected.[82] The number of agreements accepted by the Official Trustee grew from 123 in the period December 1996 to 30 June 1997, to the above mentioned 5,647 in 2001/02, thus showing debtor's increasing partiality for debt agreements. The following overall picture emerges from an analysis of debt agreements accepted by creditors in the period 1 July 1999 to 31 May 2000[83]:

(a) debt levels included in debt agreement: AU$14,100;
(b) before tax median income estimated for the first 12 months of the debt agreement: AU$24,000;
(c) duration of the agreement: three years;
(d) (Median) amount payable by the debtor: AU$11,500;
(e) number of debt agreements administered by a remunerated third party: 95 per cent;

---

[79] Usually 25 days after acceptance of the proposal for processing: Bankruptcy Act 1966 (Cth), s 185(2).

[80] Mason and Duns (n 1 above) at text accompanying nn 121–23.

[81] See ITSA, *Analysis of Debt Agreements* (n 74 above) and ITSA, *Annual Report 2001–2002*, 37 *et seq.*

[82] ITSA, *Annual Report 2001–2002*, 37, Table 26. The Annual Report does not indicate what happened to the balance of the debt agreements accepted for processing by the OT. There also appears to be a slight discrepancy in the number of debt agreements accepted for processing and rejected by creditors reported in Tables 26, 30.

[83] ITSA, *Analysis of Debt Agreements* (n 74 above) at 12. (The author has made stylistic and clarificatory adjustments to the summary.) Apparently, some of the figures have been rounded off in the original table. Detailed information appears in other parts of the analysis.

(f) average cost of the administration: AU$1,750;

(g) rate of return to creditors in the range of 64–72 per cent;

Non-Australian readers will be particularly interested in the figures in Table 4.2 showing completion and non-completion rates of Part IX debt agreements for the five-year reporting period ending in 2001.

Table 4.2: Part IX completion and non-completion rates as percentage of debt agreements accepted by creditors*

	2000/01	1999/2000	1998/99	1997/98	1996/97
Terminated by creditors	13.85%	37.02%	42.37%	42.86%	21.54%
Ended: obligations discharged	3.97%	10.70%	26.72%	33.67%	49.23%
Terminated by court order	0.00%	0.12%	0.95%	0.00%	1.54%
No result (ongoing or debtor not complying but no action by creditors)	82.18%	52.16%	29.96%	23.47%	27.69

Source: David Bergman, ITSA, Canberra, email communication to author, 30 July 2002.

These figures suggest that debts agreements in Australia, like consumer proposals in Canada, are subject to high rates of non-completion and presumably for the same reasons.[84]

8. CREDIT COUNSELLING AS PART OF THE BANKRUPTCY PROCESS

The Australian Bankruptcy Act contains no provisions obliging trustees to provide debt counselling to bankrupts or requiring bankrupts to obtain it from other prescribed sources as a condition of discharge. However, official receivers are required to give debtors prescribed information about their options before accepting declarations or bankruptcy petitions from debtors.[85] This exercise seems to involve nothing more onerous than the ITSA office providing the debtor with written information about available options; debtors are not usually interviewed by the ITSA staff before exercising their options.

There may be good reasons as well for this difference between Australia and Canada. The rate of bankruptcies is not as high in Australia as it is in Canada nor, until comparatively recently,[86] does one encounter complaints from

---

[84] ie, change in debtors' circumstances over the life of the debt agreements and excessive optimism by debtors about their ability to sustain the payments over the life of the agreement. As in Canada's case, non-completion rates can only be realistically gauged after a debt agreement has run for its projected life span.

[85] Bankruptcy Act 1966 (Cth), ss 54D, 55(3A).

[86] See, text accompanying n 27 above.

Australian creditors with the same frequency about perceived bankruptcy abuses by debtors. Another reason may be that Australia has had well-established debt counselling facilities for several decades so that there is little need to add another layer to the existing facilities.

According to Martin Ryan (citing to Jones),[87] Australian debt counselling went through three phases. The first involved the establishment of innovative programmes in the 1960s and 1970s. The second involved the recommendation that financial counselling services be extended to form part of the network of family services available in Australian communities. This recommendation was implemented in the mid- and late 1970s. The third phase involved the further implementation of the recommendation and the offering of counselling by a wider range of organisations. Ryan also stresses[88] the important role played from the early beginning by government funding at both the state and Commonwealth levels. Most of the existing counselling services in Australia are now funded by the Commonwealth government through the federal Ministry of Consumer Affairs.

Counselling services are currently available in all states, with Victoria having the highest number of outlets in 1995 at 82. Well-developed service networks also exist in New South Wales, South Australia, Queensland, and Tasmania. There are also state-based and publicly funded organisations of debt counsellors and national organisations, the Australian Financial Counselling and Credit Reform Association (AFCCRA), which serves as an umbrella organisation for its financial counselling members and as a pressure group to promote reform of the law and practices in the credit area.[89]

Martin's book also contains[90] a valuable analysis of the occupational ideologies of Australian debt counsellors, an exercise that does not appear to have a Canadian counterpart. He divides the ideologies into three groups:

(1) *Debt repayment ideology.* This is very creditor-oriented and is likely to blame debtors for their financial difficulties.
(2) *Social work (or welfare) ideology.* The emphasis here is on help and advice to the client and less on repayment of debts.
(3) *Developmental ideology.* This approach de-emphasises the client and focuses more on the wider social system. Its aim is to change the social system rather than the debtors. Debt repayments are given low priority and its proponents emphasise the need for credit law reforms and the need to develop alternative credit facilities for low-income debtors.

Finally, given the close relationship between consumer bankruptcies and the availability of consumer credit, it is worth noting that on the whole the

---

[87] M Ryan, *Social Work and Debt Problems* (Avebury, 1996) 126.

[88] *Ibid* at 127.

[89] AFCCRA publishes its own news magazine, *Sharkwatch*, and was also very active in making submissions on the Bankruptcy Legislation Amendment Bill 2002, see above 4.2.

[90] Ryan (n 87 above) at 129.

Australian states have done better than the provinces in Canada in securing the adoption of uniform consumer credit legislation and providing it with effective enforcement mechanisms. The states agreed on a Uniform Consumer Credit Code in 1994 and the Code became effective throughout Australia in 1996.[91] The Code contains detailed provisions for administration and supervision of compliance with the Code's provisions. Heavy civil penalties can be (and have been) imposed for non-compliance.[92] Several of the states have also established separate consumer credit legal centres[93] to assist consumers with legal aspects of credit problems and, where appropriate, to initiate remedial action.

---

[91] AJ Duggan and EV Lanyon, *Consumer Credit Law* (Butterworths Australia, 1999) 22–26.

[92] *Ibid* at ch 11.

[93] A good example is the New South Wales Consumer Credit Legal Centre (NSW) Inc, which publishes annual reports on its activities. During the author's visit to Sydney, he met with Denise Iosifidis, solicitor to the Centre, and is grateful to her for providing him with copies of recent ITSA Annual Reports as well as much other useful information.

5

England and Wales[1]

1. INTRODUCTION

GIVEN THE COMMON legal background of England and Canada, the rapid growth of consumer credit in both countries, and the liberalisation of their personal insolvency regimes,[2] one might have expected a similar expansion in the number of consumer insolvencies in both jurisdictions.

As Table 5.1 shows, there was indeed an impressive increase in the number of English individual insolvencies between 1987 and 2001: from 7,427 to 29,775, an increase of 301 per cent over the 14-year period, compared with the 234 per cent increase experienced by Canada during the same period. The increase in the number of English insolvencies per 1,000 head of population between 1987–2000 is equally striking: 273 per cent for England compared to 158 per cent for Canada.[3] The English figures look even more impressive when it is considered that they do not take into account the number of administration orders (AOs) made during the period under Part VI of the County Courts Act 1984.[4]

However, these statistics leave a false impression for the following reasons. The number of English individual insolvencies in 2001 (29,775) was still less than one-third of the Canadian number despite the fact that Canada's population (30 million)[5] was only 55 per cent that of England and Wales (52 million).[6] Even more striking is the fact that at the end of 2000 the number of insolvencies per 1,000 population stood at 3.1 in Canada compared with 0.56 for England, a difference of about 554 per cent. Another important difference is that until the mid-1990s consumer insolvencies in England only accounted for between 20 to

---

[1] To avoid needless repetition of country names, England and Wales will be treated as one country for the purposes of the following presentation. No disrespect is intended for readers of Welsh origin!

[2] In England, the major changes were introduced in the Bankruptcy Act 1986, which took effect in 1987. Important amendments were added in the Enterprise Act 2002 and these are summarised in 5.6 below. In Canada, so far as consumer insolvencies are concerned, the important changes occurred in the amendments to the BIA in 1992 and 1997. (The 1997 amendments, of course, reversed the earlier liberalising trend.) The detailed provisions of the English Act are discussed below.

[3] See Table 5.1.

[4] Administration orders (AOs), which are comparable to consumer proposals under Part III 2 of the BIA, are discussed in 5.4(c) below. No complete statistics are available for AOs but it appears that in the year 2000 they were running at an annual rate of around 10,000.

[5] Statistics Canada, CANSIM II, Table 051-0001.

[6] National Statistics, *Revised population estimates England & Wales 1991–2000*. (London, 27 February 2003).

England and Wales

Table 5.1: Individual Insolvencies – Selected Years*

Year	Administration Orders	Individual Bankruptcies (IB)	% of consumer debtors (CD/IB)	Individual Voluntary Arrangements (IVA)	Insolvencies (IB + IVA)	Insolvencies per 1000 capita	Insolvencies per 1000 capita (Canada)
1987	7,140	6,994	n/a	n/a	7,427	0.15	1.2
1992	n/a	32,106	22%	4,686	36,794	0.72	2.6
1995	9,294	21,933	22%	4,384	26,319	0.51	2.7
1996	10,357	21,803	26%	4,466	26,271	0.51	3.2
1997	9,936	19,892	28%	4,545	24,441	0.47	3.3
1998	8,280	19,647	n/a	4,901	24,552	0.47	3.0
1999	n/a	21,611	n/a	7,195	28,806	0.55	3.0
2000	n/a	21,550	53%	7,978	29,528	0.56	3.1
2001	n/a	23,477	n/a	6,298	29,775	n/a	3.3

*Sources: OSB, *International Insolvency Statistics* (June 2002) 5; Insolvency Service, DTI (August 1998), and author's own calculations. NB The English individual bankruptcy and IVA numbers cover business as well as consumer insolvencies; the same is true of the Canadian per capita rate in column 8. The heading in column 5 of the OSB table p5 is misleading and has been corrected by the author in Table 1 above.

30 per cent of the total number of personal insolvencies, the rest being classified as business or professional insolvencies.[7]

In the light of these qualifying data, Prof Michael Adler has expressed the view[8] that Canada has nothing to learn from England with respect to the treatment of insolvent consumer debtors. The conclusion is open to question since it is arguable that the much smaller English insolvency numbers carry important lessons of their own, as will appear later. Prof Adler's observation is absolutely correct, however, in stimulating us to enquire why there is such a large discrepancy between the English and Canadian numbers. It is believed the reasons are both positive and negative.

The much lower English insolvency figures cannot be ascribed to negligible growth in the volume of consumer credit. At the end of 1998, consumer credit debt in the United Kingdom stood at £101,481 million (approximately CAN$233,406 million)[9] compared to the Canadian balance of CAN$157,770 million, and a balance of United States$1,331.7 billion for the US.[10] On a per capita basis, with some rounding out, the outstanding per capita debt balances were: United States, US$4,932, Canada, US$3,418, and the United Kingdom, US$2,706.[11] On the strength of these figures, all other factors being the same (which they are not), one would expect the British insolvency numbers to be only about 20 per cent less than the Canadian numbers.

A second reason to query the reliability of the English personal insolvency statistics as an index of consumer welfare is that there is no shortage of chronic indebtedness in England. All the English observers agree on this.[12] Here are

---

[7] See Society of Practitioners of Insolvency (now renamed as 'R3', Association of Business Recovery Professionals), *Personal Insolvency in the UK, 6th Annual Survey* (London, 1996). However, the ratio of consumer bankruptcies to personal bankruptcies has been climbing steadily and amounted to 53% (11,598 of 21,550 personal bankruptcies) in 2000. See DTI, *Productivity and Enterprise: Insolvency—A Second Chance* (2001) 9. Another distinction is that many of the personal insolvencies are triggered by a creditor's petition although there are no official figures and the author has not been able to pin down exact numbers. They are certainly higher than the average of about 10% in Canada and Australia.

[8] M Adler, 'The Overseas Dimension: What can Canada and the United States Learn from the United Kingdom?' (1999) 37 *Osgoode Hall Law Journal* 415, 420.

[9] This is based on a conversion rate of £1=CAN$2.30, which is on the low side.

[10] See Office of the Superintendent of Bankruptcy, Programs, Standards and Regulatory Affairs, *International Consumer Insolvency Statistics* (Ottawa, June 1999) 5, 21, 11.

[11] The population figures used were: US, 270m, Canada, 30m, and UK, 60m. The UK population figure includes the Scottish population of 5m. See Government Actuary Office, *National Populations Projections 1998-Based* (London, The Stationery Office, 2000).

[12] See, inter alia, Adler (n 8 above) at 420; R Berthoud and E Kempson, *Credit and Debt: The P.S.I. Report* (London: Policy Studies Institute, 1992); J Ford and M Wilson, 'Personal Debt and Insolvency' in H Rajak (ed), *Insolvency Law: Theory & Practice* (1993) 93 *et seq*; Conaty *et al*, 'Private and Public Concerns—Unemployment, Credit and Debt in Britain: An Overview' in U Reifner and J Ford, *Banking for People* (1992) ch 37; and Fiona Maharg-Bravo, 'Concern at Record Level of Consumer Borrowing,' *Financial Times*, 27 November 2002, at 4, noting that, according to a DTI report, a quarter of all households had been in financial difficulties in the past 12 months and quoting a NCAB official to the effect that in 2001–02 the Association had handled more than a million new debt cases. For recent studies on the over-indebtedness phenomenon and its incidents, see also DTI, Consumer Affairs Directorate, *Report by the Task Force on Tackling Overindebtedness* (July 2001), Elaine Kempson, *Overindebtedness in Britain: A Report to the Department of Trade*

some illustrative data. Among council tenants, consumer credit arrears increased from 2.2 per cent to 8.2 per cent in the 1980s, the Finance Houses Association reported that the proportion of accounts two or more months in arrears increased from 5 to 7% between 1979 and 1984, and the number of court cases involving consumer credit increased from 175,000 in 1979 to 414,000 in 1987.[13] Again, the number of mortgage loans in arrears for six months or more grew from 57,600 (0.9 per cent) of outstanding mortgages to 290,080 (3.0 per cent) in 1992, and 216,230 insolvent mortgagors lost their homes during the same period.[14]

The following factors help to explain the relatively low number of personal insolvencies in England. English observers agree that there is little awareness among consumers about the availability of bankruptcy as a remedy for chronic indebtedness.[15] Unlike in Canada, insolvency practitioners do not advertise their services to consumers in business telephone directories and other popular media. They have little incentive to do so because, even if an insolvency practitioner assists the consumer to prepare her petition in bankruptcy (which is unusual), the practitioner has no control over the appointment of the trustee given that the trustee is appointed by the creditors, assuming the creditors take any interest in the trustee's appointment at all. Further, in summary administration cases, unlike in Canada, private practitioners are excluded entirely because those cases are all handled by official receivers.[16]

Another important factor is the high initial cost of filing a bankruptcy petition, which has triggered recent constitutional litigation.[17] The Insolvency Rules require the petitioner to deposit the sum of £250 to cover the administrative costs

---

and Industry (July 2001) and S Edwards, *In Too Deep: CAB Clients' Experience of Debt* (National Citizens Advice Bureaux & Citizens Advice Scotland, May 2003) (CAB UK now dealing with well over one million debt enquiries per year. Marked growth in number of new enquiries involving consumer credit—'the problem of personal indebtedness is getting worse'—para 1.6).

[13] Berthoud and Kempson (n 12 above) at 151 and Table 10.7, at 171.

[14] Ford and Wilson (n 12 above) at 97. The United Kingdom experienced a sharp recession in the late 1980s resulting in a rapid increase in the number of personal insolvencies as well as home mortgages in default.

[15] Berthoud and Kempson (n 12 above) repeatedly stressed in their seminal study that debtors rarely took the initiative in finding solutions for debt problems but usually reacted to creditor initiatives.

[16] Insolvency Act 1986 (UK) c 45 (IA), ss 275, 297(2); IF Fletcher, *The Law of Insolvency* (3rd edn, 2002) 12–004. The court may issue a certificate for summary administration (CSA) if, upon hearing the debtor's petition, the court makes a bankruptcy order and two facts are established: (1) that the debtor's unsecured debt is less than the prescribed amount (£20,000 in 1996) (the 'small bankruptcies level'), and (2) that within the preceding five years the debtor had not been adjudged bankrupt, made a composition or entered into a scheme of arrangement with creditors: IA, s 275(2). Where a certificate is issued, IA, s 297(2) provides that the official receiver shall be the trustee of the estate. The number of 'summary' cases as a percentage of total bankruptcies is on the increase. There were 12,545 summary cases in the year ending 31 March 2000 and 15,750 summary cases in the year ending 31 March 2002 and the percentage increased from 58.5% to 67.2%. (Information supplied to the author by email, 15 January 2003).

[17] *R v Lord Chancellor, ex parte Lightfoot* [1999] 2 WLR 1126, affd. English Court of Appeal, 23 July 1999 [2000] 2 WLR 318.

of the Insolvency Service as well as a court filing fee of £120[18] before the petition will be accepted. So far as the deposit is concerned, the Insolvency Rules grant no dispensation for indigent debtors. The English courts have held that the constitutional rule that delegated legislation cannot deprive a litigant of a right of access to the courts unless the enabling Act clearly confers this power does not apply to the deposit requirement under the Insolvency Act.[19] In Canada, impecunious debtors seem to have no difficulty persuading insolvency practitioners to accept payment by instalments and absence of a down-payment does not appear to be a major hurdle.[20]

Two other reasons also deserve to be noted. The first, frequently stressed by English observers of the North American scene, is that bankruptcy still carries a substantial stigma in the United Kingdom.[21] It may well be so but the Scottish experience of the late 1980s[22] show that the stigma is easily overlooked by debtors when presented with the opportunity to file bankruptcy proceedings and obtain an early discharge from debts at public expense. The other reason is that an administration order under Part VI of the County Courts Act 1984 offers a much cheaper, possibly faster, and surely less bureaucratic and intimidating form of relief for insolvent debtors whose debts do not exceed £5,000. On average, about 8,000 debtors invoke these provisions each year, although Part VI has some serious drawbacks. Amendments addressing many of them were enacted by the British Parliament in 1990[23] but have not so far been proclaimed, and may never be. Assuming the improvements are made, it seems reasonable to assume that much larger numbers of English debtors will be attracted to make use of administration orders.

---

[18] See Supreme Court Fees Order 1999, SI 1999/687, Sch 1; and County Court Fees Order 1999, SI 1999/689, Sch 1. There is also a swearing fee of £7 if the petition is sworn before an officer of the court. During the Committee stage of the Enterprise Bill (5.6 below) an amendment was moved (a) to grant exemption from the deposit and court fees for individuals on means-tested benefits and tax credits, and (b) to allow for remission of all or part of the deposit and court fees, or payment by instalments, for persons with low incomes. The amendment was ultimately withdrawn. See UK Parliament, 17th Sitting Stdg Com B, 2001–02, HC, May 14, 2002, Cols. 690–695. Existing regulations already grant dispensation from court fees to individuals and families qualifying for special assistance programmes. See Supreme Court Fees Order 1999, SI 1999/687; and County Court Fees Order 1999, SI 1999/689.

[19] *Lightfoot* (n 17 above). However, in *Lightfoot* both the trial judge and the Court of Appeal were also satisfied that Parliament had intended to confer deposit-requiring powers on the Lord Chancellor.

[20] As previously mentioned (chapter 2.4 above), in Canada, the members of CIPA have agreed with the Superintendent to accept such indigent cases for insolvency services as are referred to them for assistance by the local OSB officials.

[21] 'We also have a cultural "Victorian" view of bankruptcy. Although views have moderated in the last 20 years or so, we retain a sense of stigma about the whole thing, and cases are still routinely advertised in local newspapers etc': email from Steve Hill, a London insolvency practitioner, to author, 22 August 2002. See also 'KPMG–Bankruptcy Still a Social Stigma', Commercial Press Release, 19 February 2003, reporting on the results of a survey.

[22] See Chapter 6.1 below.

[23] See Courts and Legal Services Act 1990 (UK), s 13 5.2 and below.

2. PROFILE OF ENGLISH INSOLVENTS

For the past 10 years the British Association of Business Recovery Professionals ('R3: Rescue, Recovery, Renewal')[24] has conducted an annual *Survey of Personal Insolvency* containing data about the personal characteristics of insolvents and the final results of bankruptcy and individual voluntary arrangement (IVA) proceedings. Unfortunately, for the most part, the survey does not distinguish between bankruptcy and IVA proceedings, but it is possible to some extent to deduce differences in the characteristics of debtors in the two types of proceedings.

The survey indicates that debtors were the main source of petitions for insolvency proceedings in 2001 and accounted for 38 per cent of all bankruptcies.[25] The average age of the debtors in the sample was 45; 80 per cent of the bankrupts were male; and 63 per cent of the debtors were married.[26] Most of the debtors (42 per cent) were located in the southeast of England.[27] The majority of debtors (63 per cent) were self-employed; the majority (44 per cent of sample) were sole traders and the remaining 19 per cent self-employed with a business partner; 30 per cent of the debtors were employed; unemployed debtors accounted for just 5 per cent of the sample.[28]

With respect to their assets, 23% of the debtors' assets were under £2,500; 38 per cent of the debtors had assets exceeding £20,000, giving an overall average of £33,020.[29] Average liabilities amounted to £77,160.[30]

The most common *commercial* reasons for their failure given by the debtors were loss in market, tax liabilities and poor management. The most common *personal* reasons given were mismanagement of personal finances credit cards (20 per cent), ill-health (20 per cent) and other (19 per cent).[31] Overall, however, as a proportion of all insolvencies, the survey concludes that commercial factors were more likely to cause insolvency than domestic factors.[32] Bearing in mind the opening caveat, it seems safe to conclude that there are important differences in the profiles of English and Canadian insolvents, differences that may be ascribed at least in part to the cost barriers facing English bankrupts.

---

[24] Formerly known as the Society of Practitioners of Insolvency.

[25] R3, Association of Business Recovery Professionals, *9th Survey of Personal Insolvency* (London, March 2002) 2, 5.

[26] *Ibid* at 6.

[27] *Ibid*.

[28] *Ibid*. Apparently a majority of the debtors were engaged in manual occupations: *ibid* at 7, and also at 14. This seems surprising given the high percentage of debtors who were self-employed. The report does not provide a definition of 'manual occupations' and it may be that the manual occupational category is limited to employed debtors.

[29] *Ibid* at 9.

[30] *Ibid*.

[31] *Ibid* at 13.

[32] *Ibid*. Data focusing on the profiles of overcommitted consumers using the services of the Citizens Advice Bureaux have recently become available. See S Edwards, *In Too Deep: CAB Clients' Experience of Debt*, esp. 2.1 *et seq.* (NCAB & Citizens Advice Scotland, May 2003) and NCAB, *Oxfordshire Money Advice Project. Financial Statements Analysis* (Oxford, October 2002).

3. OTHER FEATURES OF CURRENT ENGLISH INSOLVENCY REGIME

(a) Initiation of Bankruptcy Proceedings

Apart from the deposit and court fee requirements, it is as easy in England for a debtor to initiate bankruptcy proceedings as it is for a debtor in Canada. There are, however, some procedural differences. All proceedings must be initiated by a petition, which must be filed in the bankruptcy court, and a bankruptcy order must be made by the court.[33] However, there is no requirement for a formal hearing[34] and typically the order will be made on the strength of the petition and the supporting documents. Once the bankruptcy order is made, it will be 'gazetted' and advertised in such local newspapers as the official receiver deems appropriate.[35] Insolvency practitioners are rarely involved in preparing the petition and court clerks will help with the form filling free of charge as a public service. The forms are simple and a debtor's petition is almost invariably granted.[36] Where the unsecured debts amount to less than the 'small bankruptcies' level (currently £20,000) and, if a bankruptcy order were made the value of the estate would be more than the minimum amount (currently £2,000), the court can appoint a person to investigate and report back whether the case is suitable for an IVA governed by Part VIII of the Insolvency Act. If the report is favourable and the debtor agrees, the court may then make an interim order to facilitate consideration of the debtor's proposal.[37] In short, as in Canada, the Act encourages consensual arrangements with creditors to avoid the starker bankruptcy solution.

Where a bankruptcy order is made, reference has already been made to the facilitative provision for the summary administration of small estates, the historical source of the equivalent Canadian institution. As in Canada, the consequence will be a simpler, cheaper and more expeditious administration[38] coupled with the important fact (for which there is no Canadian counterpart) that the estate will be administered by the Official Trustee without further cost to the bankrupt.

---

[33] IA, s 264(1)(b). Bankruptcy petitions can be filed in the county courts as well as in the High Court of Justice: *ibid*, s 373(1). For the details see Fletcher (n 16 above) at 6–079 *et seq*. 'Court' for these purposes means a Registrar in Bankruptcy of the High Court or the registrar or deputy registrar of the county court. See Insolvency Rules 1986, Rule 13.2. (The author is indebted to Registrar Stephen Baister of the High Court of Justice, Bankruptcy Division, London, for this information.)

[34] Practice Direction on Insolvency Proceedings, para 16, provides that the court may make the order without the applicant's attendance.

[35] Insolvency Rules, Rule 6.46(2).

[36] Email message from Steve Hill to author (1 August 2002).

[37] IA, ss 273(1), 274(2).

[38] For the details, see Fletcher (n 16 above) at 12–002/12–005. The summary administration provisions were repealed in the Enterprise Act 2002, below 5.6.

(b) Exempt Property and Income Payment Orders

Section 283(2) of the Insolvency Act implements recommendations of the Cork Committee[39] designed to overcome the rigidities of the monetary limits of the exemptions in the Bankruptcy Act 1914. In the Committee's view, the limits had outlived their usefulness and no longer reflected contemporary standards of what even a bankrupt and his family needed to live with dignity and a minimum of comfort and to enable the debtor to continue to ply his trade or profession. As a result, section 283(2) divides the exempted property into two categories, ie:

(a) such tools, books, vehicles and other items of equipment as are necessary to the bankrupt for use personally by him in his employment, business or vocation;

(b) such clothing, bedding, furniture, household equipment and provisions as are necessary for satisfying the basic domestic needs of the bankrupt and his family.

The distinctive feature of these provisions is that there is no longer a monetary ceiling so long as the exempted goods are 'necessary' to enable the debtor to earn his livelihood or to satisfy the basic needs of the bankrupt and his family. Presumably, the judgement of what is necessary rests in the first instance with the trustee, with a right of appeal to the court in case of disagreement.[40] It is open for consideration whether the subjectivity inherent in a necessity test is better than the indexing of monetary amounts applicable to exempted property introduced in Canada in some of the recent provincial legislation.[41] One is also troubled by the rigidity of a necessity test under section 283(2)(a), untempered as it is by a qualifying 'reasonably necessary' adverb.[42] From a North American perspective, a conspicuous omission from section 283(2) is the exclusion of any equity held by the debtor in his home. This is not because the Cork Committee was insensitive to the needs of providing a roof for the debtor and his family in a country that has been chronically short of affordable housing since the Second World War. Rather it is because the Committee and the British Parliament, when considering the problem, were anxious to strike a proper balance between the creditors' entitlement to have the equity realised to satisfy the estate's debts and allowing the debtor and his family sufficient time to make alternative accommodation arrangements. The result of these efforts are some very detailed provisions in sections 336–338 of the Insolvency Act which, once again, vest

---

[39] *Insolvency Law and Practice. Report of the Review Committee* (Cmnd 8558, June 1982) ch 24.

[40] IA, s 303(1).

[41] eg, the British Columbia Court Order Enforcement Act, RSBC 1996, c 78, s 71 as amended SBC 1997, c 27, s 1.

[42] The necessity test has caused difficulties in Ontario when the courts were called upon to decide whether use of an automobile was a 'necessary' tool of the trade for an employee.

much discretion in the court hearing an application by the trustee for vacant possession of the matrimonial home.[43]

As previously noted,[44] the trustee's entitlement to require the debtor to turn over the surplus portion of his income was already enshrined in the 1883 Act and was carried forward into the 1914 legislation, though perhaps not widely invoked. The role here of the 1986 Insolvency Act appears to be to refine the earlier provisions and in particular to add the court's sanction in the form of 'income payment orders' (IPOs) to make sure that the surplus income is actually paid over.[45] There are several key differences between section 310 of the Insolvency Act and the approach adopted in the 1997 BIA amendments in Canada and the current Congressional Bills in the United States to determine the debtor's surplus income. First, the English Act does not impose an explicit obligation on the trustee to apply for an IPO; presumably it is to be implied as a broader aspect of his obligation to protect creditor interests and to gather in all assets belonging to the estate.[46] If the application is made, the court 'may,' not 'must,' make such an order although no doubt the court must exercise its discretion judicially. Thirdly, in determining the amount of the IPO the court is not bound by objective criteria; rather section 310(2) enjoins the court not to make an order the effect of which would be to reduce the bankrupt's income 'below what appears to the court to be necessary for meeting the reasonable domestic needs of the bankrupt and his family.'[47]

So, once again, the British Parliament has indicated its strong preference for flexible standards over the dangers of a procrustean bed. However, it is difficult to believe that Parliament would have endorsed this degree of subjectivity if it

[43] For the details, see Fletcher (n 16 above) at 8–013 to 8–020. Mr Hill suggests that the absence of any exemption for homes, even if the debtor only has a modest equity in it, is also a significant deterrent to a debtor choosing the bankruptcy route. He also points out that even if the home is mortgaged beyond its value, because the property vests in the trustee at the outset, the trustee can effectively do nothing for 20 years and must wait for property price inflation to make it worthwhile selling at that stage. This happens regularly. The Enterprise Act 2002 (5.6 below) provides for the home to revest automatically in the debtor after three years unless the trustee takes positive steps to realise or secure his interest. Email message from Steve Hill to author (22 August 2002).

[44] See Chapter 2.6 above.

[45] Fletcher (n 16 above) at 8–025 to 8–028, IA, s 310, and Insolvency Rules 6, 189–6, 193, Forms 6.64–6.68. These provisions are modestly amended in the Enterprise Act 2002, see 5.6 below.

[46] In practice, it may be assumed that the trustee will have a strong incentive to seek an IPO since there may be few other sources to cover the trustee's fee and expenses.

[47] For a lucid analysis of the statutory provisions and supporting case law, see Gareth Miller, 'Income Payment Orders' (2002) 18 *Tolley's Insolvency Law and Practice* 43. As Prof Miller points out (at 46–48), it is now well established that there are important differences between the tests of exempted property under IA, s 283(2) and the discretion conferred on the court in making an IPO under s 310(2). In a striking passage, the court observed in *Re Rayatt* [1998] 2 FLR 264, 271 (citing the Cork Report) that it was not the object of s 310 that 'the debtor should become the slave of his creditors.' So far as the Insolvency Service is concerned, in bankruptcy cases administered by the Service the staff is directed to apply the current Financial Expenditure Survey published by the Office for National Statistics to determine the bankrupt's 'total disposable income' (TDI). When that has been established, the Service will apply for an IPO of between 50–66% of TDI, with the higher percentage being sought for higher TDIs. (Information supplied to the author by email, 15 January 2003.)

had thought it likely that the courts would be frequently called upon to resolve differences between the trustee and the debtor as to the 'reasonable domestic needs' of the debtor and his family.[48] Section 310(6) of the Insolvency Act is also relevant in highlighting Parliament's concern not to burden the debtor with an IPO for an indefinite period once the debtor has obtained a discharge. The basic rule is that an IPO is not to be made after the discharge except (i) where the court imposes an IPO as a condition of discharge on a debtor not entitled to an automatic discharge under section 279(1)(a) and (ii) where an IPO had been made before the discharge in respect of a debtor entitled to an automatic discharge under section 279(1)(b). In the latter case, the IPO cannot run for more than three years beginning with the pre-discharge date and ending after the discharge.

Information about operating experience with IPOs in England appears to be sparse. The number of IPOs (see Table 5.2) increased from 1,712 in 1996/97, or 7.8 per cent of the number of bankruptcy orders, to 2,434, or 11.0 per cent of the number of bankruptcy orders in 2000/01:

Table 5.2: Total number of income payment orders*

1996–1997	1,712
1997–1998	1,979
1998–1999	2,297
1999–2000	2,410
2000–2001	2,434

*Source: Insolvency Service, *Annual Report and Accounts 2000–2001* (London, 2000 The Stationery Office) 15.

This author has not been able to locate information about the average duration, size and debtor's and third parties' compliance with IPOs.

(c) **Discharge Orders**

Since the Canadian discharge system was borrowed from England, it may be instructive to explain what has happened to the British discharge rules over the past 25 years. In 1957, the Blagden Committee[49] criticised the technical intricacies of the discharge provisions. In 1976, the Bankruptcy Act 1914 was amended

---

[48] In a letter to the author dated 25 August 1998, Mr Peter Joyce, Inspector General of the English Insolvency Service, indicated that income payment orders were made in about 10% of bankruptcy cases.

[49] *Report of the Committee on Bankruptcy and Deeds of Arrangement Law Amendment* (Cmnd 221, 1957) paras 53–78.

to introduce an automatic discharge rule in a limited number of cases. The automatic discharge was triggered five years from the date of bankruptcy.[50]

The Cork Committee[51] recommended drawing a distinction between a liquidation of assets order (LAO) and a bankruptcy order for individual insolvents, and would have allowed a discharge from an LAO one year after an income payment order had been made. The Committee opposed an automatic discharge from a bankruptcy order but would have permitted the bankrupt to make a discharge application one year after the bankruptcy adjudication. As before, the court would have retained the right to suspend the discharge order or to make it absolute or conditional.

The British government did not adopt these recommendations. Instead, the Insolvency Act 1986 introduced a more lenient discharge system.[52] Pursuant to section 279(1), persons not made bankrupt in the preceding 15 years are entitled to an automatic discharge in regular cases three years after the bankruptcy order and after two years in summary administration cases. Where the debtor has failed to comply with his bankruptcy obligations, the official receiver may apply to the court for an order that the relevant period shall cease to run. In that case, the order may either specify a suspensory period[53] or may impose conditions to be met by the debtor before the running of time can resume.

It will therefore be seen that the current British discharge system is, on paper at least, substantially more favourable to the debtor than the Canadian system. Under the British system, only the official receiver can apply to have the running of time suspended for an automatic discharge and then only where the debtor has breached his statutory obligations. Also, the discharge order is absolute. While an income payment order may run beyond the date of the automatic discharge if the order so provides, it has a finite life span. No less important, both the making of an IPO and its amendment rest with the court. The court's discretion is not circumscribed by statutorily sanctioned surplus income standards as is true under the Canadian BIA.

(d) Non-Dischargeable Liabilities

So far as non-dischargeable liabilities and obligations of the debtor are concerned, they are listed in section 281 of the Insolvency Act and, at least on a superficial reading, appear to be much shorter than those appearing in the Canadian and US Bankruptcy Acts.[54] They cover liability for fraudulent

---

[50] The details will be found in IF Fletcher, *Law of Bankruptcy* (1978) 306–10. See also, *Report of the Committee on Bankruptcy* (above n 49) at paras 58–71.

[51] *Report of the Committee on Bankruptcy* (above n 49) at para 608 *et seq*.

[52] Fletcher (n 16 above) at 11–04. See also 5.6 below for the changes incorporated by the Enterprise Act 2002.

[53] IA, s 279(3).

[54] See comparative table, Chapter 2.10, Table 2.4 above.

conduct, a fine imposed for an offence (other than in relation to public revenue offences), family support and maintenance orders, liability under personal injury claims, and such other bankruptcy debts, not being debts provable in the debtor's bankruptcy, as are prescribed.[55] A distinctive feature of this list is the power conferred on the court in section 281(5) to release the debtor from a personal injury or family support or maintenance debt 'to such extent and on such conditions' as the court directs. This reflects an innovative attempt by the British Parliament to balance the need for continued enforcement of basic debts strongly imbued with public values against the goal of not placing insuperable obstacles in the honest debtor's ability to make a fresh start.

(e) Reaffirmation of Discharged Debts

The British Insolvency Act contains no statutory provisions dealing with the reaffirmation of discharged debts and, as in Canada, this feature of bankruptcy law continues to be governed by common law principles.[56] The subject has also attracted very little attention in England. This is not surprising given the generally low profile of consumer bankruptcies, the relatively small number of bankruptcies, and the financial hurdles facing low-income consumers seeking to use the bankruptcy route.

4. ALTERNATIVES TO STRAIGHT BANKRUPTCY

There are three major alternatives to bankruptcy under the English regime, two of which have been previously mentioned. The first, an IVA, is regulated in the Insolvency Act; the second, an administration order (AO), is, as we have seen, governed by the County Courts Act 1984. The third is a deed of arrangement. It will be convenient to address the third alternative first.

(a) Deeds of Arrangement

Deeds of arrangement are regulated by the Deeds of Arrangement Act 1914,[57] and involve assignment of the debtor's property for the benefit of the debtor's creditors. The 1914 Act suffers from near-fatal flaws. The deed of arrangement must be registered within seven days of execution, in the absence of which the deed becomes absolutely void. Even more serious was the fact that, before 'acts

---

[55] As Prof Fletcher explains (n 16 above) at 11–022, this last category of non-dischargeable debts restates a well-established common law rule applying to non-provable debts, though the IA has now qualified it.

[56] Fletcher (n 16 above) at 11–023.

[57] *Ibid* at 4–043/044.

of bankruptcy' were eliminated from the English Insolvency Act in 1986, the execution of a deed of arrangement entitled a non-assenting creditor to petition for the debtor's bankruptcy and, if a bankruptcy order was made, could result in the invalidation of the deed of arrangement and of any collection and distribution of assets under the deed.

The Cork Committee thought deeds of arrangement had outlived their usefulness and that the 1914 Act should be repealed. It was not. Nevertheless, deeds of arrangement have become almost totally obsolete and will not be considered any further.

(b) Individual Voluntary Arrangements[58]

IVAs were introduced in the Insolvency Act 1986[59] on the recommendation of the Cork Committee. IVAs are the counterpart of BIA Part III 2 consumer proposals in the Canadian Act but without the monetary ceilings in the Canadian Act. IVAs enjoy considerable popularity with English debtors and, between 1995 and 1998, clocked in at a steady 4,000-5,000 annual rate, or about 16 per cent of the total number of annual insolvencies.[60]

There are other, still more important, differences between IVAs and Canadian consumer proposals, which indicate that IVAs are more formal and more closely regulated than are consumer proposals in Canada. First, the debtor's proposal under an IVA must undergo preliminary scrutiny by an insolvency practitioner (the 'nominee') who must report to the court whether a meeting of the creditors should be held to consider the proposal.[61] If the court approves the insolvency practitioner's report, a meeting of creditors will be convened. Secondly, there is no automatic stay of proceedings. Rather the debtor must apply for an interim stay order, which is only good for 14 days.[62] A third difference is that the English creditors must approve the proposal by three-quarters in value of the creditor's claims. This is in contrast to the Canadian position where a meeting of creditors is only required if so directed by the

---

[58] For a detailed discussion of the statutory provisions, see Fletcher (n 16 above) ch 4 at 4–002 *et seq.*

[59] IA, ss 252–263.

[60] The numbers jumped to 7,195 and 7,978 IVAs in 1999 and 2000, or about 25 per cent of all insolvency proceedings: DTI, Insolvency Service, *General Annual Report for the Year 2000*, s 2.2, Table 2. The Report offers no explanation for this significant increase in the number of IVAs.

[61] IA, s 256. See further R3, *Is a Voluntary Arrangement Right For Me?* (2002) (www.r3.org.uk/pdf/A5booklet.pdf), an IVA guidance leaflet that every insolvency practitioner is required to give a debtor contemplating an IVA. The proposal may easily run to 20 pages or more and is a very technical document. (R3 has prepared standard terms and conditions for incorporation in proposals by its members, which runs to 27 pages.) This is in contrast to a consumer proposal under the BIA, which usually only runs to about half a dozen pages. For an instructive case on the duty of care owed by the nominee to the debtor, see *Pitt v Mond* [2001] BPIR 624 (Judge Roger Cooke).

[62] IA, s 252.

Superintendent of Bankruptcy or if requested by creditors holding in the aggregate at least 25 per cent in value of the proven claims.[63]

If the creditors approve the proposal, the supervisor nominated in the proposal (usually also the nominee insolvency practitioner at the earlier stage) becomes responsible for supervising the implementation[64] and may, if the IVA so provides, become involved in running the debtor's business. A further difference between an IVA and the Canadian consumer proposal is that the debtor's default under an IVA—even a prolonged default—does not result in an automatic bankruptcy order. Instead, the supervisor or a creditor must bring a bankruptcy petition.[65]

From the debtor's perspective, there also appear to be important fee differences. An English debtor faces two sets of fees: one for the nominee insolvency practitioner and a second set for the supervisor's services. Neither comes cheap and the fees are probably beyond the pocket of most low-income English debtors.[66]

(c) Administration Orders

The essential structure of Part VI of the County Courts Act 1984[67] is as follows. A debtor with multiple debts not exceeding a prescribed amount (currently £5,000), at least one of which must have been reduced to judgment, applies to the court for an AO and completes a form providing details of the debts, his income and other assets, and basic living expenses for himself and (where relevant) his family. The court staff then assesses the debtor's ability to pay off the debts by instalments, in whole or in part,[68] and notifies the creditors of the proposed order. If any creditor objects to the proposed order a hearing will take place before the judge and the judge will determine the character of the order. If there are no objections the order will go as proposed. So long as the order is in effect, a creditor whose name is included in the schedule to the order cannot present a bankruptcy petition against the debtor unless, inter alia, the debt to him

---

[63] BIA, s 66.5(2).

[64] IA, s 263.

[65] *Ibid*, s 264(1).

[66] IVA costs vary but a going rate for acting as nominee is around £1,000–£1,500; the cost of the supervisor's services will vary depending on what the supervisor is required to do and may be around £1,000 a year. Percentage fees are permissible but are extremely rare: Steve Hill, email to author (31 July 2002).

[67] County Courts Act 1984 (UK) c 28.

[68] There appears to be some uncertainty about the scope of s 112(6) of the Act although its language seems clear enough. It provides that the order may require payment by instalments or otherwise, 'and either in full or to such extent as appears practicable to the court under the circumstances of the case.' The doubt arises because of the 'composition' provision, added in s 112B in the 1990 amendments to Part VI, but not yet proclaimed. See Courts and Legal Services Act 1990, s 13(5). 'Composition' is not defined and it is not clear how it differs from the powers conferred on the court under County Courts Act 1984, s 112(6).

exceeds £1,500. Before the 1990 amendments to the Act, there was no restriction on the duration of an order.[69]

(d) Administration Orders in Practice

The Civil Justice Review Report[70] brought to light much valuable information about the actual operation of AOs, including the following facts. The average amount of total debts on an order was £2,500 but one-third of the orders were in the £3,000–5,000 range (approx. CAN$7,200–$12,000). The duration of the orders in the sample examined by the investigators varied greatly; a larger number were for 10 years or more and some had a potential duration of 70 years! Half the cases examined called for monthly payments of less than £25 (CAN$60). The smallest amount was £5 and the largest £150. The investigators also found very patchy payment records by the debtors. In 40 per cent of the examined cases, there had been no payment within the preceding two months; in half the cases there had been no payments for at least six months.

The court registrars told the Review Board that they seldom reviewed an order. If they did review it, most said they would reduce the amount of the instalments if the debtor was in difficulties but not the total amount of the debt. Of the 57 debtors with AOs interviewed by the investigators, 22 had sought advice about repaying their debts from solicitors or a Citizens' Advice Bureau (CAB). All the debtors said they were satisfied with the AO procedure. However, the investigators also found that a significant number of the debtors had difficulty completing the court forms. One-fifth of the creditors interviewed felt that the procedure was biased in favour of debtors, was slow and had not led to payment of their debts.

The Report was convinced of the utility of administration orders[71] but also saw a need to extend their scope and to simplify the procedure. The Report made the following specific recommendations:[72]

(1) The existing requirement for a judgment debt as the precondition for an order should be dropped.
(2) A judgment creditor as well as the debtor should be able to apply for an order.
(3) The registrar should be able to make an order on his own motion.

---

[69] County Courts Act 1984, s 112(9), as added in 1990 (but still unproclaimed), imposes a three-year limit or such earlier date as specified in the order.

[70] Civil Justice Review, *Report of the Review Body on Civil Justice* (Cmnd 394, June 1988) 608.

[71] 'This form of "mini-bankruptcy" has an important economic function of rehabilitating debtors in a comparatively short time and restoring them to their full economic status.' *Ibid* at 645. For a less enthusiastic evaluation see JE Davies, 'Delegalisation of Debt Recovery Proceedings: A Socio-Legal Study of Money Advice Centres and Administrative Orders' in IDC Ramsay (ed), *Debtors and Creditors: A Socio-Legal Perspective* (London, Professional Books, 1986) ch 8.

[72] *Report of the Review Body on Civil Justice* (n 70 above) at 645.

(4) The monetary limits on the making of orders should be removed.

(5) An order should run for no more than three years. If the debtor is unable to pay the debts within that time the registrar should make a composition order.

(6) Restrictions should be imposed on the future enforcement of debts where the debtor has no realisable assets or surplus income.

(7) Scheduled creditors providing essential service on an ongoing basis (such as gas, electricity or water utilities) should only be able to withdraw that services with leave of the court.

(8) In considering an AO application, the registrar should be able to consider whether bankruptcy would be a more appropriate remedy for the debtor because of the better protection it provides to debtors as well as the availability of greater sanctions for debtor misconduct.

As previously explained, many of the Report's recommendations were implemented in the 1990 amendments to the County Courts Act 1984. The amendments have not been proclaimed and the author was advised by the Lord Chancellor's Office in 1999 that the whole future of administration orders was actively under consideration at the time.[73] Since then, it appears the Insolvency Service has been brought into the discussions[74] but as of August 2002 no published decision had been reached.

5. CREDIT COUNSELLING AS PART OF THE BANKRUPTCY PROCESS

Given the limited attention paid to consumer bankruptcies in the British Insolvency Act, it would be surprising to find it addressing the issue of counselling for debtors, and it does not do so. Rather, the developments in this area have all been non-statutory. The evolution of debt counselling in England is succinctly described in the following extract from a chapter by a group of English authors:

> The Payne Committee Report [1969] identified debt as a problem influenced by social and economic forces, and not merely a question of dishonesty or bad management. At this time the growth of payment problems was noted by lawyers at a Legal Advice Centre based at the Birmingham Settlement, and in 1971 saw the launch of the Birmingham Settlement Money Advice Centre, the first debt counselling service in the UK. Although the 1970s saw a further growth in debt problems, by 1982 the National Consumer Council identified only 16 services nationally. By mid 1986 there were 100 services. However, also in 1986, the NCC reported a 96 per cent shortfall in debt counselling services. Significant problems remain in terms of providing an adequate, nationally available advice service. Issues of funding are central, and the appropriate balance between state and creditor financing unresolved. Unlike the position in some

---

[73] Letter to author from Ms Anna Lee, Lord Chancellor's Department, London, 22 October 1999.

[74] *Insolvency—A Second Chance* (n 7 above) at para 1.48.

other countries, to date creditors in Britain have not been heavily involved in support-ing debt counselling/money advice.[75]

The authors continue to point out[76] that that the major providers of debt counselling in Britain are the Citizens Advice Bureaux (CAB), local authorities, and independent advice centres. The CAB is the largest of these and has some 900 outlets nationwide, 100 of which offer specialist debt counselling services. In 1988 the National Association of CAB estimated that the Bureau had handled half a million enquiries related to debt. Within local authorities, specialised debt counselling services are sometimes provided through welfare rights units, social services or housing departments. Independent advice centres are represented by Money Advice Centres such as the one based at the Birmingham Settlement.[77]

The authors also note[78] that the approach to debt counselling by these agencies is based on broadly similar principles and involves, first, attempts to maximise the debtor's income (eg, by ensuring that the debtor is in the correct tax bracket and is receiving all welfare benefits to which she is entitled), giving priority to the payment of those debts that carry the most punitive sanction from the debtor's perspective (such as fuel debts or mortgage arrears), and negotiat-ing with creditors with respect to the other debts and, where necessary and resources permit, attending court with their client. This account may suggest that in England, unlike Australia,[79] political and cultural ideologies play no role in determining the types of counselling. While this may be true on a day-to-day basis, it is not true in a wider setting since in England too[80] social workers and their political allies are actively involved in lobbying for better protection of the needs of poor and indebted consumers.

Apart from the not-for-profit and government-sponsored debt counselling services described above, in recent years commercial debt counselling and debt management services have also become very active and advertise extensively on the Internet.[81]

---

[75] Conaty *et al*, 'Private and Public Concerns – Unemployment, Credit and Debt in Britain: An Overview' in U Reifner and J Ford (eds), *Banking for People* (1992) ch 37 at 559 (footnotes omitted).

[76] Conaty (*ibid*) at 559–60.

[77] In March 2002, the Money Advice Trust (MAT) launched a national telephone-based money advice service at new premises in Birmingham as well as a Scottish telephone-based service in Fife and a rural peripatetic service based in Cornwall. See MAT, *Annual Review of Activity for the Year ended 31 March 2002.*

[78] Conaty (n 75 above) at 561.

[79] See Chapter 4.8 above.

[80] Conaty (n 75 above) at 561 *et seq.*

[81] Email information to the author from Steve Hill (22 August 2002). A leading player is Baines & Ernst, which apparently handles a large number of debt management plans. (www.bainesandernst.com).

6. ENTERPRISE ACT 2002

For several years prior to 2002, the British government had been mulling over the desirability of introducing liberalising changes to the Insolvency Act. In March 2000, the Department of Trade and Industry (DTI) issued a consultation paper, *Bankruptcy: A Fresh Start*[82] inviting comments on some of the reforms under consideration. The impulse for putting them forward was the government's concern that a vibrant British economy was essential to improve the standard of living and maintain welfare services, that the spirit of free enterprise in England was seriously deficient, and that an important reason for the deficiency was individuals' fear of financial failure and consequent bankruptcy and the stigma attaching to bankruptcy. The consultation paper suggested relieving these concerns by introducing, among others, the following changes in the Insolvency Act[83]:

(1) reducing the period of eligibility of discharge from two years to six months, unless otherwise ordered by the court;
(2) encouraging IVAs in the post-bankruptcy period as an alternative to income payment orders;
(3) authorising the official receiver to act as nominee and supervisor of PPIs to address the high cost of servicing IVAs and the low pay-out to creditors;
(4) eliminating most of the current restrictions, disabilities and prohibitions applicable alike to honest and dishonest or irresponsible bankrupts and replacing the restrictions with a new regime of bankruptcy restriction orders (BROs) aimed only at dishonest and irresponsible debtors[84];
(5) amending section 283(2) of the Act to provide exemption on a '£1 for £1' basis in a home equity for money invested in the debtor's business[85];
(6) the consultation paper also invited comments on whether counselling or financial management instruction requirements should be imposed on a bankrupt when the official receiver believed they would be helpful.[86]

For the most part, the DTI's proposals were well received and in 2001 the government issued a White Paper[87] announcing its intention to proceed with most of the proposals, albeit several of them in modified form. The government made good with its promise in the Enterprise Bill. The Bill was introduced in the House of Commons in the spring of 2002 and received Royal Assent on

[82] The Insolvency Service, *Bankruptcy: A Fresh Start: A Consultation on Possible Reform to the Law Relating to Personal Insolvency in England and Wales* (London, Stationary Office, 21 March 2000).
[83] *Ibid* at s 7.
[84] *Ibid* at s 7.15.
[85] *Ibid* at s 8.
[86] *Ibid* at s 7.19.
[87] Secretary of State for Trade and Industry, *Productivity and Enterprise: Insolvency—A Second Chance* (Cm 5234, London, July 2001).

7 November 2002.[88] The important differences between the original proposals and the enacted provisions and other significant features are these:

(1) The basic discharge period is reduced to one year rather than six months as initially proposed. However, a shorter period will apply if, before the one year period has expired, the official receiver files a notice with the court that investigation of the bankrupt has been concluded under section 289 or that an investigation is unnecessary.[89]

(2) The existing disqualifications imposed on a bankrupt are restructured and are combined with a new bankruptcy restriction order regime.[90] Importantly, a BRO can only be made by the court.[91]

(3) The suggestion for a new home equity exemption and the introduction of counselling and financial management educational requirements have been dropped.[92]

(4) However, a new section 283A has been added to the Insolvency Act 1986 providing that a bankrupt's home shall cease to form part of the estate after three years unless the trustee has realised the debtor's interest in the home before this period or the bankrupt has agreed to buy out the estate's interest in the home.[93] A new section 313A also precludes the sale, taking of possession of the home by the trustee, or placing a charge on it if the estate's interest in the home is below a prescribed amount.[94]

(5) The Enterprise Act introduces[95] the concept of an income payment agreement (IPA) to supplement the existing provisions governing IPOs. IPAs will be made between the bankrupt and the trustee or official receiver and will require the bankrupt to pay a specific part or proportion of the bankrupt's income for a specified period. However, it is important to emphasise that, even after the 2002 amendments, the English Act still contains no automatic surplus income requirements comparable to those imposed under section 68 of the Canadian BIA.

(6) The summary administration provisions are repealed.[96]

(7) A 'fast-track' procedure is introduced to allow a bankrupt to enter into an IVA after bankruptcy and authorising the official receiver to act as nominee and supervisor of the IVA.[97]

---

[88] See Enterprise Act 2002 (UK) c 40.

[89] *Ibid*, s 256(1), amending IA, s 279.

[90] Enterprise Act 2002, ss 257, 266 *et seq* and Sch 20.

[91] *Ibid*, s 1(1), Sch 20.

[92] The proposals were dropped because they received little support from respondents: *Insolvency—A Second Chance* (n 87) at above, para 1.5.

[93] Act, s 261(1)–(3).

[94] In effect, this amounts to an exemption in the bankrupt's favour although it is not described this way in IA, s 313A.

[95] Enterprise Act 2002, s 260.

[96] *Ibid*, Sched 23, s 1, repealing IA s 275.

[97] Enterprise Act 2002, s 264 and Sch 22. Section 264(2) also allows the fast-track procedure to be extended by ministerial order to other IVA cases.

During the debate on the Enterprise Bill a private member's amendment was moved to allow the Secretary of State, by statutory instrument, to grant remission to indigent debtors from payment of bankruptcy fees. However, the amendment was not accepted by the government.[98] Consequently, it appears, bankruptcy facilities in England may remain as inaccessible to low-income consumers in the future as they have largely been in the past.

---

[98] See above n 18, and cf. the recommendations in S Edwards, above n 32, at ch 12.

6

Scotland

1. RELEVANCE OF SCOTTISH EXPERIENCE

IN THE ORDINARY course of events, there would be little justification for singling out Scotland for special treatment. Scotland has a small population (5 million) and, though Scottish bankruptcy law has a long history, it has been much influenced by English developments. This appears to be particularly true of the post-1985 period, when Scotland completely revised its bankruptcy law[2] following a comprehensive report by the Scottish Law Commission.[3] The affected features of the 1985 Act include voluntary and involuntary bankruptcies (described as 'sequestrations') for individual debtors,[4] the automatic discharge of the debtor after three years,[5] exemption of the debtor's personal and household goods (but not the debtor's home) from the trustee's reach,[6] subjection of the debtor's earnings to an income payment order,[7] and a short list of non-dischargeable debts.[8] The Bankruptcy (Scotland) Act 1985 also contains what appears to be a relatively simple system of arrangements or composition between the debtor and his creditors in the form of private and 'protected' trust deeds.[9]

What makes the Scottish experience especially noteworthy is the remarkable increase in the number of individual sequestrations between 1985/6 and

---

[1] The following discussion is based on M Adler, 'The Overseas Dimension: What Can Canada and the United States Learn from the United Kingdom?' (1999) 37 *Osgoode Hall Law Journal* 415; WW McBryde, 'The Scottish Experience of Bankruptcy' in H Rajak (ed), *Insolvency Law: Theory and Practice* (London, Sweet & Maxwell, 1993) 117; R Black (ed), *The Laws of Scotland: Stair Memorial Encyclopaedia*, vol 2 ('Bankruptcy') (Law Society of Scotland/Butterworths, 1988); Accountant in Bankruptcy (AIB), *Annual Report 1999/2000* (Edinburgh, 2000); and AIB, *Introduction to Sequestration* (Edinburgh, undated (www.oaib.demon.co.uk/Publications/ AB16_Introduction_to_sequestration.pdf). Other sources are indicated below.

[2] Bankruptcy (Scotland) Act 1985 (UK) c 66 (B(S)A).

[3] Scottish Law Commission, *Report on Bankruptcy and Related Aspects of Insolvency and Liquidation* (SLC No 68, 1982).

[4] (B(S)A), s 5.

[5] *Ibid*, s 54(1). There are some minor exceptions. The Law Commission had recommended allowing the debtor to apply for an earlier discharge but the recommendation was not accepted: *Laws of Scotland* (n 1 above) at 1438. Also, a creditor or the permanent trustee may apply for deferment of the automatic discharge (B(S)A), s 54(3).

[6] *Ibid*, s 33(1).

[7] *Ibid*, s 32(2),(3).

[8] *Ibid*, s 55(1).

[9] *Laws of Scotland* (n 1 above). Pt 19; (B(S)A), s 59 and Sch 5. One of the distinctions between a private and protected trust deed is that a private trust deed is not required to be registered whereas a protected trust deed must be registered. On the other hand, a protected trust deed enjoys substantial benefits denied to private trust deeds. While the objectives of the Scottish system are similar to IVAs made under the English Insolvency Act 1986, the mechanics of the two systems differ significantly.

1992/93—from 437 to 11,970—and the rapid decline after 1992 to the point where the number of sequestrations has stabilised at 2,000–3,000, though continuing to show annual increases.[10]

On the other hand, the number of protected trust deeds remained negligible until 1993 but has since grown fourteen-fold, from 282 in 1993/94 to 4,011 in 2001/02 (see Table 6.2).

Table 6.1: Scotland—Individual Sequestrations

1976/77	132	1989/90	2,618
1977/78	127	1990/91	5,451
1978/79	106	1991/92	8,587
1979/80	150	1992/93	11,970
1980/81	181	1993/94	4,022
1981/82	213	1994/95	2,340
1982/83	282	1995/96	2,380
1983/84	292	1996/97	2,534
1984/85	298	1997/98	2,701
1985/86	437	1998/99	3,110
1986/87	808	1999/2000	3,185
1987/88	1,401	2000/01	2,938
1988/89	1,612	2001/02	3,193

Sources: OSB, *International Insolvency Statistics* (October 1999)16, AIB, *Annual Report 1997/1998* and AIB, *Annual Report 2001/2002*.

Table 6.2: Protected trust deeds in Scotland*

1988/89	10
1989/90	12
1990/91	3
1991/92	1
1992/93	2
1993/94	282
1994/95	424
1995/96	525
1996/97	532
1997/98	890
1998/99	1,574
1999/2000	2,353
2000/01	2,943
2001/02	4,011

*Sources: OSB, *International Insolvency Statistics* (October 1999) 23; AIB, *Annual Report 2001/2002*.

[10] Note, however, that about one-third of the annual sequestration petitions are presented by creditors: AIB, *Annual Report 1998–1999*, 19–20.

Translated into an insolvency rate (ie, combining the annual number of sequestrations and protected trust deeds), the Scottish rate reached the impressive level of 2.12 per 1,000 persons in 1992.[11] In 1998, it was 0.76, or just over a quarter of the Canadian rate but substantially above the English rate.

The reasons for the rapid escalation in the number of sequestrations after 1986 were the following. Scotland introduced a completely revised Bankruptcy Act in 1985. Under the prior 1913 Act, a bankruptcy could not proceed without the appointment of a private trustee. However, insolvency practitioners were unwilling to accept appointments unless there were sufficient assets in the estate to assure payment of their fees and disbursements or unless a third party was willing to guarantee payment. As a result, many bankruptcies never proceeded beyond the making of the bankruptcy order. In other cases, administration of the estate was often not completed.[12] Debtors also faced a significant hurdle in launching a voluntary petition because of the requirement that a creditor has to give his prior approval to the initiation of the proceedings.[13] One of the effects of these impediments was that before 1985 the number of sequestrations was less than 300.

The Scottish Law Commission expressed concern that bankruptcy proceedings could not be initiated for lack of funds and recommended that the state assume responsibility for funding the trustee's services in such cases. The Commission anticipated that only about 10 per cent of the number of annual sequestrations would require subsidising at an annual cost of between £30,000–£40,000 (approx CAN$75,000–CAN$100,000).[14]

These estimates turned out to be wildly optimistic because the Commission had overlooked the great attractions of state-funded sequestrations for insolvency practitioners and their clients. The practitioners apparently adopted two techniques to launch sequestration petitions and then to secure their appointments as trustees. The first was to persuade a friendly creditor to concur in sequestration proceedings by the debtor and the making of the sequestration order. The second, and more common procedure, was for the debtor to execute a protected trust deed in favour of his creditors. Once this had been done, the 1985 Act allowed the trustee to petition for a sequestration order without the creditors' concurrence.[15] It seems that prior to 1993, the Scottish courts had no option but to grant the order.

The costs to the state of subsidising the sequestrations grew at a remarkable rate —from £13,000 in 1986–87 to £26.31 million in 1993.[16] This created a great furor. The authorities responded in two steps. First, the Accountant in

---

[11] Office of the Superintendent of Bankruptcy, *International Consumer Insolvency Statistics* (Ottawa, June 1999 and October 1999) 20.

[12] SLC Report (n 3 above) 2.33; *Introduction to Sequestration* (n 1 above) at 28.

[13] (B(S)A), s 5(1).

[14] Adler (n 1 above) at 418.

[15] *Introduction to Sequestration* (n 1 above) app 2.

[16] AIB, *Annual Report 1997/1998* (n 1 above) at 23, Table (vi).

Bankruptcy (AIB)[17] introduced 'block payments' in the 1990s for the services of private trustees. This reduced the payment in an average case from almost £3,000 to £1,540 in 1998/99 (approximately CAN$6,900 to CAN$3,540).[18] Secondly, an amending Act of 1993[19] ended a trustee's power under a protected trust deed to bring a sequestration petition without the concurrence of the creditors or the court, and also provided that after 1993 the AIB was to act as interim and permanent trustee except where the creditors had elected or appointed a private insolvency practitioner.[20]

2. UNANSWERED QUESTIONS AND CONSULTATION PAPER

It is not difficult to deduce from the above narrative that Scottish insolvency practitioners were quick to exploit the loopholes in the 1985 Act to their advantage. But this is only a partial explanation for the rapid escalation in the number of sequestrations after 1986,[21] and many questions remain unanswered. What was the profile of the debtors receiving the subsidised sequestrations (none appears to have been published)? What has happened to insolvent Scottish consumers since the 1993 Act and since the sharp decline in the number of sequestrations? Are we to assume that the current number of annual sequestrations (around 3,000–4,000) represents the realistic number of debtors requiring the benefits of bankruptcy protection and that the pre-1993 numbers were greatly inflated?

A partial answer to these questions appears in a Consultation Paper issued by the Scottish Office in July 1997.[22] The authors of the Paper were concerned that one of the unintentional effects of the 1993 amending Act was severely to restrict access to the bankruptcy system by heavily indebted consumers. This result had come about for the following reasons. The 1985 Act only allowed debtors to petition for a sequestration order if they secured the concurrence of a creditors although no creditor's, concurrence was required for a summary sequestration (ie, one in which the total assets were less than £300). Prior to 1993, debtors

---

[17] He is the Scottish equivalent to the Superintendent of Bankruptcy in Canada.

[18] AIB, *Annual Report 1998/1999*, 17.

[19] Bankruptcy (Scotland) Act 1993 (UK) c 6.

[20] Adler (n 1 above) at 419; *Introduction to Sequestration* (n 1 above) at 29, app 2, at 33–34. However, since the 1993 Act the AIB has continued to retain the services of insolvency practitioners on an agency basis: AIB, *Annual Report 1998/1999*, 21, Table (iv). Interestingly, in a substantial number of cases the AIB is also elected trustee by the creditors, presumably because his costs are lower than those of a private practitioner. Since 1993, the costs of funding appointed trustees in pre-1993 sequestrations also dropped sharply. In the fiscal 1998/99 year, the programme yielded a small surplus of £0.04 million: AIB, *Annual Report 1998/1999*, 23, Table (vi).

[21] McBryde (n 1 above) at 121.

[22] Scottish Office, *'Apparent Insolvency'. A Consultation Paper on Amending the Bankruptcy (Scotland) Act 1985* (July 1997). The Scottish Office issued a second consultative document in July 1998 dealing with desirable amendments to the 1985 Act involving protected trust deeds and other issues. See Scottish Office, *The Bankruptcy (Scotland) Act 1985. A Consultation Follow-Up: Protected Trust Deeds and Other Issues* (July 1998).

overcame the restriction by signing a trust deed and relying on a petition by the trustee under the trust deed. Such trustees had 'an unconstrained right' to petition for the debtor's sequestration.

Because of the abuses, the 1993 Act eliminated this sequestration route. Instead, the Act provided that a debtor could petition for sequestration without a concurring creditor provided the debtor was 'apparently insolvent'. Apparent insolvency is defined in section 7(1) of the 1985 Act but, in the case of a debtor's petition, only those forms of apparent insolvency brought about by a creditor's diligence (ie, warrant of execution) or statutory demand of a creditor for attachment of the debtor's earnings can be relied on. The 1993 Act does not permit a debtor's petition on the basis of a simple declaration of the debtor's insolvency.

It seems that, in the case of debtor petitions, some Scottish courts have interpreted the requirements of apparent insolvency very technically with the result that many consumer debtors are no longer eligible for sequestration relief. The Consultation Paper sought advice on how the existing hurdles could best be removed and whether the respondents supported their removal. The 1997 Paper intimated[23] that the AIB had estimated that if the authors' proposals were implemented they would result in an increase of between 2,000 and 3,000 sequestrations per annum and that the AIB would likely be appointed as interim and permanent trustee in the vast majority of cases.

At the time of this writing (August 2002), the Consultation Paper's proposals have not been implemented.[24] Even if they were implemented, an increase of 2000–3,000 consumer bankruptcies would still leave the Scottish consumer bankruptcy rate well below the Canadian level. All the same, it seems safe to claim that the Scottish experience over the past 15 years again emphasises the importance of the attitude of insolvency practitioners in making their services available to debtors on affordable terms and of the procedural requirements in the legislation in determining accessibility to the system for heavily indebted consumers.

3. DEBT ARRANGEMENT AND ATTACHMENT (SCOTLAND) ACT, 2002

The Scottish Parliament approved this important new law on 17 December 2002. The Debt Arrangement and Attachment (Scotland) Act 2002 (DAA(S)A) introduces a new approach to the treatment of consumer indebtedness in Scotland, and largley implements the recommendations of a working group

---

[23] July 1977 Paper (n 22 above) at para 23.

[24] The July 1998 Paper (n 22 above) at 3, also reports on the responses to the July 1997 Paper (n 22 above). Respondents representing consumer interests mostly supported the proposals; others, especially those from professional bodies, gave more detailed arguments not amounting to simple agreement or disagreement. Respondents representing creditors tended to oppose giving debtors liberalised means of establishing apparent insolvency.

established by the Scottish Minister of Justice in June 2000.[25] The Act falls into several parts. Part I establishes a Scottish national debt arrangement scheme to help consumers with multiple debts pay their debts in a managed way without the threat of enforcement action. Every proposal for a debt payment programme must be reviewed and approved by an accredited money adviser and also requires the approval of the debtor's creditors and of the minister or designated public agency.

Part II of the Act introduces a new regime for execution of judgments and exemptions from execution, the previous system of poinding and warrant sales having been abolished in 2000.[26] Part III of the Act introduces a special procedure for executions against goods in homes and requires court approval in the form of an 'exceptional attachment warrant'.

The Scottish Government obviously attaches great importance to the DAA(S)A. Nevertheless, to a Canadian observer the debt arrangement provisions look very much like the orderly payment of debt provisions in Part X of the Canadian BIA, but with some important differences. The Scottish scheme apparently requires the unanimous consent of creditors,[27] which is not the case with respect to Canadian creditors under part X. Also, Part X does not require the intervention of a financial adviser. British observers have also noted the important fact that the DAA(S)A does not provide for remission of any part of the debt.[28] This makes the Scottish scheme distinctly less useful than the English administration order or consumer proposals under the Canadian BIA.[29]

---

[25] *Striking the Balance: a new approach to debt management.* Report of the Working Group on a Replacement for Poinding and Warrant Sale to Jim Wallace, QC, MSP, Minister for Justice (6 July 2001).

[26] See Abolition of Poinding and Warrant Sales Act 2000. (The Act apparently only took effect on 31 Dec 2002). See also DAA(S) A, s 58, which seems to have the same effect. Reform of the law of poinding and warrant sales had also been previously recommended by the Scottish Law Commission. See Scottish Law Commission, *Report on Poinding and Warrant Sales*, SLC No 177, 2000.

[27] Arguably this requirement may be relaxed under the broad regulation making powers conferred on the Scottish Executive under the Act.

[28] S Edwards, *In Too Deep, CAB Clients' Experience of Debt* (NCAB & Citizens' Advice Scotland, May 2003), at 7.31.

[29] Above ch 2.11.

7

Scandinavia and Continental Countries of Western Europe[1]

1. TRADITIONAL CONTINENTAL PHILOSOPHY

THE APPROACH OF the continental European countries, including the Nordic countries, to the treatment of consumer over-indebtedness lies at the opposite end of the spectrum to the liberal discharge policies adopted in common law jurisdictions, not just the United States but equally those of Canada, Australia, England and Scotland, the latter of which has a mixed legal system. The reasons for this disparity rest partly in legal history and partly in the restricted role that consumer credit has played, and probably still plays, in these countries. For a long time, bankruptcy was not, and in many cases still is not, an option for consumers in Western Europe and, where it was available, unpaid debts survived the bankruptcy process for as much as 30 years. Even now, nearly 20 years after legislative relaxation of the old shibboleths, consumer access to a right of discharge remains difficult and heavily circumscribed. Dr Niemi-Kiesilainen reminds us in her excellent survey of the European legislative developments[2] that there are three basic differences between the Scandinavian, continental European and common law approaches. Thus, in all the European legislation examined by her (a) access is restricted to debtors deemed deserving of assistance; (b) all of them require a mandatory payment plan of from five to seven years and there are no facilities for an automatic discharge[3]; and (c) all of them place special emphasis on debt counselling services provided by a variety of state-sponsored or state-funded social agencies. Their dual role is to help the consumer draw up a debt adjustment plan and to mediate its acceptance by

---

[1] The following description is based primarily on J Niemi-Kiesilainen, 'The Role of Consumer Counselling as Part of the Bankruptcy Process in Europe' (1999) 37 *Osgoode Hall Law Journal* 409 (hereafter 'Counselling'); J Niemi-Kiesilainen, 'Consumer Bankruptcy in Comparison: Do We Cure a Market Failure or a Social Problem?' (1999) 37 *Osgoode Hall Law Journal* 473 (hereafter 'Developments'); J Niemi-Kiesilainen, 'Collective or Individual? Constructions of Debtors and Creditors in Consumer Bankruptcy' in J Niemi-Kiesilainen, IDC Ramsay and WC Whitford (eds), *Consumer Bankruptcy in a Global Perspective* (Hart Publishing, forthcoming); U Reifner, *Consumer Lending and Overindebtedness Among German Consumer Households*, *Expert Report to the European Commission* (Hamburg, 27 March 1998) (hereafter *Expert Report*); and U Reifner, 'The Eleventh Commandment: Inclusive Contract Law and Personal Bankruptcy' in Niemi-Kiesilainen, Ramsay and Whitford (above).

[2] Niemi-Kiesilainen, 'Developments' (n 1 above) at 475.

[3] 'All European bills emphasise that the law must not undermine the general moral imperative of paying one's debts': Niemi-Kiesilainen, 'Developments' (n 1 above) at 482.

creditors, and to wean debtors away from the use of consumer credit and to live in the future on a balanced and, usually, very tight budget.

Even the modest changes in European attitudes might not have come about but for the rapid increase in the number of consumer debtors in the 1980s and 1990s.[4] Before the 1970s and 1980s, most of the continental countries restricted the availability of consumer credit through various controls. Demand exceeded supply and defaults were rare.[5] Since then the volume of consumer credit and/or household credit has grown rapidly though not at an even rate. The UK figures were cited earlier.[6] In Germany, consumer credit increased from 15 billion ECU in 1970 to 200 billion ECU in 1998. As a percentage of PDI, average indebtedness grew from 15 per cent in 1978 to 25 per cent in 1997.[7] Table 7.1 traces the growth of consumer credit in Germany[8] between 1980 and September 1997, and shows that it increased by 200 per cent during this period, though part of this increase was presumably due to the reunion of East and West Germany in 1990.

Prof Reifner's report to the European Union summarises the impact of these developments on the German pocketbook. In 1998, an estimated 820,000 Germans were registered as insolvent and between 4–7 per cent of all households were estimated to be over-indebted. The main reasons given, in descending order of importance, for debtors' default in meeting their debt obligations were unemployment and drop in income, illness, divorce and accidents.[9] These statistics should be compared with a 2001 EU Study[10] estimating that in 1996 there were approximately 53 million over-indebted persons in the European Union equivalent to 18 per cent of the total population over 18 years old or 16 per cent of all EU households.

A profile of debtors developed from 700 files opened by German debt advice agencies also revealed the following facts.[11] The number of male debtors was greater than the number of female debtors, the percentage of married, divorced and single debtors was about equal and debtors' income was in the lowest one-third bracket of the German population. With respect to the source of their income, 25 per cent of the clients were receiving unemployment benefits and 19

---

[4] 'Debtors' is used here in the sense commonly employed by sociologists, ie individuals with accumulated debts. A substantial number of the chapters in U Reifner and J Ford (eds), *Banking for People* (Berlin, de Gruyter, 1992) contain a detailed examination of the state of indebtedness in various European countries, especially among low-income consumers. For a later study, see EU Directorate-General for Health and Consumer Protection, *Study of the Problem of Consumer Indebtedness: Statistical Aspects, Final Report* (Brussels, October 2001) (hereafter *Consumer Indebtedness*).

[5] Niemi-Kiesilainen, 'Developments' (n 1 above) at 480.

[6] See Chapter 5.1 above.

[7] Reifner, *Expert Report* (n 1 above) summary, at (5).

[8] 'Consumer credit' is defined in the Monthly Report of the German Bundesbank, *Statistical Yearbook 1996*, 26, and includes instalment credit. It is not clear what definition of consumer credit is used in *ibid* Table 1 and how it is distinguished from 'consumer credit' in the Report.

[9] *Ibid* at (6). Note however that debt counsellors gave a different analysis and listed unemployment as the cause of the debt problems in only 27% of the cases as compared with 14% to illness, 23% to inappropriate consumer decisions, and 16% to family problems. *Ibid* at 6.

[10] EU, *Consumer Indebtedness* (n 4 above) at 3.

[11] Reifner, *Expert Report* (n 1 above) at 7.

Table 7.1: Development of consumer credit and private indebtedness in Germany*

Year	Consumer credit (DM 1 million)	Instalment credit (DM 1 million)	No of house-holds in 1,000s	Population in 1,000s (from 1990 onwards for Eastand West Germany)	Gross wages and salaries (DM1 million)
1980	130.720	66.922	24.811	61.566	733.900
1981	136.296	68.751	25.100	61.682	766.800
1982	144.059	72.384	25.336	61.638	788.400
1983	155.904	75.111	25.500	61.423	803.400
1984	164.787	77.924	26.000	61.175	831.400
1985	179.520	82.846	26.367	61.024	861.900
1986	188.840	88.422	26.739	61.066	906.100
1987	200.570	93.704	26.218	61.170	945.100
1988	213.989	–	27.100	61.450	982.200
1989	232.931	109.324	27.793	62.063	1,027.100
1990	259.692	120.808	32.100	79.365	1,108.800
1991	294.962	138.063	35.256	79.984	1,354.700
1992	324.521	148.117	35.700	80.594	1,462.800
1993	345.824	151.827	36.230	81.179	1,488.300
1994	363.888	160.902	36.695	81.539	1,512.200
1995	370.600	182.100	36.938	81.818	1,559.600
1996	388.800	192.500	37.281	82.012	1,569.900
Sept 1997	397.700	200.300	37.581†	82.212†	1,579.000†

Source: Monthly Report of the German Bundesbank, *Statistical Yearbook 1996*; and U Reifner, *Consumer Lending and Overindebtedness Among German Consumer Households, Expert Report to the European Commission* (Hamburg, 27 March 1998) 28.
† Estimate.

per cent welfare payments. Most of them had received no high school education and more than 15 per cent had not completed their primary school education. About half the debtors were under 40 years old. Most of the debtors owed between 5,000–25,000 ECUs (approximately CAN$7,700–$38,500); 54 per cent of the debtors had less than seven creditors; 20 per cent had more than 10 creditors. The most important creditors were banks (30 per cent), department stores and mail order merchants (23 per cent), and the state (14 per cent).

2. RECENT CONSUMER INSOLVENCY LEGISLATION

Between 1984 and 1998, most of the Western European countries adopted some form of legislation designed to assist over-committed consumers in coping with their debt problems. Among the Scandinavian countries, Denmark was the first (1984) and was followed by Finland and Norway in 1993 and Sweden in 1994. Among the continental countries, France adopted a very restrictive law in 1989 (the loi Neiertz); Germany adopted a somewhat broader (but still very demanding) regime in 1994 as part of the complete revision of the German bankruptcy law (Insolvenzordnung),[12] which only took effect at the beginning of 1999. The Austrian legislation of 1994 appears to have been influenced by the German model. Finally, the Netherlands enacted its law as recently as 1998.[13]

Dr Niemi-Kiesilainen has helpfully summarised[14] the key features of the European legislation (see Table 7.2).[15]

Table 7.2: Four models of consumer bankruptcy*

	Scandinavia	*Germany*	*France*	*United States*
Primary aim	rehabilitation	repayment	prevention	efficiency
Nature of law	debt adjust-ment law	bankruptcy law	consumer protection law	bankruptcy bankruptcy law
Mandatory counselling	yes	yes	no	no
Filing made with	enforcement agency	court	commission	court
Access	restricted	through bankruptcy	broad	open
Exceptions to availability	broad	creditor acceptance	broad	fraud
Duration of plan	five years	seven years	moratorium	three years
Administrating party	debtor	trustee	debtor	trustee
Bearer of costs	state	debtor (waiver)	state	debtor
Applicability to home mortgages	Finland and Norway yes; Sweden and Denmark no	no	no	yes
Bar to subsequent filing	forever	10/20 years	no	six years

Source: J Niemi-Kiesilainen, 'Consumer Bankruptcy in Comparison: Do We Cure a Market Failure or a Social Problem? (1999) 37 *Osgoode Hall Law Journal* 473, at 499, together with minor adjustments made by the author.

[12] See M Balz and HG Landfermann, *Die Neuen Insolvenzgesetze* [The New (German) Insolvency Laws] (Dusseldorf, IDW-Verlag 1995). (The authors were closely involved in the drafting of the laws.)

[13] Cf N Huls, 'Prospects for Statutory Consumer Debts Arrangements in the Netherlands' in Reifner and Ford (eds) (n 4 above) ch 30. For an important empirical study of the Dutch law, see N Jungmann, in J Niemi-Kiesilainen, IDC Ramsay and WC Whitford (eds), *Consumer Bankruptcy in a Global Perspective* (Hart Publishing, forthcoming).

[14] Niemi-Kiesilainen, 'Developments' (n 1 above) at 499.

[15] *Ibid* at 497; Reifner, *Expert Report* (n 1 above) at 78–79.

Prof Reifner has also prepared a table adopting a different approach in which he classifies the legislation according to its ideological bent and compares the 'neo-classical' Anglo-American fresh start system with the conservative German system, the French state-monitored 'debt management' model, and the Scandinavian model involving debt relief and self-regulation. It has been objected that these are misleading labels since the European laws have more in common with each other than their ideological typing suggests they should have. Let us therefore say no more about the ideologies. However, it will be helpful to summarise the essential features of a representative member of each of the three types—the Danish, French and German laws—so that the reader can capture their flavour for herself.

3. REPRESENTATIVE LEGISLATIVE REGIMES

(a) Denmark: Debt Arrangement Act 1984[16]

To be eligible for consideration, the debtor must have minimum debts of US$40,000 (approx. CAN$60,000) if employed or US$15,000 (CAN$22,500) if the debtor is unemployed or retired. The court must take into account the overall circumstances of the case as well as the debtor's behaviour and the character of the debts. The debtor must propose a plan, usually with a five years' duration, longer if student loan debts are involved. All unsecured creditors are treated alike. Secured debts are outside the plan. The payment schedule is based on the debtor's surplus income over what is required for the debtor's essential expenses. Those expenses are based on the minimum social security allowances paid by the state. The debtor is sometimes allowed to stay in the family home.

The debt adjustment process is a separate proceeding from a normal bankruptcy and the debtor's application must be approved by the court before a plan can be formulated. If the application is granted, the costs of the scheme are borne by the state. The plan itself, however, is prepared by a private trustee who also administers the plan. In determining whether to approve the plan the court is not bound by the creditors' opinion.

According to Dr Niemi-Kiesilainen, only about 5,000 applications were filed in the 1980s as compared to 8,000 in 1991. However, the success rate is only about 25% and critics have complained that the approval standards are too high and that serious debt problems remain outside the new law altogether.

---

[16] Niemi-Kiesilainen, 'Developments' (n 1 above) at 488–90.

(b) France: Loi Neierz 1989, amended 1995[17]

What is distinctive about the French approach is that it uses an administrative commission supervised by the Bank of France to prepare a payment plan (*plan conventionel*) and then to administer the plan. The plan is meant to be consensual but if the creditors are unwilling to accept it the Commission may apply to the court, which can then exert pressure on the dissenting creditors. The debtor's good faith (*de bonne foi*) is a precondition to the Commission's obligation to assist the debtor, although the law provides no definition of this elusive term. There are also restrictions on the scope of the plan. The most important of them is that the principal of the debt may not be reduced except in the case of a home mortgage where the home has been sold (and presumably the selling price was less than the outstanding mortgage). Repayment of the debt may be rescheduled for one and a half times the original repayment period. Apparently the average length of a plan is 10 years.

Particular problems arise where debtors have no payment capacity.[18] The Commission's approach in such cases[19] has been to grant successive repayment extensions. The appropriateness of this solution has been questioned, particularly given the fact that the law allows for such debtors to be discharged after a three-year period.

The loi Neierz is considered a success: 90,000 applications were filed in the first 10 months after its introduction. The numbers dropped to an average of 68,000 a year between 1991 and 1994 but climbed again to 95,700 in 1997. Whatever else may be said about the French approach, it seems clear that large numbers of French debtors are anxious to find relief from their debt problems.

(c) Germany: Insolvenzordnung 1994[20]

The original report of the Commission established by the German government in the 1980s to present proposals for revising the century old German insolvency laws did not include recommendations for dealing with consumer problems and a discharge facility was only provided for business debtors. Strong pressure by consumer groups and the support of the Social Democratic opposition party led to amendments being adopted for consumer debt relief during debate on the Bill in 1991. The law was approved in 1994 but, as previously mentioned, only

---

[17] Niemi-Kiesilainen, 'Developments' (*ibid*) at 483–85; Loi No 89-1010 du 31 décembre 1989, JO 2 janvier 1990, p 18; Décret No 95-660 du 9 mai 1995, JO 10 mai 1995, p 7711; and French Senate, *Commission des lois et des finances—Rapport d'information no.60, Surendettement Prévenir et Guérir* (29 October 1997).

[18] 25–40% of the debtors fall into this category.

[19] The French courts have also resorted to this device.

[20] Niemi-Kiesilainen, 'Developments' (n 1 above) at 485–87; Reifner, *Expert Report* (n 1 above) at 81–87.

became operative at the beginning of 1999. The law adopts a two-track procedure for the relief of consumer debtors. The first, governed by article 304, involves a debt adjustment plan; the second is a bankruptcy proceeding, falling under article 286, which, if all goes well, may conclude after a interlude of seven or more years with the discharge of any remaining debts. Under the debt adjustment procedure, the debtor must negotiate with the creditors and present them with a plan. The plan must be approved by half the creditors in number and value but a secured creditor cannot be bound without its consent. The plan also requires court approval and, when that has been obtained, an insolvency manager will collect and distribute the payments and supervise the plan.

The bankruptcy procedure is apparently based on different principles and involves the debtor being required to pay his attachable income for up to seven years to a trustee manager for distribution to the creditors followed by discharge of any remaining debt if the debtor has observed all the requirements of the law. Importantly, the article 286 procedure also has a preliminary phase requiring the debtor and his creditors to engage in serious negotiations about the terms and amounts of the payments to individual creditors.[21] It also envisages the possibility of the payment plan involving all of the debtor's family with the prospect of reducing the seven-year period if other members of the household contribute payments.[22]

The new law encountered substantial teething troubles in its first year of operation. Apparently, only 13 per cent of the applications for debt release led to approved payment plans. Some of the difficulties were the following[23]: there was a long waiting list for the obligatory debt counselling mandated by the legislation; attorneys were not entitled to sufficiently high fees to be attracted to offer their services; some judges believed that the debtor must be in a position to repay a minimum amount of the debt to be entitled to enrol in a plan; and major creditors were being unco-operative in the negotiation of payment plans. The debt release provisions in article 304 *et seq* were also criticised on the following grounds[24]:

(1) The costs of the procedure have to be borne by the debtor. Since many debtors cannot afford to pay, even with legal aid, they are excluded from access to debt relief altogether.

(2) The procedure is too complex and may lead to the proceedings being terminated without the debtor's participation.

(3) The duration of the procedure—a minimum of seven years[25]—is much too long, especially when account is taken of the financial hardship suffered by the debtor during this period as well as the debtor's obligation to comply with numerous duties.

---

[21] Reifner, *Expert Report* (n 1 above) at 82.

[22] *Ibid* at 83.

[23] The information is taken from an email to the author by Dr Reifner of 6 December 1999.

[24] Reifner, *Expert Report* (n 1 above) at 85–86. See also Reifner, 'Eleventh Commandment' (n 1 above).

[25] In practice, after allowing for an initial waiting period, it may be as long as 10 years.

(4) The law is regressive in so far as it requires the debtor to accept any offer of work even if totally unsuitable for the debtor.
(5) The law takes no account of creditors' responsibility for the debtor's over-indebtedness. Banks are also given unfair priority treatment over other creditors' claims and, in particular, may continue to attach the debtor's earnings.
(6) The law is demeaning to debtors and deprives them of their dignity as human beings.
(7) The law operates unfairly against guarantors of the debtor. They may be sued by the debtor's creditors but have no right of recourse against the debtor. This means that other members of the debtor's family, and divorced or separated spouses, will suffer great hardships and may themselves have to seek bankruptcy relief!

(d) 2001 Amendments to German Law

Following publication of a consultation document by the German government in 2000, the Bundestag approved amendments to the consumer insolvency provisions on 28 June 2001.[26] The amendments went well beyond what consumer activists expected and include the following key points[27]:

(1) the trusteeship phase of the debt relief procedure begins with initiation of the insolvency proceedings and will run for six instead of seven years;
(2) the validity of pre-bankruptcy wage assignments is reduced from three years to 2 years;
(3) extra-judicial debt settlement proceedings are protected against execution efforts by individual creditors;
(4) insolvency court fees are reduced;
(5) debtors who cannot pay the court fees may postpone payment until their debts have been discharged;
(6) the conduct of the debt discharge phase of the proceedings will be in the discretion of the bankruptcy court;
(7) article 850 *et seq* of the Code of Civil Procedure, permitting enlargement of types of property that are not pledgeable, may be invoked in insolvency proceedings;
(8) small business enterprises with more than 20 creditors will still be restricted to using the commercial insolvency law to obtain debt relief.

---

[26] Ins-Änderungsgesetz 2001 (Law to Amend the Insolvency Law).

[27] H Springeneer, IFF, 'Änderungen im deutschen Verbraucherinsolvenzverfahren: Mehr als eine 'erste Repartur'?' [Changes in German Consumer Insolvency Law: More than a Minor Repair Job?] (memorandum, Hamburg, 2001). (The author is indebted to Udo Reifner for providing him with a copy of the document.)

German pro-debtor commentators feel that these amendments do not go far enough and that further substantial changes will be necessary to put German consumer insolvency law on a par with other more liberal regimes.

(e) Role of Counselling[28]

Most the European countries had a variety of debt counselling agencies[29] even before the introduction of the debt adjustment laws. Their role has been much enhanced as a result of the new legislation. Even where use of the agencies' services is not a legal requirement, it is a practical necessity because of the complex legal provisions and the need for an experienced professional to negotiate with the creditors. The role of the agencies seems to have two distinct components: (a) where there is a debt adjustment law, to assist the debtor to draw up a payment plan for presentation to the creditors and, where there is not, to prepare a voluntary payment plan; and (b) to train and educate the debtor to live within the constraints of a budget that requires the debtor to reduce his consumption to bare essentials while paying off his debts in whole or part, and to be able to live on a balanced budget after completion of the payment plan without resort to credit.

It is this last feature that warrants a particular comment. Dr Niemi-Kiesilainen has the impression[30] that in Canada rehabilitation of the debtor is achieved though the debtor's discharge from bankruptcy and that, unlike in Europe, emancipation from debt by actually paying off the debts is not part of the North American goal. She also expresses concern that the North American aim is to produce better consumers of credit whereas the European aim is to reduce the consumer's reliance on credit. She admits, however, that since payment plans are *imposed* on debtors under the European laws 'it is hard to see it [them] as emancipation from the cultural compulsion to consume excessively.'[31] These are challenging observations that merit further discussion in the concluding Part C of this study.

---

[28] For much fuller details, see Niemi-Kiesilainen, 'Counselling' (n 1 above).
[29] According to Prof Reifner, Germany alone has some 700 consumer counselling outlets.
[30] Niemi-Kiesilainen, 'Counselling' (n 1 above) at 413.
[31] *Ibid.*

Part C

Assessing the Various Insolvency Regimes and Suggestions for Changes

8

Assessment and Suggestions for Changes

1. INTRODUCTION

THE INSOLVENCY REGIMES surveyed in Part B of this study cover a broad spectrum of philosophies and approaches. This is true even though they purport to address the same phenomenon—how to help over-indebted consumers who, largely through no fault of their own, find themselves with accumulated debts they cannot hope to pay off within a reasonable time frame, if ever.

The gamut of philosophies run from the US fresh start philosophy, now heavily under attack in its home territory, on the left side of the spectrum to the dominant continental European view on the right that discharge from debts should only be available as a last resort and only after the debtor has walked the treadmill for five to seven years. In between we have Canada, Australia, England, and Scotland. Canada is closest to the United States in rate of insolvencies but much closer to Australia (or perhaps it should be the other way around) in philosophy and approach and with respect to income payment requirements.

England is a puzzle since all the evidence points to the fact that consumer indebtedness is as common there as it is in Canada and Australia. The answer rests partly in the stigma that still attaches to bankruptcy in England but more importantly, it seems, in the financial hurdles facing impecunious debtors who cannot raise the £250 deposit and £120 filing fee required to file a petition.[1] The Scottish experience shows how radically the wind shifts when the financial barriers are removed. This does not, of course, prove the case for state financed bankruptcy facilities but it casts important light on one facet of the insolvency phenomenon. Current English developments also illustrate the fact that the absence of affordable insolvency facilities does not resolve the debt problems. Rather it creates a growing market for commercially-driven debt counselling, debt settlement and debt pro-rating agencies, and also puts that much more pressure on not-for-profit debt advice and credit counselling services. Despite the historical and philosophical differences between insolvency systems—and especially the differences between common law based and continental European systems—it is important not to cast them in iron clad terms. There are signs of some convergence between the common law and European approaches. These

---

[1] As noted in Chapter 5.3 above, efforts to persuade the Blair government to grant relief from these high fees in the Enterprise Act 2002 amendments to the English Insolvency Act 1986 were not successful.

changes are seemingly fuelled, in the case of Europe, by the rapid increase in the number of over-indebted consumers and the need to make the insolvency systems more functional and efficient and, in the case of the common law jurisdictions (but especially the United States), by strong creditor pressure for means testing and restrictions on easy discharges.

Given the options presented by the different national regimes and Canada's willingness to reassess its own choices, two basic questions and a host of subsidiary issues need to be addressed. A substantial number of them were addressed in the report of the Canadian Personal Insolvency Task Force, though not, in this author's view, always satisfactorily. In any event, the following discussion is based on the the author's own perceptions of the issues and the suggestions are informed by his own interpretation of the available data and are undoubtedly coloured by his own philosophy of consumer bankruptcy.

2. THE BASIC QUESTIONS

(a) Whose Fresh Start Version?

Basically the answer to this question is whether we believe it appropriate to apply a means test to determine the debtor's ability to pay over surplus income or whether, following the philosophy enshrined in the present US Bankruptcy Code, we subscribe to the view that it is better for the debtor to determine voluntarily whether he wants to make payments in the form of a chapter 13 type plan or consumer proposal under the Canadian Act, encouraged, it may be, by various incentives.

Historically, the simpler US fresh start approach had great appeal and may have corresponded to the needs of nineteenth century US society when the economy was very volatile and incomes were subject to sharp fluctuations. It is much more difficult to justify in the contemporary environment where income is overwhelmingly the average debtor's most important form of asset. The author has dealt elsewhere[2] with some of the traditional US objections to mandatory income contributions and explained why he found many of them unpersuasive. It seems moreover that a majority of US senators and congress persons have been persuaded—influenced no doubt by intense pressure and financial inducements from the credit industry—of the need to reorient the US fresh start philosophy. However, the avenue chosen in the Congressional Bills to oblige debtors to pay over their surplus income, by denying them access to chapter 7 and leaving them with the option of a revised and much less attractive chapter 13 plan, seems contrived and disingenuous as well as being very expensive and complex. It pays lip service to the fresh start tradition while substantively

---

[2] JS Ziegel, 'The Philosophy and Design of Contemporary Consumer Bankruptcy Systems: A Canada-United States Comparison' (1999) 37 *Osgoode Hall Law Journal* 205, 245–48.

depriving it of its most distinctive component. It is therefore believed that the Canadian (and general Commonwealth) approach is the sounder one, which is not to suggest that it is free from difficulties either. Moreover, in Canada's case, it does not answer the related question whether greater clarity is needed with respect to the relationship between a straight bankruptcy under Part III of the BIA and a consumer proposal under Part III 2.[3]

The Canadian (and general Commonwealth) approach is also much to be preferred over the moralistic and onerous philosophy reflected in the current crop of European debt adjustment and consumer bankruptcy provisions. The refrain that the sanctity of legal obligations must be maintained regardless of the circumstances has a familiar ring to North American and English ears but was given its quietus in most common law jurisdictions 75 or more years ago. A puritanical philosophy is only maintainable so long as the number of over-indebted consumers is small and so long as states are willing to take rigorous steps to control access to consumer credit. If neither of these conditions obtains, short of ignoring the realities of the contemporary market place, governments have little choice but to adopt a more liberal bankruptcy policy.

Even in its heyday, the denial of discharge from personal debts made heroic assumptions about the stability of incomes and the debtor's ability to anticipate and avoid personal and financial reverses. In the current North American environment of effortless amounts of often unsolicited consumer credit purveyed through saturation advertising and unsolicited credit cards, the maintenance of a Calvinist philosophy seems unsustainable. It may be that continental Europe operates in a markedly different market milieu, though the statistics seem to belie it. But if it is true, it means that continental Europe has little to teach common law jurisdictions (just as they have little to teach continental countries) unless it is to tell us that somehow the genie of consumer credit and all its attendant problems can be kept under tight control.

(b) Social Insurance, Means Testing and Surplus Income Payments

If Canadian consumers are the victims of too much credit and personal adversities over which they have little control, we are bound to ask whether there is any justification for mandatory income contributions from the debtor. Why not simply let the consumer credit industry write off bankruptcy losses as part of the cost of doing business, and why bother with the complex mechanics of means testing and collecting small amounts of surplus income at considerable expense in order to satisfy a moral principle?

The question has been addressed in some detail earlier in this study[4] but, given its pervasive importance, some of the answers need to be restated.

---

[3] See 8.3(l) below.
[4] See Chapter 3.5(b) above.

(a) A surplus income regime does not make creditors whole. They will continue to suffer heavy losses since, on the strength of recent evidence,[5] only about 19 per cent of consumer bankrupts will make any payments and these will mostly be for small amounts.

(b) On well-established insurance principles, an unqualified fresh start rule is bound to lead to abuses. Even the staunchest supporters of the fresh start rule admit this though they differ widely on how they would address the abuses.

(c) Long US experience shows that a purely voluntary, incentive driven, chapter 13 regime is very difficult to operate and may generate new abuses of its own.

(d) US experience also shows that the absence of income payment requirements leads to great pressures on other parts of the system, notably by an ever lengthening list of non-dischargeable debts and obligations and pressure on consumers to reaffirm their debts after discharge from bankruptcy.[6]

(e) Finally, a wholly voluntary payment system encourages juggling between a straight bankruptcy order under chapter 7 and a plan under chapter 13 depending on which option offers the debtor the least painful exit from her debt difficulties and regardless of her creditors' reasonable expectations.

(c) Holding Credit Grantors Accountable

An unwillingness to abandon Canada's traditional middle of the road philosophy should not blind us, however, to the credit industry's own significant contribution to the current consumer bankruptcy malaise. There is a strong correlation between the growth in consumer credit and the increase in the number of consumer bankruptcies.[7] Unhappily, too, long experience shows that even the prospect of non-recovery of all or part of a debt is not sufficient incentive for some creditors to limit credit to creditworthy[8] borrowers and in amounts they can comfortably carry. This is a very large topic that deserves a report of its own. In Canada, the federal government and the provinces already have in place a large body of legislation regulating various aspects of consumer credit.[9]

---

[5] See Chapter 2.7 above.

[6] There is no guarantee that a surplus-income payment requirement will relieve the pressure for a larger number of non-dischargeable debts. It may, however, make it easier for legislators to resist the pressure if the debtor is not seen to be getting an easy ride.

[7] Cf RM Lawless, 'The Relationship between Non-Business Bankruptcy Filings and Various Basic Measures of Consumer Debt' www.law.missouri.edu/lawless/bus-bkr/filings.htm).

[8] See JS Ziegel, *Memorandum to the PITF* (2001); and PITF Report, Chapter 2.3 above, Annex 3 ('Reservation and Dissent by JS Ziegel'). The author is not alone in voicing his concerns over abuses in credit granting practices. See the documents cited below n 10 and, so far as credit cards are concerned, RD Manning, *Credit Card Nation: The Consequences of America's Addiction to Credit* (Basic Books, 2000). For the perceptions of an Australian financial counsellor, see J Pentland, 'Debt Collection: the Final Pusher into Bankruptcy?' (2002) 12(2) *ITSA New Directions* 10.

[9] For a short overview, see JS Ziegel, 'Canadian Perspectives on the Challenges of Consumer Bankruptcies' (1997) 20 *Journal of Consumer Policy* 197, at 206–9.

However, much of it is not designed to encourage sound credit practices and the parts that might be so construed (such as truth in lending disclosure requirements) are unenforced in practice or largely ignored by the consumer for whose benefit they were designed.

Crafting a more effective policy is no mean task. The following is a list of possible avenues worthy of exploration on the assumption that the Canadian government is willing to incorporate one or more of them as part of a balanced and well conceived future insolvency law[10]:

(a) Denial of claims to credit grantors who grant credit recklessly and without reasonable efforts to establish the debtor's capacity to repay the debt;

(b) Denial of claims by credit grantors advertising 'no down-payment' and 'no payments required for X number of months or days' unless the advertisement also carries information of equal conspicuousness concerning (a) the average percentage of purchasers eligible for the concessionary terms, and (b) the cash and credit prices of the goods or services being offered by the merchant where these relaxed terms are applied for;

(c) Following the example of HR 833 (1999),[11] requiring the monthly statements of credit card issuers to indicate how long it will take credit card holders to pay off the outstanding balance if the holder only makes the minimum monthly payments;

(d) Demoting claims to deferred creditor status[12] if the cost of the credit exceeds a prescribed percentage point above the Bank of Canada's prime rate for loans at the time of the extension of the credit;

(e) Denying secured creditor status for secured sales below CAN$500[13];

(f) Permitting the debtor, as distinct from the trustee, to redeem secured household goods acquired more than a year before the debtor's bankruptcy for the market value of the property at the time of redemption.

Another possibility, in the author's view one of great social importance, would be for the Canadian government to offer incentives for the development of non-profit low cost credit facilities for low-income consumers. This would have the added benefit of giving those consumers hands-on experience in the

---

[10] For other recent discussion of the issues, see DTI, *Tackling Loan Sharks and More! Consultation Document on Modernising the Consumer Credit Act 1974* (undated) (www.dti.gov.uk/ccp/consultpdf/loanshark.htm); and Commission of the European Communities, *Proposal for a Directive of the European Parliament and of the Council on the harmonization of the laws, regulations and administrative provisions of the Member States concerning credit for consumers* (COM(2002) 443 final; 2002/022 (COD)) esp Art 9 (responsible lending) and Art 15 (state-imposed penalties, including those for violation of Art 9).

[11] HR 833 § 112 amending the Truth in Lending Act (15 USC 1637(a)) by adding new paras (9) and (10).

[12] Cf BIA, s 138 (establishing deferred creditor status for persons standing in non-arm's length relationship to the debtor).

[13] Cf NBRC recommendation, Chapter 3.2(d) above.

handling of credit under the watchful eyes of friendly lenders not driven by profit motives.[14]

3. SPECIFIC ASPECTS OF CANADA'S INSOLVENCY SYSTEM AND
SUGGESTIONS FOR CHANGES

Canada's consumer insolvency system is basically sound but it has important weaknesses that need to be improved in material respects. The following discussion is designed to highlight the most important areas and to offer suggestions for changes in light of the rules and practices obtaining in the other insolvency systems reviewed earlier in this study.

(a) Access to the Bankruptcy System

As previously explained,[15] access to the Canadian bankruptcy system is very easy and could hardly be much easier. The current filing fee for an assignment by the debtor is only CAN$75 in the case of a summary administrations; the accompanying documentation (the debtor's statement of affairs) is also non-onerous. Moreover, the assignment in bankruptcy occurs automatically as soon as the written assignment has been received and endorsed by the official receiver. Similarly, the stay of proceedings by creditors under section 69.3 of the BIA take effect at the same time without the need for a court order.

Despite the liberality of this procedure, the question remains whether it is adequate to accommodate the needs of low-income debtors with heavy debts who lack the cash to make even a down payment for the trustee's services, much less to cover the balance of his fees. It is true most trustees offer very flexible payment arrangements although, as previously explained, there is serious doubt about their legality. In any event, judging by the frequency with which trustees object to a debtor's discharge from bankruptcy because of non-payment of fees,[16] the flexibility is apparently not sufficient. It also seems anomalous that a trustee should be able to object to a discharge unrelated to a breach of the debtor's obligations incurred after the assignment, again assuming that the trustee's objection is well based in law.

The Superintendent's informal agreement with licensed trustees was supposed to take care of such impecunious debtors.[17] However, there is little hard

---

[14] In the late 1970s, at least one of the major Canadian banks (the Royal Bank of Canada) funded front store banks in low-income communities run by local citizens under the supervision of a bank employee. Regrettably, the initiative was abandoned a few years later for reasons not known to the author. The need to develop alternatives in the UK to high cost credit for low income consumers is also stressed in Edwards, Chapter 5.1 above, n 32, at ch 9.

[15] See Chapter 2.5 above.

[16] See Chapter 2.8 above.

[17] *Ibid.*

evidence of how well the arrangement works in practice and how debtors are supposed to know about the facility. Another option, following the English, Scottish and Australian precedents, would be for the OSB to handle such impecunious cases itself, as indeed it did under the old FITA programme. However, given the financial constraints on the OSB and likely opposition from insolvency practitioners, it is safe to assume that the suggestion would not be welcomed. This is not a sufficient reason for rejecting the suggestion but it counsels caution until we have much clearer evidence of the extent of the current problem. What *does* give ground for concern is that private trustees in Canada have become such a powerful pressure group that it becomes politically very difficult for the Superintendent to introduce changes that are opposed by CAIRP.[18]

(b) Do We Need a Separate Bankruptcy Process for Small Estates?

The argument in favour of a separate process for small estates is that there is no need in their case for the heavy baggage of the BIA and its complex provisions and that a simpler process with its own nomenclature would serve debtors' needs better without harming creditors. Does the English administration order procedure offer a suitable model, especially in light of the (still) unproclaimed 1990 amendments to the County Courts Act 1984?

The answer is yes and no. The reasons favouring its adoption are that the AO procedure costs the debtor very little if anything and does not carry the stigma of bankruptcy. Nevertheless, the objections to copying the AO procedure in Canada seem greatly to outweigh its merits. This is because:

(a) as previously described,[19] the current AO procedure has many weaknesses;
(b) it is not clear that the AO involves less paper work than summary administrations under the BIA;
(c) there is no persuasive reason why creditors should receive payments from an insolvent estate without contributing to the costs of the service; and
(d) the adoption of a court (or other officially) administered insolvency service would reverse the well-established Canadian policy of privatising the administration of estates to the maximum possible extent, even assuming the court facilities were available for an AO type procedure.[20]

---

[18] What happened in the Personal Insolvency Task Force demonstrates this well. Trustees constituted the single largest and most vocal professional group and firmly resisted any changes in the BIA that would jeopardise trustees' income. The trustees also successfully persuaded the Task Force that trustees should be able to enter into binding fee arrangements with bankrupts that would be enforceable even after the bankrupt's discharge and even though the debtor had no surplus income as measured under BIA, s 68.

[19] See Chapter 5.4(d) above.

[20] Against this position, it may be argued that the orderly payment of debts machinery established since the early 1970s under Part X of the BIA establishes an important precedent in the opposite direction. However, Part X is now little used and it would require a major restructuring to breathe life back into it.

It is therefore probably better to maintain the status quo, but this is no reason not to pursue efforts to streamline and simplify summary administrations still further. The Australian experience shows[21] how much can be accomplished to simplify the administration of no-asset bankruptcies and therefore greatly to reduce their cost. It is believed a strong case can also be made in the case of voluntary assignments for changing the nomenclature of the order made after the filing from 'bankruptcy order' to 'insolvency order.' The consequences would remain the same but the lingering Victorian odour associated with 'bankruptcy' would be removed.

(c) Preconditions to Initiation of Bankruptcy Proceedings

This question has two parts. So far as the first part is concerned, a requirement that the debtor must be able to prove that she consulted an accredited credit counselling agency is a feature of the recent Congressional Bills,[22] but it has little to commend it. It would add to the debtor's financial burden if the debtor were expected to pay for the consultation, and it would provide the debtor with no new information that she does not, in Canada's case, already receive from the insolvency practitioner before insolvency proceedings are initiated. The impulse for the Congressional Bills' requirement is apparently the credit industry's concern that US bankruptcy attorneys are too quick to recommend a bankruptcy filing to their clients without exploring alternatives. In Canada, the concern is already addressed in the Superintendent's directive to insolvency practitioners[23] although admittedly this does not guarantee that the practitioner will adequately explain the various options open to the consumer, especially where some of the options may not coincide with the practitioner's own financial interests. However, debtors are not as ignorant or as helpless as they are sometimes made out to be. The grapevine among debtors works quite effectively and, in Canada, trustees regularly report that debtors are often well informed about the options open to them before they consult a trustee and decide to make a voluntary assignment in bankruptcy.

The second half of the question—whether the debtor should be required to make a voluntary debt settlement with the debtor's creditors before filing a bankruptcy petition—is based on the well-established Scandinavian and continental European models. The European partiality for this two-step approach to insolvency relief appears to rest on two pillars: (a) the existence of a large number of publicly funded debt counselling agencies with debt pro-rating capabilities, and (b) the need to protect limited judicial resources. Neither condition applies to Canada. In Canada, there is a scarcity of publicly-funded credit coun-

---

[21] See Chapter 4.3 above.
[22] See Chapter 3.9 above.
[23] See Chapter 2.14 above.

selling agencies and only those that are wholly or partly sponsored by creditors appear to have pro-rating facilities. There are also other factors that militate against the adoption of a two-step procedure in Canada. The current Canadian system, giving the debtor at the outset a choice between a straight bankruptcy solution and a consumer proposal, is more efficient and avoids the duplication of resources inherent in the continental European approach. Another reason is that long experience in common law jurisdiction has shown that non-statutory pro-rating plans can be easily abused by private operators unless they are part of a statutory regime and are adequately supervised.

(d) Conflicting Loyalties of Trustees

This issue involves two distinct but related features of the current Canadian scene. Insolvency practitioners advertise their services widely and then, when consulted by debtors, almost invariably nominate themselves or another member of the firm if an assignment in bankruptcy is recommended as a solution to the debtor's problems.[24] On the face of it, this appears to give rise to a conflict since the practitioner's advice may be coloured by self-interest. The second concern arises out of the practitioner's position *after* his appointment as trustee. Most consumers would have great difficulty distinguishing between the practitioner's first and second roles but would continue to look to him for guidance and advice and would see him as 'their' counsellor. However, the BIA—and well-established bankruptcy law principles—oblige the trustee to wear several hats, some of which are antithetical to the debtor's interests. In particular, in his section 170.1 pre-discharge report to the court, the Superintendent and the creditors, the trustee must state, inter alia, whether in his opinion the debtor could have made a viable proposal and whether the debtor has met his payment obligations under section 68 of the BIA.

Under optimal conditions, the insolvency practitioner should not be permitted to nominate himself as trustee: the US system has managed to keep the two roles quite separate. However, in the United States the debtor does not have to pay the trustee's fees (apart from a small administrative charge) and so the bifurcated arrangement can be made to work quite well. It is doubtful that the US practice could be replicated in Canada without a major restructuring of the trusteeship system and it seems safe to predict that the effort would encounter strong opposition. It will also be urged that the appearance of conflict in Canada is more apparent than real and that there is no hard evidence that the existing system of self-nomination leads to serious conflicts of interest.

This may be true in those cases (a majority) in which the debtor obtains an automatic discharge after nine months, although, given the current concerns in

---

[24] As previously explained, Chapter 2.5 above, the procedure has become so routine that the PITF Report recommends formal adoption of the debtor's nomination.

North America with corporate and securities conflicts of interest, any allegations of conflicts of interest should not be treated lightly. In any event, the infrequency of conflicts is no defence to the trustee being required to blow the whistle on his own client once he accepts the appointment of trustee and so long as the existing system of privately appointed trustees is maintained. A trustee should neither be required, nor be permitted, in the trustee's section 170 report, to pass moral or financial censure on the debtor's conduct. The trustee's report should be purely factual and objective. Any inferences from the trustee's report and any objections to the debtor's discharge from bankruptcy should be made by the Superintendent or the creditors, not by the trustee. The alternative to requiring the trustee to abstain from censuring the debtor's conduct would be to require the debtor to sign a document acknowledging the trustee's statutory obligations and relieving him from any liability for violating his duties of loyalty to the debtor.

(e) Property Excluded from Estate

For reasons previously explained,[25] the current rule in section 67(1)(b) of the BIA applying provincial law to determine the bankrupt's property exemptions is unsatisfactory, is incompatible with the federal government's legislative responsibilities, and is unfair to creditors and debtors alike. As a sound principle of bankruptcy policy, all bankrupt debtors should be governed by a uniform exemptions regime subject, it may be, to some degree of flexibility to reflect varying housing costs and other social and economic conditions in different regions of Canada. US scholars are near unanimous in their condemnation of the existing bifurcated US exemption rules and deference to state-determined exemptions.[26] Canada should learn from the US experience. Our model should be a substantially uniform list of exemptions regardless of the happenstance of the debtor's province of residence.

(f) Contents of Federally Mandated Exemptions List

If the Canadian government is willing to assume its proper constitutional role in this area, then the following options are open to it in designing the new statutory framework:

(1) to adopt a list of exemptions based on the average level of exemptions in the existing provincial regimes;

---

[25] See Chapter 2.6(b) above.
[26] See Chapter 3.4 above.

(2) to set its own level of exemptions in light of what the federal government regards as reasonable and necessary to enable the debtor and his family to maintain a basic lifestyle with a measure of comfort and dignity;

(3) to let the trustee make the initial determination of reasonableness (the English approach) with a right of appeal to the court;

(4) to allow the financial ceilings and particular categories of exempted property to be changed by regulation (the British Columbia model) or to be linked to a cost of living index; and

(5) to give the debtor a 'wild card' option in respect of each class of property enabling him to increase the exemption level for any category of property up to a maximum amount until the prescribed wild card amount has been exhausted or to apply the whole wild card amount applicable to the debtor's property to any specific category of property.

Apart from these possible configurations, the new federal regime should also make it clear (i) that the debtor is entitled to retain a motor vehicle up to a stated value for his personal, family or business and vocational use as appropriate, (ii) that the debtor, if a home owner, should be entitled to retain a reasonable amount of equity in the home, and (iii) apart from any equity allowance, if a needs-based case can be made out, a home owner and his family should be permitted to stay in the home on appropriate terms, with the court being authorised to settle the terms if they cannot be settled among the parties or by mediation. The purpose of such provisions is not to penalise the home lender but to prevent harmful dislocation of the debtor's family if it can be done without unfairness to the lender.

The PITF Report[27] made a useful start towards a more rational exemptions policy by recommending the debtor's entitlement to opt between a federally determined exemptions level and the otherwise applicable provincial exemptions. However, this will not ensure equal treatment of bankrupts across Canada because an optional federal standard will not discourage provinces from adopting exemptions more generous than the federal exemptions. In the author's view the Canadian government should not hesitate to go the whole way[28] and to apply a unified exemptions standard across Canada just as it has done with respect to determining whether the debtor must pay over surplus income under section 68.

---

[27] See Chapter 2.3.

[28] As has been done by the Commonwealth government under the Australian Bankruptcy Act and as recommended for the United States by the Bankruptcy Commissions of 1973 and 1997. However, the author's recommendation for Canada is not meant to preclude variations based on genuine provincial, urban and rural differences, though such differences can probably be best accommodated through wild card exemptions.

(g) Status of Secured Claims

A significant weakness of the existing BIA provisions is that they do nothing to protect the debtor's equity in property subject to a security interest or, where there is no equity, to enable the debtor, on terms fair to both parties, to retain property necessary for his and his family's well-being or to earn his livelihood in the case of tools, equipment or motor vehicles. To add to the current difficulties, in the case of household goods, debtors frequently do not appreciate that the merchant has retained a purchase money security interest in the item. Similarly, debtors may seriously under-estimate the risks involved in giving a general security interest in household goods (where this is permitted under provincial law) for a high cost loan, or to pledge the family home for an 'equity loan.'[29] A further difficulty is that the automatic stay triggered on the making of the bankruptcy order (section 69.3) does not apply to secured creditors and, though the trustee is free to apply for a stay, he rarely has an incentive to do so and usually there are no funds to finance the application. By all accounts, in the few reported cases where an application has been brought,[30] the courts have been reluctant to intervene. It is true the BIA gives the trustee a right to redeem the collateral[31] but in most cases this will be an empty gesture for the same reasons as the fact that the trustee has no incentive to apply for a stay of proceedings.

Many, though not all, of these problems, are addressed in the US Code and would require the following changes in the BIA if deemed appropriate:

(1) there should be an automatic stay for 30 days following the bankruptcy order unless the court lifts the stay earlier at the secured creditor's request;

(2) where the trustee has disclaimed any rights in the property the debtor will be obliged, within the 30-day period, to indicate his intention to surrender the property, to redeem it, or to reaffirm the security agreement with the secured party[32];

(3) following the earlier suggestion, the debtor should be entitled to redeem at its market value tangible personal property intended for personal, vocational, professional, family or household goods if the property is exempt property under the BIA[33];

---

[29] An equity loan is a loan on existing equity in the matrimonial loan and may exceed the value of the equity. Such loans are common in the United States and have been criticised because of the selling methods used and the fact that they may also involve a violation of US tax laws: NBRC Report, Chapter 3.2(d) above, at 238–41, and sources there cited. Equity loans are now also widely available in Canada and are popular with lenders because of the superior character of the collateral and the loans' profitability.

[30] Most, if not all, involve commercial cases.

[31] BIA, s 128(3) provides that the trustee, not the debtor, may redeem the property on payment of the debt or the value of the security as assessed by the secured party in the proof of claim.

[32] Cf 11 USC §521(2).

[33] Cf 11 USC §722.

(4) a non-possessory, non-purchase money security interest in exempt property held by the debtor for personal, vocational, family or household purposes would be automatically discharged on the making of a bankruptcy order.[34]

(h) Surplus Income Payment Requirements

Given the practical and conceptual importance of the 1997 BIA amendments and its counterparts elsewhere, it is surprising how little detailed scrutiny the operational results have received so far.[35] It is true that 85 per cent or more of bankrupts are meeting their surplus payment obligations without apparent difficulties and that there are very few requests for mediation. However, the fact that about 10 per cent of the bankrupts are paying less than the prescribed amount suggests one of two possibilities: that the LICO standard is not appropriate in all cases or that the Superintendent's standards are too rigid. Conceivably the risk of losing the entitlement to an automatic discharge also encourages debtor compliance even at the risk of some short term pain.

These and other considerations suggest adoption of the following steps:

(1) All available payment information should be collected, analysed and published by the OSB on a regular basis.
(2) The basis and appropriateness of the LICO standards used by the Superintendent to determine what is surplus income requires independent verification.
(3) The Superintendent's standards should be compared with the contributory income standards applied under the Australian Bankruptcy Act and proposed income standards under the Congressional Bills to determine what Canada can learn from them.
(4) The directive should be amended to make it clear that a debtor's non-discretionary expenses include (a) payments required to be made under purchase or leasing agreements to enable the debtor to retain exempt property; and (b) expenditures reasonably necessary for the gaining of the debtor's livelihood.
(5) Given their fundamental importance, the surplus income standards under section 68 should be established by regulation under the BIA and not by directive, and interested parties should be given ample opportunity to comment on any proposed amendments to the standards. It is also suggested that an insolvency ombudsperson should be appointed both to comment on proposed amendments to the directive and on desirable changes generally in section 68 and other parts of the BIA. The ombudsperson should not be a

---

[34] Cf 11 USC §523(f)(B) and PITF Report, Chapter 2.3 above, at ch 2(IV).
[35] The PITF Report, Chapter 2.3 above, at ch 3(I), importantly recommends clarification of the meaning of income for the purpose of s 68 and the supporting directive but does not otherwise examine actual results since the section came into effect in May 1998.

member of the OSB but should be financed from public funds. The ombudsperson should be appointed for a minimum period of three years to provide the appointee with some security of tenure and to encourage discharge of the appointee's responsibilities without fear of adverse consequences.

(6) Another very significant issue arises out of the PITF recommendation[36] that the surplus income payment period be increased from nine to 21 months. The reasons given in the Report are not very persuasive[37] but the recommendation could be justified on the footing that nine months is too short and lets a bankrupt with substantial surplus income off too easily.

(i) Discharges from Bankruptcy

The nine-months' period for automatic discharges under section 169 of the BIA is shorter than the periods used in other Commonwealth legislation but appears to work well in practice. There may be cases where the debtor needs an earlier discharge and he should continue to be free to make such an application. So far as can be determined, no compelling case has been made to bring the automatic discharge period forward to a matter of weeks (as is true under the US Code)[38] following the filing of the petition and the appointment of the trustee.

For the reasons previously indicated and to avoid conflicts of interest, a trustee's report under BIA, section 170.1 should not include adverse comments on the debtor's conduct if the trustee or a member of his firm provided advice to the debtor before the debtor's assignment.

The list of grounds on which a discharge may be refused or suspended or made conditional under BIA, section 173(1) is badly out-dated (as compared for example with the current English list as amended in 2002) and should be updated. Particularly objectionable is section 173(1)(a)[39] because its Victorian ancestry bears no relationship to current commercial and consumer realities.

(j) Non-Dischargeable Debts

The Canadian list of non-dischargeable debts is much shorter than the US list in §523 of the US Code, and for this one must be grateful. However, the Canadian list is longer than the English and Australian list and, as previously explained,[40]

---

[36]   PITF Report, Chapter 2.3 above, at ch 3(IV).

[37]   To stop debtors from shopping around to see which trustee can be relied on not to recommend an extended period of payment in the trustee's s 170.1 report.

[38]   11 USC §727(a).

[39]   This provides that the fact that the debtor's assets are insufficient to provide a dividend of 50 cents on the dollar is prima facie grounds for denying the discharge unless there is a satisfactory explanation for the shortfall.

[40]   See Chapter 2.10 above.

the basis for the inclusion of some of the items in the Canadian list and the exclusion of others is not self-evident. The list needs to be reviewed in the light of its practical impact and theoretical foundations and having regard to the extent to which it prevents the rehabilitation of debtors who may otherwise deserve it.

Particularly troubling is the impact of the 1998 BIA amendments on the non-dischargeability of student loans[41] and the fact that the amendments were adopted without prior consultation with interested parties and so soon after the 1997 amendments adding section 178(1)(g) had come into force. The 1998 amendments should be reviewed in the light of their impact and the experience of other countries with large volumes of student loans, particularly the United States, England and Australia. Serious consideration should be given to the PITF recommendation[42] to reduce the waiting period for a discharge application to five years and to allow a court to shorten the period still further in hardship cases. Regard should also be paid to the findings of observers that students are often not adequately advised before a loan is granted on the appropriateness of their study programme and their job prospects on completing the programme, and the fact that many loans are being made for courses and programmes of dubious value.[43] All this is not to deny that student loans are different from commercial loans and that student loans that are not repaid must be made good by other taxpayers. It does mean that balancing two important sets of public values is that much more difficult but is nevertheless unavoidable.

(k) Reaffirmation Agreements

This area is a black hole in Canadian law and practice because there are no reliable statistics about the frequency of debtors' reaffirmation of pre-bankruptcy debts following a discharge of the debts under BIA, section 178. Reaffirmations undoubtedly occur, particularly in relation to liened property.[44] The BIA contains no rules regulating the practice and Canadian courts are divided on what amounts to reaffirmation or novation of an agreement sufficient to satisfy the common law and civil law tests for an enforceable agreement.[45]

The BIA goes to much trouble to establish the transparency of a bankruptcy system that treats unsecured creditors alike (including secured creditors with unsecured claims), and has a strong stake to ensure that those policies are not undermined by unfair creditor pressure and uninformed consumer decisions during bankruptcy or afterwards. Some protective rules are therefore necessary

---

[41] *Ibid.*

[42] PITF Report, Chapter 2.3 above, at ch 2(I).

[43] The details will be found, inter alia, in Saul Schwartz, 'The Dark Side of Student Loans: Debt Burden, Default, and Bankruptcy' (1999) 37 *Osgoode Hall Law Journal* 307.

[44] See Chapter 2.13 above.

[45] See Chapter 2.13 above.

and should address both secured and unsecured claims. At a minimum, the BIA should provide that a reaffirmation agreement in favour of a business or professional creditor is unenforceable unless the debtor received independent advice before signing the agreement and, if the agreement was made before the debtor's discharge, that it has been disclosed to the trustee. Any other requirements, and the appropriateness of introducing court supervision of reaffirmation agreements,[46] should await the results of empirical enquiries into the scope and frequency of reaffirmation agreements in Canada.

The PITF Report[47] draws a distinction between affirmation of secured and unsecured debts. It would recognise affirmation of secured debts on a sliding scale based on the market value of the collateral and refuse recognition of unsecured debts with limited exceptions. The Report's objectives are laudable but the proposals are complex and would be difficult to police. They may also prove counter-productive in so far as they may encourage secured creditors to repossess the collateral rather than accept less than the full balance owing on the original agreement. The most serious objection to the proposals, however, is that they were made without benefit of any hard data about existing Canadian reaffirmation practices and their impact on debtors and creditors.

(l) Alternatives to Straight Bankruptcies

Most of the countries surveyed in this study have legislative provisions of recent origin providing for alternatives to straight bankruptcies. In many of the continental European countries they are the only statutory facilities granting relief to overburdened debtors. Apart from this factor, the continental legislative schemes differ greatly in scope, the roles of the players (debtors, creditors, trustees, courts and other agencies) and ultimately in the effectiveness of the schemes.

As previously described,[48] prior to 1992 Canada only had a pro-rating or debt consolidation law in the form of Part X of the BIA providing for payment of consumer debts over a maximum of five years. In that year, new Part III 2 introduced for the first time a specifically consumer-oriented proposal regime designed to provide a range of alternatives for dealing with the debt problems, including, importantly, remission of part of the debts. Part III 2 grew very slowly in popularity in the first three years of full operation and in 1996 the number of consumer proposals only amounted to 3.9 per cent of the number of straight bankruptcies. A marked change occurred in 1997 and 1998, both in the number of consumer proposals and as a percentage of the number of consumer bankruptcies. The number of proposals in those years grew by 39 per cent and 50 per

---

[46] Cf. 11 USC §524(e) and the discussion in Chapter 3.8 above.
[47] PITF Report, Chapter 2.3 above, at ch 2(V).
[48] See Chapter 2.11 above.

cent. In 1998, the number of consumer proposals (7,155) represented 9.4 per cent of the number of bankruptcies. It was 16.8 per cent in 2001. By way of contrast, with the exception of 1995 and 1996, the number of orderly payment of debts (OPD) orders has grown very little and appears to have settled down to an annual figure around the 1,500 mark.

The OSB officials must feel very encouraged by the absolute and relative growth in the number of consumer proposals since 1997. Nevertheless, the number of Canadian proposals still pales by comparison with the number of chapter 13 filings in the United States. These grew from 73,147 in 1980 to 389,398 in 1998, and in the latter year amounted to 38.6 per cent of the number of chapter 7 bankruptcies.[49] This suggests that stronger or different forces influence the popularity of chapter 13 filings in the United States as compared with the attractions of consumer proposals in Canada.

So far as Canada is concerned, the strong growth in the 1997 and 1998 numbers can be explained in several ways:[50] (a) the impact of the 1997 BIA amendments and the appreciation by debtors with sizeable incomes that straight bankruptcies and an automatic discharge will be opposed by creditors and may well attract the critical comments of the trustee in his section 170 report, and (b) the incentive to trustees to steer their clients into consumer proposals because of the improved tariff of fees introduced by the OSB in 1998. A third possibility, debtors' anxiety to protect their non-exempt assets and to avoid the stigma of bankruptcy, are not new factors although it is possible that trustees have given them greater prominence in discussions with debtors.

With respect to the US factors, attorney's self-interest and other local cultural factors are said to be very important in the choice of chapter 13 over chapter 7.[51] On the other hand, in the United States, the threat of opposition to the debtor's discharge is generally not a serious factor and, as previously noted,[52] abuse motions under section 707 of the US Code have met with mixed judicial reactions. Much more powerful driving forces favouring chapter 13 petitions appear to be the opportunities for 'lien-stripping', to cure defaults in security agreements, and to pay off the secured debts over a longer period of time if the court approves the plan. For the right debtors, the prospect of escaping otherwise non-dischargeable debts[53] must also be a very attractive reason for choosing chapter 13.

It will therefore be seen that the factors driving Part III 2 proposals in Canada are not the same as those influencing chapter 13 filings, and are likely to remain

---

[49] Office of the Superintendent of Bankruptcy, Programs, Standards and Regulatory Affairs, *International Consumer Insolvency Statistics* (Ottawa, June 1999 and October 1999) 8–9.

[50] IDC Ramsay, 'Market Imperatives, Professional Discretion and the Role of Intermediaries in Consumer Bankruptcy: a Comparative Study of the Canadian Trustee in Bankruptcy' (2000) 74 *American Bankruptcy Law Journal* 399, at 434–40.

[51] J Braucher, 'Lawyers and Consumer Bankruptcy: One Code, Many Cultures' (1993) 67 *American Bankruptcy Law Journal* 501.

[52] See Chapter 3.5(a) above.

[53] 11 USC §1328.

significantly different so long as Canada retains surplus income payment requirements and open-ended grounds for opposing discharges from bankruptcy. The questions for consideration are, what can Canada learn from the chapter 13 regime and usefully adapt to Canadian conditions?

In the author's view, the following features deserve serious consideration:

(1) *Increased limits.* It is widely agreed that the current ceiling of CAN$75,000 for consumer proposals is too low to accommodate self-employed debtors and middle class consumers. There appears to be strong support for increasing the ceiling to CAN$250,000 on the assumption that the change will not adversely affect the interests of creditors. If secured creditors are included in an amended BIA, Part III 2 regime, this much again should be allowed to meet those exigencies.[54]

(3) *Inclusion of secured creditors.* The current exclusion of secured creditors in consumer proposals is based on historical grounds and can no longer be justified. This is because secured creditors are subject to stay of proceedings orders in straight bankruptcies and may be included in a debtor's proposal or plan of arrangement in BIA, Part III 1 (commercial proposals) and in the Companies' Creditors Arrangement Act. It is anomalous therefore that secured creditors should be treated differently in consumer proposals than they are treated in commercial reorganisations. However, mere inclusion of secured creditors in Part III 2 proposals will accomplish little without additional changes. The reason is that if Canadian courts follow the traditional rule of putting each secured creditor into its own class,[55] secured creditors will be able to veto any proposal not to their liking and consumers will be no better off than they are now. This suggests either that Part III 2 should be amended to dispense with the need for creditor approval (the chapter 13 approach) so long as the court finds the proposal fair and reasonable and provided that the other bench-marks for the protection of secured creditor interests are observed, *or* that the court should be able to override creditor objections to a proposal[56] if the court finds the objections unreasonable and is satisfied that the proposal will leave the secured party as well off as it would be in straight liquidation proceedings. Since it is safe to assume that secured creditors will vigorously oppose the first alternative (which is not to suggest that the second one will have plain sailing either), the second alternative seems the more attractive.

(3) *Better treatment of non-dischargeable debts?* There is no obvious reason for Canada to follow the US precedent and to treat non-dischargeable debts more favourably in a proposal than in a straight bankruptcy. The

---

[54] PITF Report, Chapter 2.3 above, at ch 1(VII), recommends increasing the ceiling to CAN$100,000 for business-related debts and removing the ceiling altogether for non-business-related debts.

[55] This is what BIA, s 50(1.4) currently requires for commercial proposals.

[56] Cf 11 USC §1325(b).

circumstances are different in Canada from those in the United States. In the United States, the drafters of the 1978 Code felt it necessary to give debtors this additional incentive to opt for chapter 13 filing because of the ease of obtaining a fresh start under chapter 7. This has never been true in Canada and is even less true since the introduction of the surplus income payment requirements in 1997. In Canada, the attractions (and disadvantages) to a debtor of choosing between the straight bankruptcy and proposal routes are more easily matched and introducing the distorting effects of two levels of non-dischargeable debts could do more harm than good.

(4) *Consequences of debtor's non-compliance.* Canada can learn, however, from chapter 13 in giving the court greater flexibility in dealing with the consequences of the debtor's non-compliance with the terms of the plan. It is counter-productive to retain the existing BIA provision[57] imposing automatic annulment of the proposal where the debtor is in default of payments for more than three months without taking into account the circumstances leading to the default.[58] It is therefore suggested that, like her US counterpart,[59] the Canadian judge should have the power (a) to modify the terms of the proposal because of changed circumstances, (b) to declare the debtor bankrupt if that appears to be the best alternative, or (c) to excuse the debtor from having to make further payments under the proposal if there are no reasonable prospects of the debtor being able to resume payments in the foreseeable future.

(5) *Addressing the high failure rate.* In the absence of reliable data, one must be cautious about making dogmatic statements about the failure rate of accepted Canadian consumer proposals. Nevertheless, it is probably safe to assume that it is around 30 per cent and that it may be higher. This is much less than the 60 to 70 per cent chapter 13 failure rate in the United States, but there is no room for complacency in Canada. The OSB strongly supports consumer proposals and, since 1998, trustees have also had strong fee incentives to recommend them to debtors.

The difficulty is that it is too easy for debtors to over-estimate their capacity to honour the agreement over a typical three to four year life span, and to exercise the discipline necessary to go without other amenities for the debtor and the debtor's family during this period. The difficulties are compounded because it appears many trustees are encouraging proposals based on LICO surplus income standards, although this requirement does not appear in the BIA. It is one thing to require a debtor to tighten his belt for a nine-month period in a straight bankruptcy; it is quite another to expect the debtor to maintain the regime for thirty-six months or longer.

---

[57] BIA, s 66.31(1).

[58] Where inspectors have been appointed, current BIA, s 66.21 confers on them a limited authority to approve an amendment to the proposal. However, inspectors are almost never appointed in consumer proposals and this useful provision has no had practical impact.

[59] 11 USC §1328(b)(1).

There is no easy answer to this conundrum. In the United States, the high chapter 13 failure rate has prompted one commentator[60] to call for repeal of the chapter. No one has recommended such radical surgery in Canada for consumer proposals under the BIA. Nevertheless, the following step could be adopted to discourage ill-considered proposals. The administrator should be required to certify that he has reviewed the terms of the proposal and believes them to be made in good faith and that, having fairly considered the debtor's financial circumstances and future prospects, the administrator is of the view that the debtor will be able to maintain the proposed payments for the projected period.

(m) Debtor Counselling

Canada still appears to be the only common law jurisdiction that makes debtor counselling a formal condition of the debtor's eligibility for discharge in case of a bankruptcy or the successful completion of a consumer proposal.[61] However, the divide is not as sharp as may appear at first sight. As already noted,[62] provisions in recent Congressional Bills require the debtor to have consulted a counselling agency before initiating bankruptcy proceedings and, if EOUST certifies it to be feasible, requiring the debtor to take a course in financial management following the debtor's discharge. In addition, all the countries surveyed in this study have very extensive facilities for debt counselling, both voluntary and as an adjunct to the delivery of government-sponsored social services. The continental European legislation also frequently envisages counselling agencies being heavily involved in preparing debt adjustment plans and in assisting debtors to comply with the plans' frequently very onerous terms.

Nevertheless, in considering the future of debtor counselling under the BIA, it is still relevant to consider whether counselling should be retained as a mandatory requirement. That question should be addressed in conjunction with a number of other questions, ie. the role of counselling, the duration of counselling and the effectiveness of counselling. Each of these issues is briefly discussed below.

(1) *Should counselling be mandatory?* The case supporting its mandatoriness at least requires a showing that the great majority of consumer bankruptcies are due to debtors' mismanagement of their budgets. However, the empirical findings are generally that unemployment and other events beyond the debtor's control are the single most important events although it is true that trustees also frequently list financial mismanagement as an important

---

[60] See WC Whitford, 'Has the Time Come to Repeal Chapter 13?' (1989) 65 *Indiana Law Journal* 85.

[61] See BIA, ss 157.1 and 66.13(2)(b) and Directive 1R2, 21 December 1994.

[62] See Chapter 3.9 above.

contributing cause.[63] There is also an issue of discrimination. No penalty is imposed under current Canadian law on creditors who adopt lax credit standards and there is no requirement for creditors to take classes on how to run their businesses responsibly. Similarly, there is no requirement for the directors of limited liability companies to take remedial courses in financial management if their companies have to close their doors. This is so even though trustees in commercial insolvencies frequently report that a company's bankruptcy might have been avoided with more skilful management by its officers and directors.

(2) *The role of counselling.* There appear to be two principal differences between the continental and Scandinavian model for counselling, as described by Dr Niemi-Kiesilainen,[64] and the role set forth in the OSB directive in Canada. In Canada, the debtor is only required to attend two one-hour sessions of instruction and education. Neither of them is directly linked to the bankruptcy proceedings, the cause of the bankrupt's difficulties or, in the case of a proposal, the terms of the proposal. The continental model, on the other hand, envisages an ongoing relationship between the debtor and the counselling agency for the duration of the plan, which may be as long as seven years. The counsellors are also actively involved in the preparation of the debt adjustment plan and its supervision after the plan has been approved by the creditors and by the court or other governmental agency. Secondly, if Dr Niemi-Kiesilainen's description can be taken at face value,[65] the continental form of counselling is much more socially directed than is the common law model. The author has queried[66] how realistic the continental model is in suggesting that the goal of counselling is to educate the consumer to live without consumer credit. Even if this question can be answered satisfactorily, there is another and equally pressing question—is it reasonable to deprive our fellow citizens of access to consumer credit and electronic payment facilities because they are poor? Instead of excluding poor people entirely from the benefits of consumer credit, does society not have an obligation to establish low cost alternatives for this segment of the population?

(3) *Duration and effectiveness of counselling.*[67] Given the requirement of only two counselling sessions and even assuming superb instruction and effective teaching materials, it is unlikely that the current Canadian approach leaves

---

[63] It is also clear that trustees do not agonise over the precise cause of the debtor's misfortune and do not feel it incumbent on them to grill the debtor for precise details. They put down a cause because they are required to do so in their s 170 report and not because they see themselves as social investigators. It also appears that the OSB, in aggregating the data from the s 170 reports, often classifies the trustees' answers more broadly than the answers themselves warrant.

[64] See Chapter 7.3(e) above.

[65] *Ibid.*

[66] *Ibid.*

[67] It is convenient to consider these two questions together.

more than a symbolic impact on the debtor.[68] At a minimum, to ensure its success one would require ongoing contact between the debtor and the counsellor to make certain that the debtor's problems were being properly addressed and that the debtor was not sliding back into serious debt. Even then, assuming a fully reformed, rehabilitated and discharged bankrupt, one would have to make heroic assumptions about the ability of such debtors to resist the blandishments of credit card companies and the allure of non-down payment offers from a myriad of sources, not to mention high cost alternative lenders ready to extend credit to discharged bankrupts.

4. CONCLUSION

The National Bankruptcy Review Commission commented in its report to Congress[69] that the Commission saw its most challenging task as trying to balance the competing interests striving for attention. A sceptic might observe that no balancing of any kind can take place unless there is agreement about the objectives of modern bankruptcy law, the interests deserving of attention and the relative weights to be assigned to them. The skeptic might also add that economic clout and having the right political connections often count for more in answering these questions than does rational analysis of the issues under consideration.

This study shows that differences about basic values continues to divide even members of the same legal family, and that even where there is consensus about the goals there may be sharp disagreement about the appropriate means for their attainment.

Canada established its basic values in the Bankruptcy Act 1919 in embracing a qualified fresh start policy while also offering debtors a compositional alternative. The 1992 and 1997 legislation have essentially maintained and updated this middle of the road posture, though there is much room for argument whether the median line is always correctly placed and whether it veers too much to the left or to the right. This study has highlighted many bumps in the road that need to be removed and above all the damage inflicted by too readily accessible consumer credit. The debate over the correct values will no doubt continue, as it should. There should be no disagreement, however, on the need for better and more complete data on the operational effects of all aspects of the existing insolvency system if future decisions are to be more than guesswork or unabashed power struggles.

---

[68] This is amply supported by recent US literature generated in response to the counselling provisions in the Congressional Bills. See also J Braucher, 'An Empirical Study of Debtor Education in Bankruptcy: Impact on Chapter 13 Completion Not Shown' (2001) 9 *American Bankruptcy Institute Law Review* 557.

[69] See Chapter 3.2(d) above.

Bibliography

1. BOOKS AND THESES

BALZ, M and LANDFERMANN, H-G, *Die Neuen Insolvenzgesetze* [The New (German) Insolvency Laws) (1st edn, 1995, 2nd edn, IDW-Verlag, Dusseldorf, 1999).

BERTHOUD, R and KEMPSON, E, *Credit and Debt: The P.S.I. Report* (Policy Studies Institute, London, 1992).

CANTLIE, SJ, *An Autonomy-Based Account of Bankruptcy Discharge* (LLM Dissertation, University of Toronto, 1992).

CALDER, L, *Financing the American Dream: A Cultural History of Consumer Credit* (Princeton University Press, New Jersey, 1999).

COLEMAN, PJ, *Debtors and Creditors in America: Insolvency, Imprisonment for Debt, and Bankruptcy, 1607–1900* (State Historical Society of Wisconsin, Madison, 1974).

COOTER, R, and ULEN, T, *Law and Economics* (3rd edn, Addison-Wesley, Don Mills, Ontario, 2000) app 'The Economics of Risk and Insurance'55–70.

DUGGAN, AJ, and LANYON, EV, *Consumer Credit Law* (Butterworths, Sydney, 1999).

DUNCAN, L, *The Law and Practice of Bankruptcy in Canada* (Carswell, Toronto, 1922).

——and HONSBERGER, JD, *Bankruptcy in Canada* (Canadian Legal Authors Ltd, Toronto, 1961).

FLETCHER, IF, *The Law of Insolvency* (3rd edn, Sweet & Maxwell, London, 2002).

GROSS, K, *Failure and Forgiveness: Rebalancing the Bankruptcy System* (Yale University Press, New Haven, 1997).

HOULDEN, LW, and MORAWETZ, GB, *Bankruptcy and Insolvency Law of Canada* (3rd edn, Carswell, Toronto, 1992).

—— and ——, *The 2002 Annotated Bankruptcy and Insolvency Act* (Carswell, Toronto, 2001).

HULS, N, *et al*, *Overindebtedness of Consumers in the EC Member States: Facts and Search for Solutions* (Éditions Stoy-Scientia, Diegem, Belgium, 1994).

JACKSON, TH, *The Logic and Limits of Bankruptcy Law* (Harvard University Press, Cambridge, Massachusetts, 1986).

LESTER, VM, *Victorian Insolvency: Bankruptcy, Imprisonment for Debt, and Company Winding-up in Nineteenth-Century England* (Clarendon Press, Oxford, 1995).

MANN, BH, *Republic of Debtors. Bankruptcy in the Age of American Independence* (Harvard University Press, Cambridge, Mass., 2002).

MANNING, RD, *Credit Card Nation: The Consequences of America's Addiction to Credit* (Basic Books, New York, 2000).

MASSE, C, *Étude de L'Efficacité Sociale des Programmes Juridiques d'Aide aux Débiteurs Surendetettés* (Le Groupe, Montreal, 1974).

NIEMI-KIESILAINEN, J, RAMSAY, IDC, and WHITFORD, WC (eds), *Consumer Bankruptcy in a Global Perspective* (Hart Publishing, forthcoming).

PARKER, AA, *Credit, Debt, and Bankruptcy Handbook* (6th edn, 1986, 7th edn. Self-Counsel Press, Vancouver, 1988).

POSNER, RA, *Economic Analysis of Law* (5th edn, Aspen Law & Business, New York, 1998).

RAJAK, H, (ed), *Insolvency Law: Theory and Practice* (Sweet & Maxwell, London, 1993).

RAMSAY, IDC, (ed), *Debtors and Creditors: A Socio-Legal Perspective* (Professional Books, London, 1986).

REIFNER, U and FORD, J (eds), *Banking for People* (de Gruyter, Berlin, 1992).

ROSE, D (ed), *Lewis' Australian Bankruptcy Law* (11th edn, LBC Information Services, NSW, 1999).

Roundtable on Recent Consumer Bankruptcy Developments, *Materials for Distribution, 21 July 1999* (Faculty of Law, University of Toronto, Convenor: JS Ziegel).

RYAN, M, *Social Work and Debt Problems* (Avebury, 1996).

SCHOR, JB, *The Overspent American: Upscaling, Downshifting, and the New Consumer* (Basic Books, New York, 1998).

SKEEL Jr, DA, *Debt's Dominion: A History of Bankruptcy Law in America* (Princeton University Press, New Jersey, 2001).

STEWART, W, *Belly Up: The Spoils of Bankruptcy* (McClelland & Stewart, Toronto, 1995).

SULLIVAN, TA, WARREN, E and WESTBROOK, JL, *As We Forgive Our Debtors: Bankruptcy and Consumer Credit In America* (Oxford University Press, 1989).

——, —— and ——, *The Fragile Middle Class: Americans in Debt* (Yale University Press, New Haven, 2000).

Symposium, 'Consumer Bankruptcies in a Comparative Context' (1999) 37 *Osgoode Hall Law Journal 1* (ed Jacob Ziegel).

TABB, CJ, *The Law of Bankruptcy* (Foundation Press, Westbury, New York, 1997).

TELFER, TGW, *Reconstructing Bankruptcy Law in Canada: 1867 to 1919: From an Evil to a Commercial Necessity* (University of Toronto, SJD Thesis, 1999).

WARREN, C, *Bankruptcy in United States History* (Harvard University Press, Cambridge, Massachusetts, 1935).

WARREN, E, and WESTBROOK, JL, *The Law of Debtors and Creditors* (4th edn, Aspen Law & Business, Gaithersburg, New York, 2001).

2. REPORTS AND MONOGRAPHS

(a) Australia

GALLAGHER, Chief Executive and Inspector-General in Bankruptcy, *Analysis of Debt Agreements* (ITSA, July 2000).

ITSA, *Annual Report by the Inspector-General in Bankruptcy on the Operation of the Bankruptcy Act, 2001–2002* (Commonwealth of Australia, Canberra, 2002)

ITSA, *Profiles of Debtors 2002* (Commonwealth of Australia, 2002).

O'NEILL, L, *The Income Contribution Scheme in Bankruptcy* (ITSA, Canberra, 2002).

Senate Legal and Constitutional Legislation Committee, *Bankruptcy Legislation Amendment Bill 1995* (Canberra, 1995).

(b) Canada

Advisory Committee on Bankruptcy and Insolvency, *Proposed Bankruptcy Act Amendments* (Minister of Supply and Services Canada, Ottawa, 1986).

Alberta Law Reform Institute, *Creditors' Access to Future Income Plans* (Consultation Memorandum No 11, June 2002).

BRIGHTON, JW, and CONNIDIS, JA, *Consumer Bankrupts in Canada* (Consumer and Corporate Affairs Canada, Ottawa, 1982.)

CAMPBELL, C, *Increased Rate of Consumer Bankruptcy in Canada – Socioeconomic Influences (1977-1997)* (Corporate Law and Policy Directorate, Industry Canada, Ottawa, January 2002).

Canadian Consumer Council, *Recommendations to the Minister of Consumer and Corporate Affairs on the Consumer Bankruptcy Aspects of the Report of the Study Committee on Bankruptcy and Insolvency* (Ottawa, 1972).

CEBRYK, N, *Consumer Bankruptcies: Contributing Key Factors* (Informetrica Limited, Ottawa, August 1999).

Corporate and Insolvency Law Policy Directorate, *Consumer Insolvency Issues: A Discussion Paper* (Industry Canada, Ottawa, April 2002).

FINNEY, R, and SCHWARTZ, S, *Student Loans in Canada: Past, Present, and Future* (C.D. Howe Institute, Toronto, 1996).

FORDE, D, and ROBERTS, L, *A National Assessment of Bankruptcy Counselling Services* (Sociometrix, Winnipeg, 1994).

INAMDAR, S, BLACK W, and KRIEGLER, AJ, *Moody's Canadian Credit Card Index* (Moody's Investors Service, 23 August 2002).

Industry Canada, *Report on the Operation and Administration of the Bankruptcy and Insolvency Act and the Companies' Creditors Arrangement Act* (Ottawa, September 2002).

National Council of Welfare, *Poverty Profile 1994* (Minister of Public Works and Government Services, Ottawa, Spring 1996).

Office of the Superintendent of Bankruptcy, *5 Year Review Issues, Personal Bankruptcies, Breakdown by Personal Surplus Income Code by Division Office* (PSRA/6 Year Review).

——, *National Insolvency Forum: Toronto Regional Report* (undated, distributed in Nov/Dec 1999).

——, *Personal Insolvency Task Force: Final Report* (Ottawa, August 2002).

Office of the Superintendent of Bankruptcy, Programs, Standards and Regulatory Affairs, *International Consumer Insolvency Statistics* (Ottawa, June 1999).

PAQUET, B, *Low Income Cutoffs from 1992 to 2001 and Low Income Measures from 1991 to 2000* (Statistics Canada, November 2002, Cat. No. 75F0002MIE2002005).

SCHWARTZ, S, and ANDERSON, L, *An Empirical Study of Canadians Seeking Personal Bankruptcy Protection* (Industry Canada, Ottawa, 1998).

Special Joint Committee of the Senate and the House of Commons on Consumer Credit and Cost of Living, *Report on Consumer Credit* (Queen's Printer, Ottawa, 1967).

Special Senate Committee, *Poverty in Canada* (Information Canada, Ottawa, 1972).

Tassé Committee, *Report of the Study Committee on Bankruptcy and Insolvency Legislation* (Ottawa, 1970).

L'Union des Consommateurs, *La Proposition de consommateur. Tendances des Impact sur les Débiteurs Canadiens* (Québec).

(c) England and Wales

Association of Business Recovery Professionals (previously known as Society of Practitioners of Insolvency), *9th Survey of Personal Insolvency* (London, 2002).

Board of Trade, Bankruptcy Law Amendment Committee, *Report of the Committee on Bankruptcy Law and Deeds of Arrangement Law Amendment* (Cmnd 221, London, 1957).

Civil Justice Review, *Report of the Review Body on Civil Justice* (Cmnd 394, Lord Chancellor's Department, June 1988).

Cork Committee, *Report of the Review Committee on Insolvency Law and Practice* (Cmnd 8558, London, June 1982).

Department of Trade and Industry, *Insolvency: A Second Chance* (Cmnd 5234, London, July 2001).

——, *Consultation Document: Tackling Loan Sharks and More. Consultation Document on Modernising the Consumer Credit Act 1974* (www.dti.gov.uk/ccp/con-sultpdf/loanshark.htm) (1 January 2003).

Edwards S, *In Too Deep: CAB Clients' Experience of Debt* (National Citizens Advice Bureaux & Citizens Advice Scotland, May 2003).

Insolvency Service, *Annual Report and Accounts, 2000–2001* (Stationery Office, London, July 2001).

——, *General Annual Report for the Year 2000* (Stationery Office, London, 2000).

——, *Bankruptcy: A Fresh Start: A Consultation on Possible Reform to the Law Relating to Personal Insolvency in England and Wales* (Stationery Office, London, 21 March 2000).

Justice Society, *Insolvency Law: An Agenda for Reform* (London, 1994).

KEMPSON, E , *Overindebtedness in Britain: A Report to the Department of Trade and Industry* (July 2001).

National Citizens Advice Bureaux, *Oxfordshire Money Advice Project. Financial Statement Analysis* (Oxford, October 2002).

National Consumer Council, *Credit and Debt, the Consumer Interest* (Stationery Office, London, 1990).

Secretary of State for Trade and Industry, *Productivity and Enterprise: A World Class Competition Regime* (Cmnd 5233, London, July 2001).

Society of Practitioners of Insolvency, *Personal Insolvency in the U.K., 6th Annual Survey* (London, 1996).

(d) European Union

BETTI, G, *et al*, *Study of the Problem of Consumer Indebtedness: Statistical Aspect: Final Report* (submitted to the Commission of the European Communities Directorate-General for Health and Consumer Protection, October 2001).

Commission of the European Communities, *Proposal for a Directive of the European Parliament and of the Council on the harmonization of the laws, regulations and administrative provisions of the Member States concerning credit for consumers* (COM(2002) 443 final; 2002/022 (COD)).

Guarantee Foundation, *Debt Advice Networking: Ways Forward* (European Conference on Money and Debt Advice, Hameenlinna, Finland, 1997).

(e) **France**

French Senate, *Commission des lois et des finances—Rapport d'information no.60, 1997/1998, Surendettement Prévenir et Guérir* (29 october 1997).

(f) **Germany**

REIFNER, U, *Lending and Indebtedness Among German Consumer Households*, Expert Report to the European Commission (Hamburg, 27 March 1998).
REIFNER, U, VEIT, S and SIEBERT, D, *Überschuldung von Verbrauchern in Deutschland am Beispiel von Konsumentenkrediten, Gutachten im Auftrag der Arbeitsgemeinschaft der Verbraucherverbände eV (AgV* [Over-indebtedness of German Consumers with Particular Respect to Consumer Credit. Report for the Executive of the union of consumers associations] (Hamburg, May 1998).

(g) **Scotland**

Accountant in Bankruptcy, *Annual Report 2001/2002* (Edinburgh, 2002).
Scottish Law Commission, *Report on Bankruptcy and Related Aspects of Insolvency and Liquidation* (SLC No 68, 1981).
——, *Report on Diligence and Debtor Protection* (SLC No 95, 1985).
——, *Report on Poinding and Warrant Sale* (SLC No 177, 2000).
Scottish Office, *'Apparent Insolvency': A Consultation Paper on Amending the Bankruptcy (Scotland) Act 1985* (July 1997).
——, *The Bankruptcy (Scotland) Act 1985: A Consultation Follow-Up: Protected Trust Deeds and Other Issues* (July 1998).
Striking the Balance. A New Approach to Debt Management, Report of the Working Group for Poinding and Warrant Sale to the Minister for Justice (6 July 2001).

(h) **United States**

BERMANT, G, and FLYNN, E, *Incomes, Debts, and Repayment Capacities of Recently Discharged Chapter 7 Debtors* (Executive Office for United States Trustee, January 1999).
Commission on the Bankruptcy Laws of the United States, *Report* (HR Doc. no 93-137, 93rd Congress, 1st Session, (USGPO, 1973).
Credit Research Center, Krannert School of Management, *Consumers' Right to Bankruptcy: Origins and Effects* (Monograph No. 23, Purdue University, West Lafayette, Indiana, 1982).
Ernst & Young, *Chapter 7: Bankruptcy Petitioners' Ability to Repay: The National Perspective, 1997* (Washington, March 1998).
——, *Chapter 7: Bankruptcy Petitioners' Repayment Ability under H.R. 833: The National Perspective* (Washington, March 1999).

Federal Judicial Center, *Implementing and Evaluating the Chapter 7 Filing Fee Waiver Program, Report of the Committee on the Administration of the Bankruptcy System of the Judicial Conference of the United States* (Federal Judicial Center, Washington DC, 1998).

National Bankruptcy Review Commission, *Bankruptcy: The Next Twenty Years, Final Report* (Washington, 20 October 1997).

United States General Accounting Office, *Report to Congressional Requestors, Personal Bankruptcy: Analysis of Four Reports on Chapter 7 Debtors' Ability to Pay* (Washington, June 1999).

United States Senate, 106th Congress, 1st Session, Bankruptcy Reform Act of 1999, S.625, *Report of the Judiciary Committee* (11 May 1999).

Visa U.S.A. Inc., *Consumer Bankruptcy: Causes and Implications* (Visa Consumer Bankruptcy Reports, July 1996).

(i) Miscellaneous Reports

International Federation of Insolvency Professionals, *Consumer Debt Report: Report of Findings and Recommendations* (London, May 2001).

3.   ARTICLES AND UNPUBLISHED PAPERS

ADLER, M, 'Reactions to Empirical Studies' (1999) 37 *Osgoode Hall Law Journal* 127.

——, 'The Overseas Dimension: What can Canada and the United States Learn from the United Kingdom?' (1999) 37 *Osgoode Hall Law Journal* 415.

AUSUBEL, LM, 'Credit Card Defaults, Credit Card Profits, and Bankruptcy' (1997) 71 *American Bankruptcy Law Journal* 249.

——, 'Personal Bankruptcies Begin Precipitous Drop: 1999 Update' (Short Report) (Department of Economics, University of Maryland, September 1999)

BARLETT, DL, and Steele, JB, 'Soaked By Congres' *Time Magazine,* 15 May 2000, 64.

BERMANT, G, and FLYNN, E, 'Explaining the (Complex) Causes of Consumer Bankruptcy' (2001) 20(7) *American Bankruptcy Institute Journal* 20.

——, and ——, 'Planning for Change: Credit Counseling at the Threshold of Bankruptcy' (2001) 20(7) *American Bankruptcy Institute Journal* 20.

BERRY, RE, and McGREGOR, SLT, 'Counselling Consumer Debtors under Canada's Bankruptcy and Insolvency Act' (1999) 37 *Osgoode Hall Law Journal* 369.

BHANDARI, JS, and WEISS, LA, 'The Increasing Bankruptcy Filing Rate: An Historical Analysis' (1993) 67 *American Bankruptcy Law Journal* 131.

BLOCK-LIEB, S, GROSS, K, and WIENER, RL, 'Lessons from the Trenches: Debtor Education in Theory and Practice' (2002) 7 *Fordham Journal of Corporate & Financial Law* 503.

BOSHKOFF, DG, 'The Bankrupt's Moral Obligation to Pay his Discharged Debts: A Conflict between Contract Theory and Bankruptcy Policy' (1971) 47 *Indiana Law Journal* 36.

——, 'Limited, Conditional, and Suspended Discharges in Anglo-American Bankruptcy Proceedings' (1982) 131 *University Pennsylvania Law Review* 69.

BRADING, R, 'Australia Needs Chapter 13 Protection' (2002) 12(2) *ITSA New Directions* 19.

Braucher, J, 'Lawyers and Consumer Bankruptcy: One Code, Many Cultures' (1993) 67 *American Bankruptcy Law Journal* 501.

——, 'Increasing Uniformity in Consumer Bankruptcy: Means Testing as a Distraction and the National Bankruptcy Review Commission's Proposals as a Starting Point' (1998) 6 *American Bankruptcy Institute Law Review* 1.

——, 'An Empirical Study of Debtor Education in Bankruptcy: Impact on Chapter 13 Completion Not Shown' (2001) 9 *American Bankruptcy Institute Law Review* 557.

——, 'Options in Consumer Bankruptcy: An American Perspective' (1999) 37 *Osgoode Hall Law Journal* 155.

——, 'Means Testing Consumer Bankruptcy: The Problem of Means' (2002) 7 *Fordham Journal of Corporate and Financial Law* 407.

Brighton, W, 'Reactions to Recent Canadian Empirical Studies on Canadian Bankruptcy' (1999) 37 *Osgoode Hall Law Journal* 137.

Buckley, FH, and Brinig, MF, 'The Bankruptcy Puzzle' (1998) 27 *Journal of Legal Studies* 187.

Buckwold, TM, 'Holding the High Ground: The Position of Secured Creditors in Consumer Bankruptcies and Proposals' (1999) 37 *Osgoode Hall Law Journal* 277.

Buckwold, TM, and Cuming, RCC, 'The Personal Property Security Act and the Bankruptcy and Insolvency Act: Two Solitudes or Complementary Systems?' (1997) 12 *Banking and Finance Review* 467.

Carruthers, BG, and Halliday, TC, 'Professionals in Systemic Reform of Bankruptcy Law: The 1978 U.S. Bankruptcy Code and the English Insolvency Act 1986' (2000) 74 *American Bankruptcy Law Journal* 35.

Comment, 'A Reformed Economic Model of Consumer Bankruptcy' (1996) 109 *Harvard Law Review* 1338.

Countryman, V, 'Bankruptcy and the Individual Debtor—and a Modest Proposal to Return to the Seventeenth Century' (1983) 32 *Catholic University Law Review* 809.

Culhane, MB, and White, MM, 'Taking the New Consumer Bankruptcy Model for a Test Drive: Means Testing Real Chapter 7 Debtors' (1999) 7 *American Bankruptcy Institute Law Review* 27.

——, and ——, 'Debt After Discharge: An Empirical Study of Reaffirmation' (1999) 73 *American Bankruptcy Law Journal* 709.

——, and ——, 'But can She Keep the Car? Some Thoughts on Collateral Retention in Consumer Chapter 7 Cases' (2002) 7 *Fordham Journal of Corporate & Financial Law* 471.

Cuming, RCC, 'Canadian Bankruptcy Law: A Secured Creditor's Heaven?' (1995) 24 *Canadian Business Law Journal* 17.

Curnock, CA, 'Insolvency Counselling: Innovation Based on the Fourteenth Century' (1999) 37 *Osgoode Hall Law Journal* 387.

DAL PONT, G, and GRIGGS, L, 'The Journey from Ear-Cropping and Capital Punishment to the Bankruptcy Legislation Amendment Bill 1995' (1995) 8 *Corporate and Business Law Journal* 155.

DAVIES, JE, 'Delegalisation of Debt Recovery Proceedings: A Socio-Legal Study of Money Advice Centres and Administrative Orders' in IDC Ramsay (ed), *Debtors and Creditors: A Socio-Legal Perspective*, (Professional Books, London, 1986) ch 8.

DEKANY, AC, *Consumer Debt Counselling in Canada* (major research paper for Osgoode Hall Law School, LLM Programme, September 1999).

DOMOWITZ, I, and EOVALDI, TL, 'The Impact of the Bankruptcy Reform Act of 1978 on Consumer Bankruptcy' (1993) 36 *Journal of Law and Economics* 803.

EISENBERG, T, 'Bankruptcy Law in Perspective' (1981) 28 *UCLA Law Review* 953.

ELLIS, D, 'The Influence of Legal Factors on Personal Bankruptcy Filings' (February 1998) *Bank Trends* (Washington DC).

FERRON, JM, 'The Constitutional Impairment of the Rights of Secured Creditors in Canada and the United States' (1986) 60 *Canadian Bankruptcy Reports (New Series)* 146.

——, 'A Bankruptcy Policy' (1990) 78 *Canadian Bankruptcy Reports, New Series*, 284.

FORD, J, and WILSON, M, 'Personal Debt and Insolvency' in H Rajak (ed), *Insolvency Law: Theory and Practice* (Sweet & Maxwell, London, 1993).

FORD, R, 'Imprisonment for Debt' (1926) 25 *Michigan Law Review* 24.

GALLAGHER, T, 'Reforms to Bankruptcy Legislation' (2000) 10(2) *ITSA New Directions in Bankruptcy* 7.

GRAVER, HP, 'Consumer Bankruptcy: a Right or a Privilege? The Role of the Courts in Establishing Moral Standards of Economic Conduct' (1997) 20 *Journal of Consumer Policy* 161.

GROSS, K, 'As We Fleece Our Debtors' (1998) 102 *Dickinson Law Review* 747.

——, 'Testimony of Professor Karen Gross Regarding Debtor Education, Before the House Subcommittee on Commercial and Administrative Law (12 March 1998)' (1998) 52 *Consumer Finance Law Quarterly Report* 180.

——, 'Demonizing Debtors: A Response to the Honsberger-Ziegel Debate' (1999) 37 *Osgoode Hall Law Journal* 263.

——, 'On the Merits: A Response to Professors Girth and White' (1999) 73 *American Bankruptcy Law Journal* 485.

——, 'Developing a Model for Assessing Financial Literacy Education: Thinking Through Multiple Lenses for Multiple Purposes' in J Niemi-Kiesilainen, IDC Ramsay and WC Whitford (eds), *Consumer Bankruptcy in a Global Perspective* (forthcoming).

GRUNDY, HP, 'Synopsis of the Canadian Bankruptcy Act' (1920–21) 1 *Canadian Bankruptcy Reports Annotated* 325.

GUARDIA, ND, 'Consumer Credit in the European Union' (European Credit Research Institute, Report No 1, February 2000).

HARRIS, SL, 'A Reply to Theodore Eisenberg's Bankruptcy Law in Perspective' (1982) 30 *UCLA Law Review* 327.

HEATH, P, 'Consumer Bankruptcies: A New Zealand Perspective' (1999) 37 *Osgoode Hall Law Journal* 427.

HOFFMAN, HB, 'Consumer Bankruptcy Filers and Pre-Petition Consumer Credit Counseling: Is Congress Trying to Place the Fox in Charge of the Henhouse?' (1999) 54 *Business Lawyer* 1629.

HONSBERGER, J, 'The Nature of Bankruptcy and Insolvency in a Constitutional Perspective' (1972) 10 *Osgoode Hall Law Journal* 199.

——, 'The Nature and Purpose of Bankruptcy' (1973) 16 *Canadian Bankruptcy Reports, New Series* 209.

——, 'Bankruptcy Administration in the United States and Canada' (1975) 63 *California Law Review* 1515.

——, *The Historical Evolution of and the Bankruptcy and Insolvency Process in Canada* (Draft Discussion Document for Industry Canada, unpublished manuscript, 1994).

——, 'Philosophy and Design of Modern Fresh Start Policies: The Evolution of Canada's Legislative Policy' (1999) 37 *Osgoode Hall Law Journal* 171.

HORRMAN, G, 'Debt Recovery in the Federal Republic of Germany: the Example of Consumer Credit' in IDC Ramsay (ed), *Debtors and Creditors: A Socio-Legal Perspective* (Professional Books, London, 1986) ch 7.

HOWARD, M, 'A Theory of Discharge in Consumer Bankruptcy' (1987) 48 *Ohio State Law Journal* 1047.

——, 'Shifting Risk and Fixing Blame: The Vexing Problem of Credit Card Obligations in Bankruptcy' (2001) 75 *American Bankruptcy Law Journal* 63.

——, 'Book Review: TA Sullivan, E Warren and J Lawrence, The Fragile Middle Class: Americans in Debt' (2001) 17 *Bankruptcy Developments Journal* 425.

HULS, N, 'Overindebtedness and Overlegalization: Consumer Bankruptcy as a Field for Alternative Dispute Resolution' (1997) 20 *Journal of Consumer Policy* 143.

JACOBY, MB, SULLIVAN, TA, and WARREN, E, 'Rethinking the Debates Over Health Care Financing: Evidence from the Bankruptcy Courts' (2001) 76 *New York University Law Review* 375.

JONES, EH, and ZYWICKI, TJ, 'It's Time for Means Testing' (1999) *Brigham Young University Law Review* 177.

JUNGMANN, N, 'Why Do Debtors Drop Out of Debt Counselling and How Do They Manage Afterwards?' in J Niemi-Kiesilainen, IDC Ramsay and WC Whitford (eds), *Consumer Bankruptcy in a Global Perspective* (Hart Publishing, forthcoming).

KUMAR, J, Mason, R, and Ralston, D, 'Personal Bankruptcies: Causes and Implications for the Credit Industry' (1999) 17 *Economic Papers* 18.

LANDER, DA, 'Snapshot of an Industry in Turmoil: The Plight of Consumer Debt Counseling' (2000) 54 *Consumer Finance Law Quarterly Report* 330.

——, 'Recent Developments in Consumer Debt Counselling Agencies' (2002) 21(1) *American Bankruptcy Institute Journal* 14.

LAWLESS, RM, *The Relationship between NonBusiness Bankruptcy Filings and Various Basic Measures of Consumer Debt.* (www.law.missouri.edu/lawless/bus-bkr/filings.htm).

LOPUCKI, LM, 'Common Sense Consumer Bankruptcy' (1997) 71 *American Bankruptcy Law Journal* 461.

MARANTZ, RG, 'The Bankruptcy and Insolvency Act: The New Look after Forty Years' (1993) 8 *Banking and Finance Law Review* 195.

——, and CHARTRAND, RH, 'Bankruptcy and Insolvency Law Reform Continues: the 1996–1997 Amendments' (1997) 13 *Banking and Finance Law Review* 107.

MARTEL, E, 'The Debtor's Discharge from Bankruptcy' (1971) 17 *McGill Law Journal* 718.

MASON, R, 'Consumer Bankruptcies: An Australian Perspective' (1999) 37 *Osgoode Hall Law Journal* 449.

MASON, RF, and DUNS, J, 'Developments in Consumer Bankruptcy Law in Australia' in J Niemi-Kiesilainen, IDC Ramsay and WC Whitford (eds), *Consumer Bankruptcy in a Global Perspective* (Hart Publishing, forthcoming).

MCBRYDE, B, 'The Scottish Experience of Bankruptcy' in Harry Rajak (ed), *Insolvency Law: Theory and Practice* (Sweet & Maxwell, London, 1993).

MCCOID II, JC, 'The Origins of Voluntary Bankruptcy' (1988) 5 *Bankruptcy Developments Journal* 361.

MCGREGOR, SLT, and BERRY, RE, 'Changing Trends in Canadian Demographics: Comparison of 1982 and 1994 National Studies' (1999) 18(4) *Insolvency Bulletin* 37.

MILSTEIN, AS, and RATNER, BC, 'Consumer Credit Counselling Service: A Consumer-Oriented View' (1981) 56 *New York University Law Review* 978.

MYATT, A, and MURRELL, D, 'Another Day Older and Deeper in Debt? Is there a Financial Crisis in Canadian Households?' (1998) 6(4) *Canadian Business Economics* 50.

NIEMI-KIESILAINEN, J, 'Changing Directions in Consumer Bankruptcy Law and Practice in Europe and USA' (1997) 20(2) *Journal of Consumer Policy* 133.

——, 'Consumer Bankruptcy in Comparison: Do We Cure a Market Failure or a Social Problem?' (1999) 37 *Osgoode Hall Law Journal* 473.

——, 'The Role of Consumer Counselling as Part of the Bankruptcy Process in Europe' (1999) 37 *Osgoode Hall Law Journal* 409.

PAULUS, CG, 'Germany: Lessons to Learn from the Implementation of a New Insolvency Code' (2001) 17 *Connecticut Journal of International Law* 89.

PENTLAND, J, 'Debt Collection: the Final Pusher into Bankruptcy?' (2002) 12(2) *ITSA New Directions* 10.

POSNER, EA, 'Contract Law in the Welfare State: A Defence of the Unconscionability Doctrine, Usury Laws, and Related Limitations on the Freedom of Contract' (1995) 24 *Journal of Legal Studies* 283.

PRICE, Z, 'The Bankruptcy Abuse Prevention and Consumer Protection Act' (2002) 39 *Harvard Journal on Legislation* 237.

RADIN, M, 'The Nature of Bankruptcy' (1940) 89 *University of Pennsylvania Law Review* 1.

RAMSAY, IDC, 'Models of Consumer Bankruptcy: Implications for Research and Policy' (1997) 20 *Journal of Consumer Policy* 269.

——, 'Individual Bankruptcy: Preliminary Findings of a Socio-Legal Analysis' (1999) 37 *Osgoode Hall Law Journal* 15.

——, 'Market Imperatives, Professional Discretion and the Role of Intermediaries in Consumer Bankruptcy: a Comparative Study of the Canadian Trustee in Bankruptcy' (2000) 74 *American Bankruptcy Law Journal* 399.

REA, SA, 'Arm-Breaking, Consumer Credit, and Personal Bankruptcy' (1984) 22 *Economic Inquiry* 188.

REIFNER, U, 'The Eleventh Commandment: Inclusive Contract Law and Personal Bankruptcy' in J Niemi-Kiesilainen, IDC Ramsay and WC Whitford (eds), *Consumer Bankruptcy in a Global Perspective* (Hart Publishing, forthcoming).

SCHWARTZ, S, 'The Empirical Dimensions of Consumer Bankruptcy: Results from a Survey of Canadian Bankrupts' (1999) 37 *Osgoode Hall Law Journal* 83.

——, 'The Dark Side of Student Loans: Debt Burden, Default, and Bankruptcy' (1999) 37 *Osgoode Hall Law Journal* 307.

STEHL, RL, 'The Failings of the Credit Counseling and Debtor Education Requirements of Proposed Consumer Bankruptcy Reform Legislation of 1998' (1999) 7 *American Bankruptcy Institute Law Review* 133.

SULLIVAN, JP, 'More than a Shirt on Your Back: New Exemptions for Debtors under the Court Order Enforcement Act', (1998) 56 *Advocate (Vancouver)* 389.

SULLIVAN, TA, WARREN, E, and WESTBROOK, JL, 'Limiting Access to Bankruptcy Discharge: An Analysis of the Creditors' Data' [1983] *Wisconsin Law Review* 1091.

——, ——, and ——, 'Law, Models, and Real People: Choice of Chapter in Personal Bankruptcy' (1988) 13 *Law and Social Inquiry* 661.

——, ——, and ——, 'Consumer Debtors Ten Years Later: A Financial Comparison of Consumer Bankrupts 1981–1991' (1994) 68 *American Bankruptcy Law Journal* 121.

——, ——, and ——, 'The Persistence of Local Legal Culture: Twenty Years of Evidence from the Federal Bankruptcy Courts' (1994) 17 *Harvard Journal of Law and Public Policy* 801.

——, ——, and ——, 'Consumer Bankruptcy in the United States: A Study of Alleged Abuse and of Local Legal Cultures' (1997) 20 *Journal of Consumer Policy* 223.

Symposium, 'The Economics of Bankruptcy Reform' (1977) 41(4) *Law and Contemporary Problems* 1.

Tabb, CJ, 'The Scope of the Fresh Start in Bankruptcy: Collateral Conversions and the Dischargeability Debate' (1990) 59 *George Washington Law Review* 56.

——, 'The Historical Evolution of the Bankruptcy Discharge' (1991) 65 *American Bankruptcy Law Journal* 325.

——, 'The Death of Consumer Bankruptcy in the United States?' (2001) 18 *Bankruptcy Developments Journal* 1.

Telfer, TGW, 'The Canadian Bankruptcy Act of 1919: Public Legislation or Private Interest?' (1995) 24 *Canadian Business Law Journal* 357.

——, 'Access to the Discharge in Canadian Bankruptcy Law and the New Role of Surplus Income: A Historical Perspective' in CEF Rickett and TGW Telfer (eds), *International Perspectives on Consumers' Access to Justice* (Cambridge University Press, forthcoming).

Treiman, I, 'Act of Bankruptcy: A Medieval Concept in Modern Bankruptcy Law' (1938) 52 *Harvard Law Review* 189.

Warren, E, 'A Principled Approach to Consumer Bankruptcy' (1997) 71 *American Bankruptcy Law Journal* 483.

——, 'The Changing Politics of American Bankruptcy Reform' (1999) 37 *Osgoode Hall Law Journal* 189.

——, 'Bankrupt Children' (2002) 86 *Minnesota Law Review* 1003

——, 'The Market for Data: the Changing Role of Social Sciences in Shaping the Law' [2002] *Wisconsin Law Review* 1.

——, 'What is a Women's Issue? Bankruptcy, Commercial Law, and Other Gender-Neutral Topics' (2002) 25 *Harvard Women's Law Journal* 19.

Wedoff, ER, 'An Updated Analysis of the Consumer Bankruptcy Provisions of H.R. 833 Bankruptcy Reform Act of 1999, as Passed by the House of Representatives' (1 November 1999) (www.abiworld.org/legis/bills/106anal/wedoff833ana820.html).

Weistart, JC, 'The Costs of Bankruptcy' (1977) 41 *Law and Contemporary Problems* 107.

Westbrook, JL, 'A Comparative Empirical Research Agenda in Consumer Bankruptcy' (1992) 21 *Canadian Business Law Journal* 30.

——, 'Comparative Empiricism' (1999) 37 *Osgoode Hall Law Journal* 143.

White, MJ, 'Personal Bankruptcy under the 1978 Bankruptcy Code: An Economic Analysis' (1987) 63 *Indiana Law Journal* 1.

White, MJ, 'Economic versus Sociological Approaches to Legal Research: The Case of Bankruptcy' (1991) 25 *Law and Society Review* 685.

White, MJ, 'Why It Pays to File for Bankruptcy: A Critical Look at the Incentives Under the US Personal Bankruptcy Law and a Proposal for Change' (1998) 65 *University of Chicago Law Review* 685.

Whitford, WC, 'Has the Time Come to Repeal Chapter 13?' (1989) 65 *Indiana Law Journal* 85.

——, 'The Ideal of Individualized Justice: Consumer Bankruptcy as Consumer Protection, and Consumer Protection in Consumer Bankruptcy' (1994) 68 *American Bankruptcy Law Journal* 397.

——, 'Changing Definitions of Fresh Start in U.S. Bankruptcy Law' (1997) 20 *Journal of Consumer Policy* 179.

WHITFORD, WC, 'Secured Creditors and Consumer Bankruptcy in the United States' (1999) 37 *Osgoode Hall Law Journal* 339.

WOODWARD, WJ, and WOODWARD, RS, 'Exemptions as an Incentive to Voluntary Bankruptcy: An Empirical Study' (1983) 88 *Commercial Law Journal* 309.

ZIEGEL, JS, 'Consumer Bankruptcies' (1972) 20 *Chitty's Law Journal* 325.

ZIEGEL, JS, 'Canadian Bankruptcy Reform, Bill C-109, and Troubling Asymmetries' (1996) 27 *Canadian Business Law Journal* 108.

ZIEGEL, JS, 'Canada's Phased-in Bankruptcy Law Reform' (1996) 70 *American Bankruptcy Law Journal* 383.

ZIEGEL, JS, 'Canadian Perspectives on the Challenges of Consumer Bankruptcies' (1997) 20(2) *Journal of Consumer Policy* 199.

ZIEGEL, JS, 'The Philosophy and Design of Contemporary Consumer Bankruptcy Systems: A Canada-United States Comparison' (1999) 37 *Osgoode Hall Law Journal* 205.

ZIEGEL, JS, 'The Modernization of Canada's Bankruptcy Law in a Comparative Context' (1999) 4 *Canadian Bankruptcy Reports (4th)* 151.

ZIEGEL, JS, 'Financing Consumer Bankruptcies, *Re Berthelette*, and Public Policy' (2000) 33 *Canadian Business Law Journal* 294.

ZIEGEL, JS, *et al*, 'Consumer Bankruptcies and Bill C-5: Five Academics Claim the Bill Turns the Problems on their Head' (1996) 13 *National Insolvency Review* 81.

Index